Library of
Davidson College

State and Society
in
Contemporary Europe

State and Society in Contemporary Europe

edited by

Jack Hayward & R. N. Berki

St. Martin's Press · New York

© Jack Hayward and R. N. Berki 1979
All rights reserved. For information, write:
St. Martin's Press, Inc. 175 Fifth Avenue, New York, NY 10010
Printed in Great Britain
First Published in the United States of America in 1979

ISBN 0-312-75604-6

Library of Congress Cataloging in Publication Data
Main entry under title:

State and society in contemporary Europe.

Includes index.
1. Europe—Politics and government—1945–
Addresses, essays, lectures. 2. Europe, Eastern—
Politics and government—Addresses, essays, lectures.
I. Hayward, Jack Ernest Shalom. II. Berki, R. N.
JN94.A3S7 1979   320.9'4'055   78-26049
ISBN 0-312-75604-6

Contents

Contributors — vii

Preface — ix

INTRODUCTION State and Society: An Antithesis of Modern Political Thought *by R. N. Berki* — 1

PART I STATE AND SOCIETY IN WESTERN EUROPE

CHAPTER 1 Interest Groups and the Demand for State Action *by Jack Hayward* — 23

CHAPTER 2 Political Parties and Government Decision-Making *by Michael Wheaton* — 42

CHAPTER 3 The Functions of the Modern State *by Neil Elder* — 58

CHAPTER 4 Trade Unions in Western European Politics *by M. S. Joseph* — 75

PART II STATE AND SOCIETY IN EASTERN EUROPE

CHAPTER 5 Party, State and Groups in Eastern Europe *by Georg Brunner and Hannes Kaschkat* — 95

CHAPTER 6 State and Nationality under Communism *by Terry McNeill* — 118

CHAPTER 7 The State and the Economy in Eastern Europe *by Hans-Hermann Höhmann* — 141

CHAPTER 8 Yugoslavia: A Special Case *by Robert K. Furtak* — 158

PART III THE INTERNATIONAL CONTEXT

CHAPTER 9 Great-Power Involvement in European Systems *by Stephen Kirby* — 181

CHAPTER 10 The European Economic Community: Expectations and Realities of Integration *by Jürgen Wohlfahrt* 203

CHAPTER 11 COMECON: Inter-State Economic Co-operation in Eastern Europe *by Alexander Uschakow* 218

CHAPTER 12 The Multinational Enterprise: A 1977 Perspective *by Roger Williams* 237

CONCLUSION The State of European Society *by R. N. Berki and Jack Hayward* 253

Index 265

Contributors

R. N. BERKI,
   Senior Lecturer in Politics, University of Hull

GEORG BRUNNER,
   Professor of Law & Political Science, University of Würzburg

NEIL C. M. ELDER,
   Senior Lecturer in Politics, University of Hull

ROBERT FURTAK,
   Professor of Political Science, University of Freiburg

JACK HAYWARD,
   Professor of Politics, University of Hull

HANS-HERMANN HOHMANN,
   Senior Research Associate of the Federal Institute of East European & International Studies, Cologne

M. S. JOSEPH,
   Former Lecturer in Politics, University of Hull

HANNES KASCHKAT,
   Lecturer in Law & Political Science, University of Würzburg

STEPHEN KIRBY,
   Lecturer in Politics, University of Hull

TERRY MCNEILL,
   Lecturer in Politics, University of Hull

ALEXANDER USCHAKOW,
   Lecturer in Law, University of Cologne

MICHAEL WHEATON,
    Lecturer in European Studies, University of Hull

ROGER WILLIAMS,
    Professor of Government, University of Manchester

JÜRGEN WOHLFAHRT,
    Lecturer in Law, University of Würzburg

Preface

Our collaborative enterprise developed out of the academic link that has existed for over four years between members of the Politics Department of the University of Hull and of the Institut für Rechtsphilosophie, Staats- und Verwaltungsrecht of the University of Würzburg. This firm institutional relationship was itself born of the personal friendship, dating back to their schooldays in Hungary, between Professor Georg Brunner and Dr Robert Berki. As a result of discussion arising out of visits from members of both institutions, it was felt that there was an important gap in the teaching and research literature with regard to the presentation of an analytical and comparative study of the relationship between state and society in both East and West Europe. Furthermore, it was considered important to avoid this Eurocentric study becoming unduly insular and introverted. So, an international dimension was envisaged, to be given equal weight with the sections devoted to East and to West Europe.

Although the editorial responsibility for this volume has been assumed in Hull, we wish to acknowledge the considerable intellectual contribution made by Georg Brunner at virtually all stages of the venture. We would particularly emphasise our debt to him in the preliminary planning of the project, the recruitment of our German contributors and in the friendly frankness with which he offered constructive critical comments upon many aspects of our joint endeavours. Finally, he and Frau Ursula Brunner were admirable hosts in Würzburg where we had our conference in August 1977 to discuss most of the draft papers making up this book.

Our main focus has been on the relationship within and between the political and administrative institutions of the major European states and the leading extra-governmental organisations, particularly trade unions and industrial enterprises, emphasising the developments in the 1970s. Our initial hypothesis was that many of the specific policy problems of industrial society derived from the difficulty of adapting traditional institutional relationships to new circumstances. Furthermore, because these relationships are no longer meaningfully discussed solely within the context of particular nation-states, an important part of our work has been to examine how the international context impinges upon the activities of states, political parties, national and multinational firms and trade unions. The vicissitudes of international collaboration being what they are, two of our initial German contributors dropped out, with the consequence that we have given insufficient coverage to the relationships of firms to their respective national governments. We consider that the evidence assembled documents the general breakdown of the sharp traditional distinction on the European continent between the 'public' and the 'private', what belongs to the state and what belongs to society. There have been invasions of the state's domain by social forces, as well as intrusions into the social domain by interventionist states. These tendencies have occurred differentially as between East and West Europe and between countries on each side of the communist and non-communist political divide. Our contributors, each in their own way, without conforming to any methodological or ideological straitjacket, have addressed themselves to particular manifestations of these contemporary tendencies.

We wish to thank the Anglo-German Foundation for the Study of Industrial Society for a grant to meet the lion's share of the costs of the conference held at the University of Würzburg in August 1977. It provided our contributors with an invaluable opportunity to comment upon each other's work and reduced some of the imperfections which undoubtedly remain in this book. To have attempted such an immense task will perhaps be regarded as foolhardy by some critics but we remain convinced that ambitious failure is more instructive than facile success. We gratefully acknowledge that the cost of translating the papers by German contributors was met from a grant by the Volkswagen Foundation to Professor Brunner. Finally, we wish to thank most warmly Miss Janet Braim of the Department of Politics and Miss Enid Savill of the Institute of European Studies at the University of Hull for the care with which they prepared the final version of this book for publication.

Many a friendship has been a victim of the attempt to collaborate. The editors are happy to place on record that theirs has survived intact the vicissitudes of this enterprise.

J.E.S.H.   R.N.B.
University of Hull
February 1978

INTRODUCTION

INTRODUCTION

State and Society: An Antithesis of Modern Political Thought

R. N. Berki

The signification of the terms 'state' and 'society', in common parlance as well as the academic study of politics, appears straightforward enough. 'State' is a singular noun and by it we customarily mean an institutional structure whose primary and distinctive function is the maintenance of authority in a given territorial unit, or, to adopt the hallowed Weberian definition, whose distinguishing mark is its successful claim to exercise a monopoly of legitimate physical coercion in such units. The state, then, has to do with government, law, legislation and law enforcement. 'Society', on the other hand, is a collective noun and by it we usually mean a plurality of groupings and formations of human beings, to be found within states as well as outside them, quite often straddling state boundaries. Society has to do with all kinds of purposes and all forms of cohesion and co-operation. We could name as its most important constituent parts, with the present exercise in view, nations and nationalities, social classes, economic enterprises, political parties, interest groups — this list is, of course, far from being exhaustive. It is, at any rate, obvious that state and society, understood in the above sense, could usefully serve as our probably least involved, and most commonsensical, organising concepts in an endeavour to comprehend even such a complicated object of investigation as the socio-political order of contemporary Europe.

However, while all countries of Europe are organised as states surrounded by societies, thus displaying at least a certain amount of formal similarity, the differences between these societies and states are equally, if not more, conspicuous. We need not go further than noting what is undoubtedly the most significant of these differences, that obtaining between Western liberal-democratic countries on the one hand, and the socialist or communist countries of Eastern Europe on the other. The basic distinction between these two major types of European order could indeed be expressed by reference to the concepts state and society, though the exercise is not as easy as it might look at first. We cannot, that is to say, adequately grasp this distinction as long as we are content to remain on the level of descriptive investigation, simply noting the respective features of states and societies in East and West. This would merely yield paradoxes. It could be said, for example, that in the East, with its monolithic power and authority structures and centralised economies, the state is strong and society is weak. Conversely in the West, with its pluralistic structure of power and authority and private economic enterprise, the state could well appear weak and society the stronger partner. Now observations of this kind are certainly valid up to a point, but they do not tell us the whole story and might, in addition, force us into untenable theoretical positions. For, to counter the above statements, it could be equally validly pointed out that in the West the law and government do in fact enjoy the highest status and exercise supreme authority, whereas in the East this status and authority is enjoyed and wielded by a political party on behalf of a social class, subordinating to itself both law and government. Is it, therefore, the case that in the West the state is strong and society weak, and in the East the state is weak and society strong?

One way out of this seeming tangle, it will be argued here, lies through an effort to extend our perspective from the plane of institutional structures such as states and social formations to the cultural attitudes and political philosophies lying behind them and, *ex hypothesi,* explaining their relationship as well as their respective strengths and weaknesses. We need, in other words, to embark on a brief excursion into the realms of modern history and modern political thought, noting some prevailing and relevant epistemological, methodological and normative concerns, in order to make sense of both state and society. In the mirror of modern political thought these two entities are being revealed as the institutional counterpart of two opposed philosophies of man as member of the human community; state and society thus, on the appropriate level of reflection and analysis, appear as two terms of a deep-lying antithesis of modern political consciousness. This antithesis can, in the first place, explain the most significant of the secular distinctions between the two halves of contemporary Europe, and in the second place it also sheds light on characteristic approaches to the study of politics in West and East.

The two contrasted attitudes, principles or philosophies will be called here, respectively, transcendentalism and instrumentalism. This theoretical distinction itself is, indeed, not new, but we shall endeavour to develop some well-known pairs of concepts[1] in a way that will illuminate some issues relevant here. Transcendentalism can also be regarded as statist orientation, while instrumentalism may be seen as societal orientation.

Transcendentalism, then, refers to the belief that man primarily belongs to a *moral* community, or, to put it the other way round, that the community has a paramount moralising function and is, therefore, logically speaking 'prior' to its members. Individuals, it is held, are united together in the service of common and moral goals. The association has a 'public' character or personality, meaning that its 'interest', though not unrelated to, nevertheless expresses more than the aggregate of the interests of its members. The public interest does not merely delimit but also defines the proper pursuits of individuals who belong to it. And association here means uniformity: individual members are equally under the authority of the common body which is always morally supreme; there are no exceptions, and differential rewards, if any, are justified only on the grounds of service. Law — the body of rules accepted in the association — is seen as the expression of the collective reason and will of the membership. The conduct of the common affairs of the association, its ongoing business, is 'politics'; this is understood here primarily or exclusively in terms of leadership and education. Transcendentalism thus exudes an air of collective heroism and dynamism; it connotes the high ideals of duty, service, the sublimation of energies. It is an idealistic principle, since it understands men not as they are, but as they ought to be. It can, as we shall see later, be construed as the underlying philosophical basis of either conservative or radical political ideologies. In the former case the state is presented as a superior, mystical, 'transcendental' entity; in the latter it is attempted to 'transcend' both state and society in fact.

The principle and attitude expressed by what we are here calling instrumentalism, by contrast, embodies the belief that man primarily belongs to an *interest* community, in other words that the group's existence and functions are external to individuals and are not directly related to their moral feelings and aims. Individuals become or continue as members of associations because they see that the latter as 'instruments' promote their own individual private aims; the essence of membership is that it is volitional and conditional. The association thus created has no moral (as distinguished from legal) personality; the common or 'public' interest is no separate, let alone superior, category but private interest writ large; it is simply the sum of individual interests. Consequently the 'authority' of the association derives solely from the 'rights' of its members. The law here is conceived in terms of rational agreement among the membership, a necessary concomitant to as well as a compromise with the pursuit of private aims. The emphasis is thus not on uniformity but on diversity; over and above the equality imposed by membership, differential rewards, be they of wealth, status or power, will be readily countenanced and justified on grounds of innate ability, luck, merit or personal connections. The common affairs or 'politics' of the association will be seen here in terms of 'business', that is, the adjustment of private pursuits and the reconciliation of various interests. Instrumentalism hence has an air of freedom, diversity, plurality, colourful and 'healthy' conflict about it; it is unheroic and its dynamism is confined to that of its self-assertive members. Essentially it is a realistic principle, as it focuses on people in their immediate reality, not in the light of moral ideals; the political changes it inspires will tend on the whole to be small-scale and gradual. Like transcendentalism, it too can be seen to nourish both radical and conservative ideological positions.

The two principles, however, also display basic similarities, which are as important to notice as their contrast. They both, after all, derive from the common European heritage of political thought, thus bearing the imprint of classical as well as medieval ideas. In the first place we ought to observe that transcendentalism and instrumentalism are both democratic, albeit only in the somewhat remote sense of accepting the notion that authority ultimately comes from the people. The former, however, sees the people's sovereignty reside in their collective capacity, in their unified will and reason. It embodies, therefore, a democratic principle that tends (to remain with the classical terminology) to lean towards 'monarchy' in that in this perspective the (temporary) transfer of actual power to one man or a small body of men would often be readily accepted, even advocated. The democratic character of the latter on the other hand, lies in its placing sovereignty in the people understood as a collection of morally self-sufficient individuals, members of lesser groupings whose collective political will is the outcome or end result of mutually adjusted interests. Here, therefore, we find a leaning towards 'aristocracy' in that it will frequently be admitted — either in a tacit or in an explicit form — that the 'interest' of certain individuals or groups weighs more heavily than that of others. Transcendentalism, in other words, places more emphasis on 'sovereignty', whereas instrumentalism accentuates the 'contractual' basis of government. Further, both these principles can be said to be 'egalitarian' in the sense that they both stipulate the equal applicability of the rules of the association. Equality in terms of the former, however, is understood primarily as aspiration to substantive equality, as common subjection, common destiny; it is the equality of the fraternal gathering, the monastery, the barracks or the battlefield. Equality is thus approximated to fraternity. For the latter, on the other hand, equality signifies merely an initial formal condition; with rewards it is equity (or proportional equality) and not absolute equality that will be stressed; it is the egalitarianism of the race-track or the market-place. Thus, here equality is approximated to freedom.

Furthermore, these two principles must also be seen as being essentially interrelated and complementary; they are not just opposed derivations from the same cultural roots. This means that European political development in the modern age, on the institutional as well as intellectual levels, could well be seen as so many and varied attempts to find the right blend or combination. In abstract terms it would of course be quite easy to establish what this right and desirable combination could look like. It would follow from the blending of moderate aspects of transcendentalism and instrumentalism.

Institutionally this could be formulated as a relationship of *co-ordination* or a situation where neither the 'state' nor 'society' is smothered by its opposite number, where they are partners, not antagonists, where there is a clearly defined public interest which, however, does not trample on the plurality of private interests, where both freedom and equality obtain, mutually delimiting and reinforcing each other. Pure or extreme forms of both these principles, however, lead in the institutional realm to a relationship of *subordination* — when either the state or society is subordinated to its partner. We have, therefore, two possible 'deviant' cases. Extreme transcendentalism or the subordination of society to state means also in effect the denial of the distinction between the two principles; it is thus manifested in political oppression, the enforcement of uniformity. The subordination of state to society or extreme instrumentalism means drawing the distinction between the two principles too rigidly and sharply; it can thus be manifested in plutocracy, weak or class-based government, corporatism and 'neo-feudalism'. These are, of course, ideal types that will not be encountered in their purity. However, we should have no difficulty in recognising systems or formations that tend in either of these two extreme directions. And the relevance of this conceptual framework to the socio-political order in the two halves of contemporary Europe, to be sure, is quite obvious.

Before we come to the contemporary scene, however, let us briefly sketch in the historical background. The development of modern Europe has signified the simultaneous emergence of the modern 'state' and modern 'society'. Institutions, that is to say, appeared in European countries and in North America (an extension of Western Europe in the political sense) that could be recognised primarily in terms of either one or the other of the two structures and justified on the basis of either of the two philosophical principles. It is impossible to say, and therefore useless to ask, which came first, institutions or their theoretical recognition and conscious advocacy. We have already argued the inadequacy of a purely empirical, institutional approach. A wholly idealist, philosophical approach would obviously be equally one-sided and erroneous. Nobody ever succeeded in consciously devising states or societies. Nobody, however, would have been able to hit upon and sustain the empirical distinction, were it not itself deeply imbedded in our intellectual development. At any rate, institutions roughly answering the description 'state' and 'society', supported by the two contrasted attitudes, emerged on the horizon everywhere. Their *relative* importance, however — again measured in both secular and intellectual terms — varied from place to place. The development of modern Europe has thus assumed an enduring pattern where variation can usefully be explained by the relative strength of state and society as institutions, and as expressed through the relative position of predominance afforded to either of the two basic principles. This can be measured by popular attitudes as well as outstanding works of political philosophy.

Geography here provides us with a rough-and-ready guide — though it is important not to over-simplify matters. By and large, the state and transcendentalism assumed predominance in the East and society and instrumentalism in the West, Central Europe being as always the battle-ground where the struggle for supremacy has repeatedly been fought. Between Russia and North America as the two extremes — seen through a perspective that is at least as old as Tocqueville's — there is a detectable variation in the development of such major political units as the Habsburg Empire, the Germanic kingdoms, Spain, France and Great Britain. The enlightened despots Katherine, Frederick the Great and Joseph II achieved modernisation in their respective domains through establishing strong centralised bureaucracies. In France the Revolution of 1789 abolished absolute monarchy, eliminated aristocratic privileges and enhanced the ideals of freedom, equality and popular sovereignty. The modern French state, however, in its Jacobin-republican as well as Napoleonic-imperial varieties, has retained and even strengthened the principle and no less the practice of centralised authority.

In Britain, by significant contrast, instead of enlightened monarchy we find an enlightened aristocracy assuming the leading role as the chief agent of modernisation, aided and later supplanted by emerging commercial groups: sea-faring merchants, manufacturers, entrepreneurs of all kinds. In the British North American colonies the role of the 'enlightened bourgeoisie' was even greater from the mid-eighteenth century onwards. In Britain and America we must also note the importance and vigour of the independent Protestant churches, clubs, chartered companies, friendly gatherings, which, as conscious representatives of various particular 'interests', acted so as further to dilute political power and diminish central authority. In Britain, political 'parties', representing the first serious intrusion of modern 'society' into the realm of 'state' proper, appeared as early as the mid-seventeenth century when they were at first associated with religious division. In the United States, 'parties' or 'factions' were immediately related to the various economic 'interests' that, as for example Madison was to argue, were all legitimate parts of the modern polity; so was, in the eyes of American republican thinkers, the principle of federated authority. Thus statist and societal orientation in thought as well as in fact came to be the chief contending expressions of modern European politics. Both kinds of development — to add one more instance of characterisation — continued directly the medieval experience, but whereas transcendentalism appears as the modern equivalent of medieval *religion,* stressing unity and bestowing a halo on authority (characteristically strong in countries where Greek Orthodoxy, Roman Catholicism and the Roman Law tradition held their longest sway), instrumentalism grew out of medieval institutions like the guild, the independent city and feudal landed property, stressing as it has done local and professional autonomy.

Popular attitudes, insofar as one can generalise in such a vast and chaotic field of investigation, have been by and large visibly influenced by these two major modes of development, and have influenced them in turn: they have thus materially contributed to the perpetuation of the state-society antithesis. In the East, people have tended on the whole to be state-oriented: they have traditionally looked to the fountain of central authority for inspiration, protection and assistance. This is epitomised not only in the proverbial attitude of the mouzhik who sought succour with the Tzar, his 'father', against the wicked landlord, but also in the conduct of merchants and craftsmen seeking protection and funds for industrial investment from the state. While 'politicians', like traders, have in this area been traditionally assigned a low status, civil servants as well as teachers have been highly respected. In the West on the other hand, the politically most articulate strata have been society-oriented in their actions and opinions, looking to themselves and to the immediate group (the neighbourhood, the local chapel, friends, business and professional colleagues) for material as well as spiritual assistance. This has been expressed in a variety of characteristic ways, like suspicion of 'officialdom' and a low view of 'intellectuals', 'rugged' or 'fierce' individualism, insularity, parochialism, the apotheosis of selfishness, and in general a 'god's-in-his-heaven-all-is-well-with-the-world' kind of confident indifference to anything beyond one's doorstep, beyond one's own 'interest'. The counterpart of the mouzhik on this side is the (no doubt equally stereotyped) figure of the mid-Western farmer.

We can easily illustrate these two contrasting principles in the development of modern political thought, but we shall alas have to confine our attention here to a handful of instances. The most eminent transcendentalist or statist thinkers have been continental Europeans. Perhaps clearest expression to the principle was given in the eighteenth century by Rousseau who argued that the foundation of human society meant 'the total alienation of each associate, together with all his rights, to the whole community', where 'at once, in place of the individual personality of each contracting party, this association creates a moral and collective body'. Living in society, he goes on, 'produces a very remarkable change in man, in substituting justice for instinct in his conduct, and giving his actions the morality they had formerly lacked'.[2] Fichte, more rigorously than Rousseau, contended that 'natural right' would be inconceivable without the presupposition of the 'state'; 'the state itself', he argues, 'becomes man's natural abode and its laws should be none other than realized natural rights'.[3] He thinks that 'it is the state alone which unites an indeterminate mass of people into an *enclosed whole,* a universality ... through it alone is rightful property established'.[4] De Maistre, though a critic of Rousseau's democratic egalitarianism, yet voices the very same attitude to state and society; in his view

> the word *people* is a relative term that has no meaning divorced from the idea of sovereignty; for the idea of a *people* involves that of an

aggregation around a common centre, and without sovereignty there can be no political unity or cohesion.[5]

Hegel, the first modern thinker to draw a sharp distinction between 'state' and 'bourgeois' or 'civil society' allowing a legitimate sphere of operation to each, yet clearly regards the state as definitely superior; the state he pronounces to be the 'substantial unity' which is

> its own absolute, unmoved purpose in which freedom attains to its highest right, so that this final purpose has the highest right against individuals whose *highest duty* is to be members of the state . . . *Unification* as such is itself the true content and purpose, and it is the destiny of individuals to lead a universal life . . .[6]

Friedrich List, founder of the school of 'national' or 'political' economy in opposition to the 'cosmopolitical' doctrines of Quesnay, Adam Smith and J.B. Say, stresses the need in successful production for 'a confederation or union of various energies, intelligences and powers'.

> We have [he argues] proved historically that the unity of the nation forms the fundamental condition of lasting prosperity; and we have shown that only where the interest of individuals has been subordinated to those of the nation, and where successive generations have striven for one and the same object, the nations have been brought to harmonious development . . . .[7]

Mazzini, spokesman of democratic nationalism, argues that human association cannot properly function unless it is realised 'among brothers, believing in the same ruling principle, united in the same faith, and bearing witness by the same name'.

> There is no true association except among equals. It is only through our country that we can have a recognized *collective* existence . . . "The true country is a community of free men and equals, bound together in fraternal concord to labour towards a common aim.[8]

Instrumentalist thinkers, however, have been equally forceful in putting their point of view and, similarly to expressions of the statist principle, here too we find a cross-section of various ideologies. Mention should in the first place be made of Burke, the intellectual mouthpiece of the enlightened English aristocracy. His political philosophy, in direct contrast to the statist universalism of Rousseau, is a plea for the primacy of the immediate group: 'to be attached to the subdivision, to love the little platoon we belong to in society, is the first principle (the germ as it were) of public affections.'[9] His view also embodies the 'weighted' egalitarianism implicit in the instrumentalist principle:

> Nothing is due and adequate representation of a state, that does not represent its ability, as well as its property . . . The characteristic essence of property, formed out of the combined principles of its acquisition and conservation, is to be *unequal.*[10]

In the great social 'partnership all men have equal rights; but not to equal things'. Bentham's political thought goes in much the same direction, although in his case the motives, perspective and idiom are rather different. In his view 'the principal object' of the law in general 'is to give security to rights', and it is the concrete ends of security, subsistence, abundance and only then equality that constitute 'the only legitimate and universal end of government'. And: 'as to absolute equality, in relation to property, such equality is neither possible nor desirable'.[11] Yet another aspect of instrumentalism can be seen clearly enunciated by Bentham's intellectual partner, James Mill, in whose opinion the *rationale* of society is the protection of the weak against the strong, an objective that 'it is plain, can best be attained when a great number of men combine, and delegate to a small number the power necessary for protecting them all. This is Government.'[12]

We are now getting as far removed as possible from the view, characterising the transcendentalist principle, that the community embodies a moral purpose. Again, from a different background, Pierre-Joseph Proudhon claims to have substituted for 'authority and politics' the 'notion of economics' which is 'alone capable of leading to a rational, practical conception of social order'. Strong advocate of 'mutualism' and federalism, he enjoins us to see government 'simply as a phenomenon of social existence, the external embodiment of our rights, the educating of one of our faculties'.[13] Two further illustrations from the twentieth century may be added. Harold Laski has argued that 'the structure of social organization must be federal if it is to be adequate. Its pattern involves, not myself and the State, my groups and the State, but all these and their interrelationships.' His 'solution' to the problem of authority 'insists on unification made through a process of so associating interests that each, in the solution effected, finds sufficient concession to itself to experiment with the result'.[14] G.D.H. Cole, early exponent of 'functionalism' and advocate of 'guild socialism', has likewise contended that it is the 'consciousness of a want requiring co-operative action for its satisfaction' that 'is the basis of *association*'. The state's claim to 'represent' fully the individual is, in his opinion, a false one, to be combated. In truth,

> social organization, however vast and complicated it may be, leaves the individual intact and self-subsistent, distributing his loyalties and obligations among a number of functional bodies, but not absorbed in any or all of them . . . .[15]

In sum, then, to cut a long and interesting story short, it appears that the instrumentalist principle has infused, in its radical form, all modern political theories of anarchism, syndicalism, corporatism and federalism; its more moderate or conservative form (which is more relevant in the present context) has given concrete shape to theories of 'liberal' or 'representative democracy'. In this perspective, it ought perhaps to be added here, the development in liberal-democratic thought from advocacy of the 'minimal' state to acceptance of the 'welfare' state has no great theoretical significance. Democratic socialism, no less than liberalism or conservatism, still embodies the instrumentalist principle, the characteristic assumptions of which have in addition also entered into the mainstream of present-day Western political science — a point on which we shall enlarge somewhat below. Transcendentalism, in turn, in its conservative form can be found incorporated in modern versions of theocracy, in varieties of political idealism and nationalism (though nationality as a societal phenomenon does not properly belong here), populism, fascism and national socialism. The radical development of transcendentalism is best represented by Marxism. As the theoretical links between conservative statist orientation and Marxism are not obvious, and certain terminological difficulties stand in our way, the point requires a word or two in explanation.

Marx, to say the least, had scant respect for the state understood simply as an institution or organisation with a definite personnel. Neither did he cherish or accept the traditional notion of authority as a norm, or indeed any kind of justification of social entities couched in 'moral' terms. No less than classical, early English liberals (of the stamp of Smith, Godwin, Paine, Bright and Cobden) he took the view that the state was merely a derivative and secondary institution, one destined to grow less and less important with the further development of 'society'. In contrast to the liberals, of course, he had a hostile attitude to this society and its political organ, the state, expecting them to be overthrown by the imminent proletarian revolution. The state, in the renowned phrase of the *Communist Manifesto,* was contemptuously dismissed by him and Engels as being the 'managing committee of the bourgeoisie'; it was seen merely as the necessary political adjunct to the class struggle, achieving seeming independence in certain temporary circumstances (like the France of Louis Bonaparte), but ultimately amenable to understanding only by severe reduction: society is master, the state its servant. And if the existing state had such short shrift, it was dealt (seemingly) the death-blow in Marx's and Engels' futuristic pronouncements: the state, with its centralised force and bureaucracy and its ethos of service and submission, was to be completely abolished in the 'higher phase of communism'.

However, to understand the Marxian position aright we have to probe more deeply below the surface of catchy phrases and oft-repeated ringing pronouncements. The truth is that Marx had a definitely high regard for the underlying *principle* or *ideal* of the state, as distinguished from its existing imperfect institutional form of appearance; his vision merely took further, and translated into a different terminology, the political egalitarianism of

Rousseau, the philosophically sublimated expression of Hegel, the moralistic nationalism of Mazzini. It was *because* he believed in a true state that he regarded the existing institution with such hostility; the latter, in his view, was an abject falsification and thus a particularly harmful impediment to progress. This view is clearly stated in his earliest writings from the so-called Jacobin-democrat phase, when his chief preoccupation was a critique of Hegel's (superior but limited) state. In his manuscript *Critique* Marx complains that in all states except democratic ones the 'constitution' rules 'without really ruling', 'without materially permeating the content of the remaining, non-political spheres'. But

> in democracy the constitution, the law, the state itself, insofar as it is a political constitution, is only the self-determination of the people ... Up till now the *political constitution* has been the *religious* sphere, the religion of national life, the heaven of its generality over against the *earthly existence* of its actuality.[16]

It can hence be cogently argued that the later Marxian formulations, like communism and classless society, are merely different expressions for the heavenly ideal of state. Marx's vision of man as a social or species-being, in union with his fellows consciously organising production and having transcended the narrow horizon of bourgeois right, i.e. having completely succeeded in *internalising* morality and authority, is that of the transcendentalist principle in its most purified form.

Marx bequeathed his sublime but utterly idealistic vision to the most able of his followers, and amongst them to Lenin who developed the original doctrine in a number of significant ways. Communism as a purified transcendentalist ideal he accepted whole-heartedly, as witness the well-known passages in *The State and Revolution*. Lenin's main importance, however, lies in his new application of this principle to revolutionary political strategy, with special reference to the vanguard proletarian party which in his conception assumes the form of a perfect synthesis of state and society. Historically as well as theoretically speaking, of course, 'party' should be seen as the societal principle of politics par excellence, as it expresses a particular interest (not opposed to but constitutive of the public interest). Lenin wholly agrees with this view in general, but his party as the representative of the class interest of the proletariat becomes nevertheless a novel and unique phenomenon in that its constituent, the working class, is pronounced the potential bearer of the interest — even further, moral personality — of the whole polity. Thus since the class destiny of the proletariat is to transcend and abolish class (i.e. particular) interest altogether, the role of the Leninist proletarian party is to be the *exclusive* fountain head and bearer of moral and political authority. Society then, we might say, is elevated, taken up into and at the same time comes to possess and devour the state, losing in the process its own societal character: the party, in substance though not in organisational form, becomes the super-state. From this ultra-statist vantage-point, then, Lenin peremptorily condemns all kinds of societal aspirations, displaying his greatest wrath for the societal, instrumentalist tendencies of the working class itself. 'Trade-unionist politics of the working class', he declares, 'is precisely *bourgeois politics* of the working class.'[17] And his revolutionary party, led by professional cadres and organised according to the principles of democratic centralism, is bound together certainly not by an aggregation of individual interests, but by internal moral ties, thus obviating the need for any formalistic political structures. As Lenin puts it,

> the only serious organizational principle for active members of our movement must be: the strictest secrecy, the strictest selection of members, the preparation of professional revolutionaries. Once these qualities are present, something more than 'democratism' is generated, namely a full comradely trust among revolutionaries.[18]

As we well know, Lenin's professional revolutionaries did succeed in assuming political leadership in Russia in 1917, and their complete hegemony was consolidated in the Stalinist state-party bureaucracy by the end of the 1920s. 'After Lenin's death the emphasis shifted increasingly, both in theory and in practice, from society to the state. State socialism gradually developed into statism.'[19] The right-wing statist power-centres of fascism and national socialism having been eliminated in the Second World War, the scene was now set for the most dramatic confrontation so far of the transcendentalist and instrumentalist principles. In the Cold War period, at any rate, the traditional geographical distinction between the relative preponderance of state and society came to assume the rigid form of a clear boundary-line between hostile alliances. The Cold War era, very significantly in our present context, also meant the decline, nay nadir, of continental Europe. The Soviet Union and the United States, both European in culture yet representing Europe only as its polar opposites — the extreme caricatures, we might be tempted to say, of the traditional pattern of European political development as unity-in-diversity — took the leadership in terms of political-military power as well as intellectual influence. And the Cold War of governments was also the Cold War of ideas. This pattern, emphasising division rather more than unity, has remained with us ever since — in very broad, macroscopic terms only. In a somewhat simplified formulation this means that countries in Eastern Europe, the Soviet Union and her allies, are to be seen as *state-led societies,* whereas the United States and her West European allies (and socially kindred, though politically 'neutral' states) are essentially *society-led states.* To employ the similar terminology used by Brzezinski and Huntington in their comparative study of Russia and America, the Soviet pattern exemplifies an 'ideological' political system that antedates and attempts to mould society, while in the West we have an 'instrumental' political system that 'merely reflects the established social patterns and is designed to protect the existing character of society . . .'[20] And the authors conclude:

> The Soviet political system was created to serve as an instrument of communist rule and reform. The American political system was created to provide a loose governmental framework for American society.[21]

The confrontation is, in other words, between revolutionary idealism stemming from a statist orientation and conservative realism expressing an orientation towards society.

Now it is not our purpose here to describe, and even less to evaluate, the actual events of the Cold War era and the succeeding period, or to pass summary moral judgment on the nature of Marxist and liberal-democratic government. Instead it might be of interest to note briefly certain aspects of the development of political thinking in this latter half of the twentieth century, notably characteristic methodological preoccupations which, it appears, have thrown into sharp relief the continuing theoretical antithesis of state and society. The political theories of East and West, in spite of their marked internal differentiation (especially in the 1960s and 70s), remain respectively theories of state and theories of society, with their opposed conceptual frameworks, value-patterns and favoured methods of analysis and investigation. The relatively simpler case of Marxist intellectual development leaves little doubt in this regard. In the Soviet Union the dictatorship of the proletariat has now been officially replaced by the state of the whole people, which, nevertheless, is still expected to wither away on the arrival of communism — unlike the party (i.e. the super-state), which is to continue as the concrete embodiment of morality and higher consciousness. Marxist thinkers in West and East have shown great sophistication in formulating advanced cultural theories (Lukás, Gramsci), reviving Left Hegelian critical philosophy (the Frankfurt School) and redesigning structuralist social science (Althusser, Colletti). Yet Marxism has not thereby lost its essentially statist orientation, afflicted by the one-sidedness and limitations germane to that principle.

Liberal-democratic political theory in the West, though undoubtedly showing more variety and thus being less amenable to concise verdicts, in its turn still retains its basically societal orientation — with the characteristic limitations germane to *that* principle. If anything, indeed, Western political thought has become more pronouncedly instrumental or societal in character since the rather simple-minded liberal-democratic formulations prevalent in the nineteenth century. Here development has been marked by a number of important changes such as the introduction of numerical and statistical techniques in empirical investigation and the increasing complexity of theory (as witness particularly the work of Parsons, Easton, Lasswell, Deutsch and Kaplan). The main attention of Western scholars has also moved from institutions and organisation (taken to near-perfection by Max Weber) to behaviour; after the thoroughgoing investigation of political parties the limelight has fallen on 'pressure groups'. There have been successive attempts at redefining the essential nature of liberal-democracy itself, in terms — significantly in view of some of the concealed premises of the instrumentalist principle at the time of its inception — mainly of consensual elites, acceptable forms and levels of social inequality and the desirability of the *absence* of mass-participation in politics (Mosca, Michels, Schumpeter, Lipset). As a recent student of European politics has put it, liberal-democratic political culture today combines the traditional model of the 'active citizen' 'with other attitudes of passivity, uninvolvement, even a shade of deference'.[22] Confirmation of this point is found also in the aforementioned study by Brzezinski and Huntington where the authors admit that in the American 'instrumental' system 'access to political power is through the medium of organized social and economic influence and interests', also adding that here upper-middle-class participation in politics has been highest.[23] A useful distinction can be drawn here between various power-elite and conflict theories (Pareto, Veblen, Burnham, Wright Mills, Dahrendorf) on the one hand, which are methodologically akin to Marxism without sharing its purified state-ideal, and modern theories of interest-group pluralism (Bentley, Truman, Latham, Polsby, Riesman, Dahl) on the other, which to date represent the instrumentalist point of view in its most fully developed form and (to be sure, rather one-sided) emphasis.

The one-sidedness of both the transcendentalist and instrumentalist approaches have some rather amusing aspects: these could be commented upon briefly. A perfectly simple but nonetheless important point to observe is that Marxists and liberal-democratic theorists *see* the same things when they describe modern society (how could it be otherwise?), but they see them from different angles and with a view to opening up different vistas. An interesting pastime (often engaged in by commentators in the past) would be here to match the verbally opposed but substantively identical definitions offered by the two camps. 'Totalitarian', for example, has largely the same substantive meaning as 'democratic centralist,' while liberal-democratic 'consensus' in the Marxist idiom reads 'hegemony'. Most remarkable is the notorious ambiguity attaching to the notion of power, which Marxists and their opponents inescapably define in diametrically opposed ways. The more obvious and perhaps less important point here is that Marxists habitually refer to society when they talk about power, while Western theorists refer usually to the state. The less obvious but more important point is that the liberal-democratic understanding of power pronounces on the ability to effect *changes,* whereas for Marxists power signifies the ability to *keep* things as they are. Why this is so should be clear once we grasp the essential distinction between the transcendentalist and instrumentalist principles. There is, on the one hand, the revolutionism of the former for which it is a mystery how society could go on existing in the West, by its own momentum and without overt political coercion. On the other hand, we have the conservatism of the latter, exhibiting an innate suspicion of all changes and initiatives from above, from an agency beyond society itself.

Marxism sees all issues through the eyes of state as it were: its approach to state and society is characteristically through a doctrine of 'political' economy. While Marxists (in Eastern Europe at any rate) equate their own rule with the supremacy of the whole over its parts, they sharpen the conflicts and disagreements of the West into the essentially societal struggle of classes. As a recent East European author has expressed the first point, 'unlike all the states of the past, the dictatorship of the proletariat is not opposed to the people but represents their fundamental interests and therefore, carries in itself the future possibility of embracing the whole population'; he also adds that the new 'state embracing the whole of the population' is 'of the same type'.[24] And even the subtlest among Western Marxist theorists are quite incapable of conceiving the Western state as a self-subsistent agency, the embodiment of a *fundamental* (and not derivative) modern principle of association — if they were not thus incapable, of course, they would cease to be Marxists. The one-sidedness of their position comes through even the most ingenious devices of verbal acrobatics. The eminent structuralist writer Nicos Poulantzas, for example, while emphatically asserting that the state is not a 'thing' or a 'mere tool of the dominant classes', then goes on to argue that

> the task of the state is to maintain the unity and cohesion of a social formation divided into classes, and it focuses and epitomizes the class contradictions of the whole social formation in such a way as to sanction and legitimize the interests of the dominant classes of the formation...[25]

Ralph Miliband, another eminent Western Marxist, has argued recently that 'political equality, save in formal terms, is impossible in the conditions of advanced capitalism. Economic life cannot be separated from political life'.[26] What, one would be tempted to ask here, could political equality conceivably mean if not formal equality? Substantive equality refers and can only refer to economics, not politics, to the texture of society and not the single surface of the state. Miliband, like Marxists in general, draws a merely *verbal* distinction between state and society, only to cancel it out immediately in his *substantive* argument.

But while Marxists thus err in obscuring this important distinction, Western political scientists have tended, for a large part, to elevate it into an unscalable wall. They see things through the eyes of society, which means that they tend to be oblivious — verbal acrobatics notwithstanding — of the close interrelationship and complementariness of society and the state. Here, not even the widely accepted substitution of the concept 'political system' for state, though undoubtedly advantageous in many ways, can be seen to have brought about an appreciable change in orientation. David Easton, for example, pioneering advocate of the notion 'political system', yet insists that political science is not interested in power relations in general nor in all kinds of allocation of values, only those that are 'authoritative', i.e. that people 'consider that they must or ought to obey'.[27] Now this could either be defined so widely as to include all 'economic statuses and roles' and 'other advantages available in society', which Easton very significantly insists on keeping separate, or so narrowly as to be severely restricted to the traditional liberal-democratic notion of state. Systems theorists, no doubt, pay more than mere lip-service to the idea of interdependence of the various social systems, yet they are at the same time emphatic in asserting that boundaries must be kept clear and that the political system must be considered autonomous for analytical purposes. Beer and Ulam, for example, have argued that 'political science, like the political process, has a certain autonomy. That is to say, it cannot be reduced to, or explained away by, the concepts and laws of economics . . .'[28] In another seminal work of political science it has been argued that 'on election day' (only?) citizens 'are crossing the boundary from the economy to the polity'.[29] Many advances made in thinking on the part of society-oriented studies, therefore, amount to little more than verbal advances; here it is interdependence that is given *formal* recognition, only to be cancelled out *substantively* once the argument gets under way.

Instrumentalism, the belief that only society, in the sense of an interest-community, is 'natural' to man while the state or 'authority' is only a secondary structure, to be tolerated but kept at bay, is manifested in Western political science in many interesting ways. Two of these will be noted here briefly. One relates to the notion of totalitarianism, which, born in an atmosphere of war, hot and cold, and worked out by such eminent thinkers as Arendt, Talmon, Friedrich and Brzezinski, and Schapiro, still retains its popularity among political scientists today. We are not commenting here on the applicability or otherwise of this notion to the empirical investigation of, say, East European Marxist countries. The point to note is that totalitarianism essentially refers to the penetration of all aspects of social life by state control or total suppression of society by the state. The judgment itself presupposes the *normative* separation of the two entities.

This notion then appears as almost the exact obverse of the Marxist purified state-ideal. While Marxism cannot conceive of society in the Western sense as a legitimate principle of association at all, Western political science cannot entertain the idea that society *itself* can be oppressive; if something is bad, baneful, evil, it must be the state. It is of more than passing interest (and amusement) to contrast this characteristically Western, society-oriented explanation, with its heavy and often exclusive emphasis on the formal *political* features of the countries it calls totalitarian, with the frantic endeavour of anti-Soviet Marxists to explain Soviet rule itself in *societal* terms.[30]

Second and last, we should note the influential tendency in Western (especially Anglo-American) political thinking to explain the liberal-democratic state itself in societal terms, the motivation for which, as has been remarked above, must be accounted for by the underlying belief that only society, and not the state, is ultimately legitimate. In order to justify authority, therefore, one has to approximate it to the scope and pursuit of social agencies, in practice most often economic ones. Marxist political economy has thus its counterpart in Western economic politics, a departure which has clear methodological and normative implications. A few examples will suffice to illustrate the point. Gabriel Almond, an influential pioneer of the study of comparative politics, has drawn a celebrated distinction between four major types of political system. At the top of his list, unmistakably connoting his normative preferences, is to be found the Anglo-American political system, which, Almond asserts, has 'a multi-valued political culture, a rational-calculating, bargaining and experimental' culture where 'the political system is saturated with the atmosphere of the market'. With barely concealed disdain he looks upon the polities of France, Germany and Italy as 'significant survivals' of older cultures, complaining that here 'political actors come to the market not to exchange, compromise and adapt, but to preach, exhort, convert, and transform the political system into something other than a bargaining agency'.[31] (Who, we might well ask, has really done the transformation, the spiriting away of the supposedly independent character of the 'political system'?) Charles Lindblom, an economist by training and exponent of the pluralist theory of politics, has forcefully argued in favour of partisan mutual adjustment or bargaining among interested parties as the most rational policy-making process — in effect restoring, even enhancing, the cherished invisible hand of traditional society-oriented political thought. It is relevant to note here Lindblom's belief — an integral aspect of the instrumentalist principle — that most of us in the West would 'probably sanction any degree of inequality necessary to maintain a government based on consent rather than a high degree of repression'.[32] Again, the basic contrast between the two philosophies could not be put more succinctly. And finally Andrew Shonfield has stated, at the end of his massive study of recent changes in the role of the state in capitalist economies, that 'what is therefore required is the opposite of a bully state — rather a wheeling and dealing type of public authority constantly seeking out allies, probing and manoeuvring for the active consensus'.[33] For him, too, the ideal still remains a state which derives from conscious wants and whose task is confined to the protection and adjustment of societal interests.

It will, however, be appropriate to end our brief survey at this juncture. The purpose of the exercise was to introduce the following studies of the contemporary scene in Europe, and not to conclude on any of the substantive issues raised. The main objective was to illuminate the historical and theoretical background. For this reason it was considered advantageous to highlight the contrasts more than the similarities, to be more polemical than accommodating, more concerned with modes of argument than with the patterns of institutional relationships, remaining thereby perhaps rather more anachronistic than contemporary. Exactly *how* anachronistic the foregoing traditional perspective in terms of state and society is, will be among the tasks of the various contributions in the main body of this book to ascertain. Things today are, to say the least, in an exciting state of flux. In Eastern Europe transcendentalism has been visibly diluted by the intrusion of the societal features of limited private enterprise, the profit motive and market institutions. And Western Europe in turn has witnessed a steady erosion of the formerly more rigid distinction of state and society, with governmental, technocratic and commercial bureaucracies tending to melt into one vast structure. Organised interest-group activities at the highest (national and supra-national) level have been more and more engaging the attention of observers. And finally after successful partial integration within the two blocs we have seen East and West cautiously but steadily building up links of economic contact and co-operation. Are these and similar changes significant from the point of view of the study of politics? Is the elusive dream of 'one Europe' dimly beckoning on a still very distant horizon? Or is the conflict of East and West, of the two opposed philosophical principles, destined nevertheless to continue, under different guises perhaps? Some answers at least to these and related questions will be advanced in the ensuing chapters.

NOTES AND REFERENCES

1. Of greatest relevance are the dichotomies employed by Tönnies and Weber ('community' and 'association'); Talmon ('liberal' and 'totalitarian' democracy); Weldon (the 'organic' and 'mechanistic' theories of the state); and Oakeshott ('teleocracy' and 'nomocracy'). As

contrasted, however, to the approach of these authors, our attitude to the two opposing philosophies purports to be value-neutral as far as possible.
2. J.-J. Rousseau, *The Social Contract* (1762), trans. with intro. by G.D.H. Cole, London, Dent, 1963, pp. 13, 15.
3. J.G. Fichte, *Grundlage des Naturrechts* (1796), *Sämtliche Werke*. Berlin, von Veit, 1845, vol. III, p. 149.
4. *Der geschlossene Handelsstaat* (1800) in *ibid.*, p. 401 (unless otherwise stated, emphasis in direct quotes is in the original).
5. *The Works of Joseph de Maistre*. ed. J. Lively, London, Allen and Unwin, 1965, p. 98.
6. G.W.F. Hegel, *Grundlinien der Philosophie des Rechts* (1821), *Werke*, Frankfurt, Suhrkamp, 1970, vol. 7, p. 399.
7. F. List, *The National System of Political Economy*. (1841), trans. by S.S. Lloyd, London, Longmans, 1928, p. 132.
8. G. Mazzini, *The Duties of Man* (1844), *Life and Writings*. London, Smith, Elder & Co., 1891, vol. IV, pp. 237, 277, 278.
9. E. Burke, *Reflections on the Revolution in France* (1790), intro. by A.J. Grieve, London, Dent, 1960, p. 44.
10. *ibid.* p. 48.
11. J. Bentham, *Constitutional Code*, reprinted in C.W. Everett, *Jeremy Bentham*. New York, Dell, 1966, pp. 236, 245.
12. J. Mill, *An Essay on Government* (1819), Cambridge University Press, 1937, p. 5.
13. P.-J. Proudhon, *Selected Writings*, ed. and intro. by S. Edwards, London, Macmillan, 1970, p. 95.
14. H.J. Laski, *A Grammar of Politics* (1925), London, Allen & Unwin, 1948, pp. 262, 263.
15. G.D.H. Cole, *Social Theory*. London, Methuen, 1920, pp. 34, 140.
16. K. Marx, *Contribution to the Critique of Hegel's Philosophy of Law* (1843), K. Marx and F. Engels, *Collected Works*. London, Lawrence and Wishart, 1975, vol. 3, pp. 30, 31.
17. V.I. Lenin, *What is to be done?* (1902), trans. by S.V. and P. Utechin, London, Panther, 1970, p. 127.
18. *ibid,* p. 188.
19. S. Stojanovic, *Between Ideals and Reality*. New York, Oxford University Press, 1973, p. 42.
20. Z. Brzezinski and S.P. Huntington, *Political Power: USA/USSR*. London, Chatto and Windus, 1964, p.72.
21. *ibid,* p. 409.
22. G. Smith, *Politics in Western Europe: A Comparative Analysis*. London, Heinemann, 1972, p. 8. Cf. also L. Davis, 'The Cost of the New Realism', in H.S. Kariel (ed.) *Frontiers of Democratic Theory*. New York, Random House, 1970, p. 223.
23. Brzezinski and Huntington, *op. cit.*, pp. 91, 103.
24. G. Antalffy, *Basic Problems of State and Society*. Budapest, Akadémiai Kiadó, 1974, pp. 86, 96.
25. N. Poulantzas, *Classes in Contemporary Capitalism*. trans. by D. Fernbach, London, New Left Books, 1975, p. 78.
26. R. Miliband, *The State in Capitalist Society: The Analysis of the Western System of Power*. London, Quartet Books, 1973, p. 237.
27. D. Easton, *The Political System: An Inquiry into the State of Political Science*. New York, Knopf, 1953, p. 132.
28. S.H. Beer and A.B. Ulam (eds.) *Patterns of Government: The Major Political Systems of Europe*. New York, Random House, 1962, p. 30.
29. G.A. Almond and G.B. Powell, *Comparative Politics: A Developmental Approach*. Boston, Little, Brown & Co., 1966, p. 20.
30. For a useful summary of these contrasting views, see D. Lane, *The Socialist Industrial State: Towards a Political Sociology of State Socialism*. London, Allen and Unwin, 1976.
31. G.A. Almond, 'Comparative Political Systems', *The Journal of Politics*. vol. XVIII, no. 3, 1956.
32. C.E. Lindblom, *The Intelligence of Democracy: Decision-Making through Mutual Adjustment*. New York, Free Press, 1965, p. 260. Cf. also R.A. Dahl and C.E. Lindblom, *Politics, Economics and Welfare*. New York, Harper, 1953, pp. 48-9.

33. A. Shonfield, *Modern Capitalism: The Changing Balance of Public and Private Power*, London, Oxford University Press, 1965, p. 389.

SELECT BIBLIOGRAPHY

Barker, E., *Principles of Social and Political Theory*, Oxford, Clarendon, 1951.
Bendix, R., *Nation-Building and Citizenship: Studies of our Changing Social Order*, New York, Wiley, 1964.
Bendix, R. (ed.), *State and Society: A Reader in Comparative Political Sociology*, Berkeley, University of California Press, 1973.
Kariel, H. S., (ed.) *Frontiers of Democratic Theory*, New York, Random House, 1970.
Weber, Max, *The Theory of Social and Economic Organization*, New York, Oxford University Press, 1947.

PART I

State and Society in Western Europe

CHAPTER 1

Interest Groups and the Demand for State Action

Jack Hayward

PRIVATE NEEDS AND PUBLIC INTERVENTION: FIXING THE AGENDA OF
PLURALISTIC POLITICS

The problem with approaching the interface between state and society in terms of traditional concepts like group pressure or state intervention is that they are implicitly unilateral. In reality their relationship is reciprocal and interactive. Our starting point should therefore be in part a recognition that 'in many respects the contemporary state itself creates the society, the public defines what is private . . . Conversely, the society is insulated from the state by the very fact of state action, and the private is preserved from the public by public action.'[1] On the other hand, the state is, in many ways, a creature of its social context. Its role is circumscribed in large measure by the manner in which, at a particular place and time, it is perceived that the state should operate. We take for granted that the state is necessarily in some ways and to a certain extent non-neutral and interventionist. It tries and sometimes succeeds in exerting pressure upon the constituent elements of society, promoting the creation of certain groups and particular political demands, while curbing others. However, we also assume that it will have to sustain sometimes irresistible counter-pressures by society from which it looks to receive indispensable support. The central paradox of the modern state is that it has become active, more comprehensively and in new ways, without having the increased strength to sustain its more ambitious role.

Both the terms 'state' and 'society' have a misleadingly monolithic ring about them. It is a cardinal virtue of the pluralistic paradigm that it disaggregates both of these concepts into the empirical reality of individuals united by institutional structures or shared interests. This highly differentiated view of the political process suffers from a lack of emphasis upon aspects of phenomena that may be united at a deeper level, regarding the distinct as necessarily separated. Nevertheless, it avoids the exclusive concern with disembodied abstraction and does not take formal assertions of the self-evident existence of a 'public interest' at face value. It explores which of a number of rival publics predominates in general or in particular and does not assume that there is more than a minimal common interest between the members of any particular public, such as the citizens of a state.

To give pride of place to the interest-group demands from within society as the principal determinant of the political agenda clearly presumes that one is operating according to the canons of the pluralist paradigm, rather than either the organisational elites or the social class paradigms. While recognising that both society and state are becoming decreasingly pluralistic, one may continue to rely principally upon the pluralist paradigm with respect to First World countries for two reasons. Firstly, it may be the case that, despite the decreasing credibility of the pluralist paradigm, it remains descriptively a less distorted way of defining and interpreting the complex interrelationships of private and public, state and society, elites and masses. Secondly, because the normative dimension cannot be excluded, it implies a certain commitment to a liberal conception of the political process, which may be preferred to the claims of organisational elitism and those of class conflict. This does not mean that one automatically takes on board the liberal dictum that 'Everyone knows his own best interest', interest being regarded simply as a randomly generated datum of individual consciousness. Nor does one necessarily need to subscribe to the view that if individuals do not perceive an interest, they have no interest. 'The pluralist paradigm focuses upon the condition of mobilisation of particular groups and individuals for political action and upon the strategies of influence and the outcomes of action in particular situations.'[2] It should be recognised that the main weakness of the pluralistic-subjectivist focus on interpersonal relations between political actors is that it takes individual, and by extension group, wants and preferences as the starting point of inquiry, without seeking out their historical, institutional or socio-economic origins.

While the pluralist paradigm will be utilised, the insights provided by two rival paradigms should be borne in mind because they help to correct the weaknesses of the approach selected. The organisational elite paradigm conceives of both state and society as highly bureaucratised, with the state regarded as 'a cluster of large-scale organisations, each based upon a separate institutional sector, the elites of which have come to manipulate and control their political base',[3] whether interest groups or social classes. To the extent that this paradigm views the organisational elites not as forming an integrated whole but as a mosaic of semi-autonomous bureaucracies with their own clienteles, it can be regarded as complementary to the pluralist paradigm, although very different in its emphasis.

The Marxist, social class paradigm stresses the framework of economic accumulation based upon the socio-economic structure, which generates incompatible sets of interests called classes, defined from this perspective as 'aggregates of individuals whose life chances are similarly affected by their common position in the division of labour'.[4] In this paradigm, class is not an empirically falsifiable descriptive category but a heuristic assumption. Certain variants of the Marxist paradigm place great and partially autonomous emphasis upon political and ideological structures as against an exclusive reliance upon economic structures. Furthermore, in the writings of Poulantzas and his school,[5] the analysis of the activities of fractions of classes reintroduces a type of interest-group pluralism that reduces the contrast with the pluralist paradigm. So an unsectarian pluralism, conscious of its limitations, can take heart from the fact that some of its severest critics have been compelled to play down the significance of horizontal conflicts between social classes and to recognise the importance of sectional interests, reintroducing a vertical emphasis into the study of state-society relations. Each of the three paradigms of state-society relationships discerned by Alford is thus only partial. Nevertheless, until a problematic synthesis is attained, one may be forgiven for basing oneself upon the paradigm that appears to be most sensitive to the diversity and mutability of human experience considered over decades rather than centuries.

Given that demands for state action or inaction emerge within an environment that regulates expectations of what it is possible and desirable that governments should do, our starting point will be the existence of a society industrialising itself by capitalist methods, in which liberal democracy is becoming accepted as the legitimate way of taking political decisions. There has been a flagrant contradiction between the fact that the people, who were increasingly being recognised as sovereign, were made up of a mass of frequently ill-fed, ill-clothed, ill-housed, ill-educated families, prone to insecurity, disease and unemployment. The intervention of the state, hitherto regarded as a constraint upon freedom, was increasingly considered to be a way of achieving protection, first for those too weak to survive the rigours of a competitive market and then as a way of securing a common minimum of provision to satisfy the basic human needs of all citizens. Self-help had been tried and proved to be successful for only a fortunate few. By the end of the nineteenth century, the tide of the French *Loi Le Chapelier* and the British Combination Acts, which a century earlier had repressed associations of producers as conspiracies against the public interest, was in full retreat. Because many of the groups who needed protection were too weak or ill-organised to champion their neglected interests, it was particularly through the trade union movements and through social democratic parties that their demands were pressed.

However, even after they became an accepted part of the pluralist institutional structure, underprivileged groups were inclined to adopt the more or less violent tactics of direct action, though this was characteristic of France and Italy rather than of Britain and Sweden. It took some time for latent groups to become mobilised into effective associations for the explicit purpose of representing group interests, although this might simply be a by-product of a primary purpose, such as the trade union's desire to strengthen the worker's bargaining power vis à vis his employer. As the processes of industrialisation and urbanisation were pioneered in Britain, it was natural that pressure for increased public intervention should manifest itself in a particularly insistent and pervasive form in Britain, appearing on the margins of the official political institutions of parliament and government.[6] What may have begun as collective bargaining between worker and employer organisations speedily became collective bargaining between both of these organisations and the government, at first sporadically on specific issues and then increasingly on a semi-permanent and general basis.

However, there have been marked differences between the major economic interest groups in their attempts to influence public policy-making. The farm organisations have remained the most parochial and circumscribed in their perspectives, being generally content not to become involved closely in the making of national economic policy. Solidly anchored in particular farm product organisations, they have sought the state's help to protect them from the effects of a highly competitive market and the vagaries of the weather. As long as agriculture was the concern primarily of a semi-subsistence peasantry, though it occupied a large part of the working population and had an impressive electoral weight (leading to the creation of peasant parties, of particular significance in Scandinavia) it was a latent force utilised by others for their purposes. The belated impact of the agricultural revolution, largely concluded in Britain in the early nineteenth century but still incomplete in extensive parts of Western Europe in the 1970s, produced a rapid decline in the farm population. This introduction of capitalism into agriculture was the price that was paid to secure farm incomes — for those who remained on the land — that were at all comparable to incomes being earned in the industrial and service sectors, where the surplus farm population would have to seek employment. While this painful process of geographical and occupational mobility did not occur without some violent unrest — notably in France in the early 1960s — the farm organisations, usually controlled by the farmers who would prosperously survive the transmutation to a market-oriented agriculture, have made a show of resistance to public policy. They have usually been resigned to slowing the process down and extracting the maximum financial concessions in return for controlling the more desperate of their condemned members. The new relationship that they could expect to enjoy with the state (or with the EEC, for those covered by the Common Agricultural Policy) was foreshadowed by the National Farmers Union in Britain, which had become virtually 'incorporated' into government during and since the Second World War, thanks to the embrace of the Ministry of Agriculture.[7]

> He who would understand politics in the large may ponder well the status of labour: a numerically great force in a society adhering to the doctrine of the rule of numbers, yet without proportionate durable political power as a class.[8]

Thus far, the worker would appear to be in the same position as the peasant farmer but the labour movement has not become resigned to the role of a victim of industrialisation. While anarcho-syndicalists in France, Italy and Spain have — apart from brief outbursts — tended to impart to the mainstream trade unions an inclination towards demagogic defeatism, in other countries such as Federal Germany, the Netherlands and Sweden, there is an acceptance of the trade unions as 'social partners' of the government. In part, this difference in behaviour is correlated with the extent of centralisation of the labour movement. For, despite doctrinal commitments and organisational structures implying centralisation, the French union movement (including the Confédération Générale du Travail (CGT) and the British Trades Union Congress (TUC) are decentralised in practice; while the German and Swedish unions attain a high degree of centralised control, enabling the national leadership to enter into commitments that will be honoured. The British trade unions are somewhat nostalgic about their old 'outlaw' status, preferring to avoid legal regulation while at the same time being closely involved in politics through the Labour Party, which acts as a privileged channel for the satisfaction of their demands. The partisan affiliations of the continental unions are less close, at least on the surface, although the Leninist conception of the union as subordinate to the party of the working class ensures that Communist-led trade unions are concerned to promote the demands of their members only when these do not conflict with the party's tactics and strategy. If the development of Eurocommunism has led to a diversification in the behaviour of Communist-led unions, the trade unions with religious (generally Catholic) affiliations have in some cases become secularised to the point where they have ceased to presume any link with their origins. This, notably, is the case with the French Confédération Française Démocratique du Travail (CFDT). It also challenges the capitalist system as such and so cannot be content simply with making piecemeal demands to secure the satisfaction of this or that claim on behalf of its members. Union demands are not insatiable merely because they always want 'more'; in the case of the anti-capitalist unions, they can never be content because they want to see the replacement of the present wealth-producing system by an entirely different one.

When we turn to employer organisations, there is no comparable problem of their relationship to the state, except when the state is controlled by a government seeking to reorganise the wealth-producing system. While farm and labour interests may secure representation in parliamentary assemblies, their governmental contacts tend to be with relatively weak sponsor ministries, Agriculture and Labour, so that their demands are less likely to succeed within the decision-making processes. Business organisations — especially if one considers the less publicised local and regional levels at which chambers of commerce operate — tend to enjoy much more effective and discreet contacts with government agencies and field services. At the centre, as well as usually being able to operate through more powerful sponsor ministries and having their *entrée* into the powerful finance ministry and even to the prime minister, the peak organisations — Confederation of British Industry, Conseil National du Patronat Français, Bundesverband der Deutschen Industrie, Confindustria, Svenska Arbetsgivareföreningen — the trade associations or *Verbände,* the major banking and industrial firms, usually enjoy privileged access and recognition from the public authorities. The need to attain 'quasi-unanimity' hampers the work of peak organisations in particular,[9] but a complex reciprocal legitimation and exchange of services occurs between the business organisations and their ministry which is seldom rivalled by any other interest group. Admittedly, the more demagogic business organisations, representing the mass of small shopkeepers and craftsmen, ranging from the self-employed in family businesses to those who employ only modest numbers, tend to be treated with the patronising contempt reserved for peasants and proletarians, except when they are sufficiently well-organised and militant to command respect. The process of industrialisation is leading to the transformation of many formerly independent businessmen into sub-contracting satellites of the larger firms. This means that — as in the case of the peasantry — provided their transformation can be achieved without too much disturbance, they can be treated with benign neglect. It is usually sufficient to handle them with fiscal leniency and protect them from the full rigours of competition, slowing down but not halting their demise as independent entrepreneurs.

These major interest groups remain in close touch with government. This is not always true of the many traditional and newborn professional associations of lawyers, doctors, teachers, architects, town planners and so forth, which have grown in number and diversity alongside the expanding role of the state. Furthermore, there are hundreds of thousands of voluntary associations, which may from time to time make demands upon the state.

Even in a country like France, not noted for the richness of its associative life, it has been estimated that over the decade 1967-76 an average of about 25,000 voluntary associations — mostly local in character — were established annually, compared with a mere 1000 annually in the interwar period. To take a particular example, since the 1960s the industrialised countries of non-communist Europe have witnessed the rapid growth in associations to protect various aspects of the environment from pollution. Because they have not as a rule yet acquired the status of the major sectional vested interests, entitling them to be officially involved in the making of public policy, they are compelled to rely heavily on the weapon of the weak: public campaigning.[10] Sometimes, they have used elections — especially local elections, as was the case in France in 1977 — to attract attention to their demands, forcing the ecological issue onto the political agenda by proving their capacity to mobilise some of the voters who had become disenchanted with the conventional political parties. At other times disruptive direct action has been used against road developments or nuclear installations, recalling the tactics adopted by the Campaign for Nuclear Disarmament in Britain in the years after 1957. However, whereas the latter campaign proved unsuccessful, many of the more modest recent public campaigns have met with success.

This contemporary preoccupation with the preservation of the environment from the side-effects of industrialisation and urbanisation is just part of a wider shift of emphasis away from the types of demand centred on economic issues to those centred upon social and cultural issues. Seen in historical perspective, the initial pressures in the eighteenth and nineteenth centuries had a strong civil and religious rights emphasis, with the struggle to secure a variety of freedoms which could be defended in a court of law. While this struggle has continued into the twentieth century, political rights became an increasing preoccupation, with manhood suffrage focusing attention in the nineteenth and women's suffrage in the twentieth century. However, universal suffrage did not, of itself, destroy social and economic inequalities; it simply ignored them. While the substantial increases in public expenditure that have accompanied the attempt to deal with particular public needs in response to popular pressure (now armed with the vote) are indicative of the acceptance of a wider role for the state, important issues of principle remain controversial. Are the social rights to employment, health, education in youth and security in old age, for example, entitlements to a socially guaranteed *minimum* of public provision, with opportunities to attain a higher level of provision left to the personal exertions of each individual and family? Or are such rights to be regarded as implying a comprehensive, classless, 'common good', *maximum* provision for all? This is a central issue between the proponents of a narrowly defined liberal democracy and those who seek to press the consequences of democracy to the fullest social democratic extent.

THE DIRECT REPRESENTATION OF INTERESTS

Although interest groups may channel their demands into the political process through the political parties, they do not necessarily use a partisan mediator and frequently press their case directly upon the political and administrative decision-makers. Particularly where the capacity of political parties to aggregate interests is low, because they are too numerous, undisciplined and ideologically intransigent to perform this function, the interest groups' peak organisations may be capable of achieving a more effective aggregation of sectional interests. They have themselves frequently to reconcile highly divergent interests and this accustoms the peak organisations to take a broader and longer-term view of their members' interests than is generally recognised. On the other hand, the more specific groups may find that given the diversified and fragmented nature of modern government, they are able to establish close and stable bilateral relationships with the relevant part of the state apparatus charged with regulating their activities. At this point the organisational elite paradigm becomes highly relevant to the understanding of the official half of the clientelistic relations that develop betwen parts of the state bureaucracy and particular sectional interests. It is not a case of public versus private interest but of agreement and disagreement about what the public interest amounts to in a particular case. Because of the bureaucracy's greater capacity to cast a veil of secrecy over its own disagreements — with Britain at one extreme of pathological secretiveness and Sweden at the opposite extreme — it is normally at an advantage in dealings with interest groups. However,

> the dividing line in regard to a proposed solution seldom runs between administrators and representatives of private interests; instead both groups are split and some members of each group align with some of their counterparts. A lack of unanimity in the bureaucracy leads to further fragmentation of power and most of the time will lend more weight to outside pressures.[11]

Bureaucratic elite perception of the pressures exerted by interest groups varies between countries. A study undertaken in the 1970s enables us to compare the attitude of senior civil servants in five countries towards interest groups. Table 1.1 shows that senior Italian officials are clearly the most likely to think that the public interest will be threatened by interest groups, but even in their case only a quarter consider that close contact with

TABLE 1.1　　　　　　　*Bureaucratic perception of interest groups (%)*[12]

	Britain	Germany	Sweden	Netherlands	Italy
1. Agree with view that the general welfare of the country is seriously endangered by the continual clash of particularistic interest groups.	21	24	25	57	89
2. Relations of close collaboration between a ministry and the groups or sectors most affected by its activity are improper and unnecessary.	4	2	5	14	24

their interest-group clientele is undesirable. The Netherlands occupies an intermediate position, with over half Dutch senior civil servants regarding interest-group conflicts as menacing the public good but only one in seven being opposed to intimate links with their own particular groups. Dutch senior officials regard employer organisations as less influential than trade unions and more influential than farm organisations but at the same time two-thirds of Dutch senior officials do not consider that there is any conflict of interest between government and private enterprise.[13] This reminds us of the class dimension, which shapes the way in which the state's permanent servants — and sometimes masters — differentiate between interest groups to the extent that they do or do not conform with basic social values. Where there is a substantial consensus over these values, as is the case in Britain, Germany and Sweden, there is less fear of interest-group conflict, as well as an almost unanimous readiness to accept a close, permanent and formal collaboration between senior officials and their interest-group clientele.

The case of France — not dealt with in the study referred to — is particularly significant because it involves the clash between a self-assertive state, where senior civil servants are profoundly imbued with a sense that they incarnate the public interest, and militant interest groups, who readily identify the public interest with their sectional interests. A survey of heads of division (*directeurs*) of Paris ministries in 1968-70 indicates that there was frequent contact between them and interest-group representatives: 26 per cent on almost a daily basis, with a further 44 per cent replying that such meetings took place 'very often' (making 70 per cent in all); while only 11 per cent said that they never had any meetings with interest groups. The *directeurs* considered that the main advantages of such contacts were that they facilitated the implementation and — to a lesser extent — the formulation of policy, as well as enabling the government to anticipate opposition.

Lesser advantages were the opportunity to acquire information from the interest groups and the ability to explain to the groups decisions that had already been taken. If the virtue of contact with the interest groups consisted essentially in disarming opposition to *faits accomplis,* the principal disadvantages were that the leakage of information led to the mobilisation of opposition to the action contemplated by the government; that constant pressure prevented the 'correct decision' being taken; lastly, officials resented the 'time wasted' by such meetings.[14]

However, we have seen earlier that the various interest groups cannot expect the same reception from the public authorities. Suleiman has acutely perceived the significance of the French distinction between 'pressure groups' and 'lobbies' on the one hand, and the 'professional organisations' on the other.[15] What is the criterion by which the former are dismissed as sinister sectional interests, unrepresentative, retrograde and demagogic, which threaten the public interest, while the latter are respectable, representative and dynamic? It is simple. Those groups that collaborate with the embodiments of *raison d'état* and act as their (junior) social partners have attributed to them the seal of legitimacy. The leaders of such acquiescent pressurised groups become state-sanctioned notables. They can at best persuade their spending-sponsor ministry to identify to some extent with the group's goals and absorb some of its values, in return for giving the division or ministry support in intra-administrative conflicts or vis à vis the politicians. At worst, the group may become a semiautonomous extension of the state apparatus, providing assistance in the implementation of public policies over which it has little or no influence. Weak and fragmented groups are much more at the mercy of the state's officials, whereas the major economic interests, notably big business, are able to hold their own. Thanks to a common educational background in the *grandes écoles,* the frequency with which senior officials from the *grands corps* move into public and private corporations in mid-career, the ability to mobilise substantial financial resources and to hire the staff to present well-argued memoranda in support of their case, big business — in sharp contrast with small business, as well as other interests — not only gets a hearing; it gets its way more frequently than other French interest groups under the Fifth Republic. This may not be so important in terms of detailed concessions as in the general presumption — characteristic of capitalist countries — that the state must sustain the instruments by which wealth is accumulated; upon which public expenditure, when it is not directly servicing the wealth-producing system, is regarded as being little better than parasitical.

In sharp contrast with the French style of administrative—interest group relations but exemplifying the close connections between big business and government departments, the close *clientela* relationships traced by La-

Palombara in the early 1960s between the Italian Ministry of Industry and Commerce and Confindustria illustrates a situation of reverse dependence in which the ministry was colonised by an interest group. The Italian state was doubly weak. The appearance of Christian Democratic hegemony was dissipated by factionalism, while a plethoric but incompetent bureaucracy relied upon the outside interests for indispensable information, expertise and political support. The fragmentation of political control attained such proportions that it was not so much a case of the ministry sponsoring demands from a major interest group but of the group using its influence on behalf of the ministry.[16] However, in Italy as elsewhere, the Treasury and Finance Ministries tend to be less permeable by pressure-group influence than are the sponsor-spending ministries, with their close clientele relationships, particularly when one descends to particular specialist divisions within the ministries. Furthermore, Confindustria in the 1970s was not the power it was in the 1950s. It was always a rather exceptional case, closely approximating in its heyday to what Marxists have regarded as the normal relationship between economic power and political—administrative power in capitalist society.

As a corrective to the tendency of functional representation to assume a bilateral, informal and ad hoc character (thereby accentuating the fragmentation of an ever—extending frontier between state and society) since the end of the First World War various European countries have experimented with functionally representative Economic Councils. Such Councils provided the major interest groups with an opportunity to engage in multilateral bargaining, a higher, horizontal level of interest aggregation than was possible in the limited forms of relationship that had developed spontaneously. Those who had ambitious hopes of this institutional innovation, expected that it would substitute for the irresponsible and intransigent assertion of sectional interest, habitually placated by improvised expedients, a disposition to arrive at comprehensive compromises in a longer-term perspective. A new breed of socio-economic statesmen would emerge who would be less partisan than their political counterparts. Realists, they would be more willing to confine their demands upon the state to the state's capacity to satisfy them. It was furthermore presumed that in return for receiving seats on such a Council, the mischief-making potentialities of interest-group leaders would be curbed. In return for an institutionalised participation in the political process, the interest groups might not challenge the decisions it produced. The Weimar Republic Wirtschaftsrat led the way after the First World War but the post-Second World War Federal German Republic has been the only one of the six original EEC members to refuse to establish an Economic Council, although the influential Bavarian Senate is functionally representative. In contrast, the French National Economic

Council, set up in 1925, survived its abolition by the Vichy regime to re-emerge as an Economic Council in the Fourth Republic and an Economic and Social Council in the Fifth Republic.[17]

There has been a great deal of uneasiness about the institution of such formal functionally representative bodies because they appear to challenge the democratic basis of legitimate authority: universal suffrage. When they are given constitutional status, as was the French Council in 1946 and the comparable Italian National Council of Economy and Labour in 1957, it is as a consultative third chamber of parliament. (In the French case, there was an abortive attempt by General de Gaulle in 1969 to amalgamate the second and third chambers, which stirred up so much hostility on the part of the interest groups that this contributed to the popular rejection of the proposal at a referendum and de Gaulle's resignation.) The competence of these Councils varies, but they rely primarily on their capacity to initiate consideration of issues, rather than simply waiting for the government to consult them. However, the Italian Council has seldom utilised its right to initiate legislation and the French Council does not have such a power. They differ in the range of issues with which they concern themselves. All take part in the processes of economic planning but the Dutch Social and Economic Council (created in 1950) devoted much of its time — for a while with some success, acting in conjunction with the Foundation of Labour — to the specific problems of a national incomes policy. There have always been isolated voices in Britain calling for the establishment of such a Council, aimed at institutionalising the new powers that be, but thus far Britain has been content with the much more modest National Economic Development Council (established in 1962). Unless one is prepared to go as far as Yugoslavia in the direction of functional representation, which is tantamount to saying that one desires an entirely different political regime, most people would agree that to tempt powerful interest-group leaders into a weak second or third chamber is merely tinkering with political institutions; it will have no significant effect on the major problem, which is adapting state institutions to the needs of contemporary society.

CONFRONTATION, CONSULTATION AND CO-OPTATION

In the British heartland of political liberalism, state 'intervention' into what are regarded as the private affairs of the individuals who constitute society has been resisted since the seventeenth century. Writing against a background of an anachronistic but pervasive traditionalist paternalism in politics and corporatist regulation in the British economy, Jeremy Bentham asserted the intrinsic incompetence of government to know what was in the individual's interest.

> It is a standing topic of complaint that a man knows too little of himself. Be it so: but is it so certain that the legislator must know more? . . . It is only with respect to these broad lines of conduct in which all persons or a very large and permanent description of persons may be in a way to engage, that he [the legislator] can have any pretence for interference; and even here the propriety of his interference will, in most instances, lie very open to dispute.[18]

While this liberating message doubtless contributed to the removal of the statutory and corporate constraints upon the new forces of bourgeois industrialism that were to produce increased wealth and personal liberty as well as increased squalor and personal insecurity, the democracy that it brought in its wake generated a demand for more state intervention. Far from the state meddling where it was not wanted, it was very reluctantly that the most liberal of European countries responded to the insistent popular demands. Despite Herbert Spencer's attempt to defend a 'limited liability' view of the state against the ill-informed legislators who pander to the desires of an ignorant electorate by taxing the deserving rich to help the undeserving poor,[19] the gradual inroads of piecemeal reform championed by radicals and socialists partially deprived the propertied classes of their power and in part helped to perpetuate that power. Notwithstanding periodic attempts at counterattack, this process of 'dynamic conservatism' has continued with only the briefest setbacks throughout the twentieth century in Britain.

Particularly when what was involved was not merely a clash between particular individuals and the state but a conflict among classes or major sectional interests, the path of peaceful parliamentary reform was frequently either not available or not efficacious. The state could not plausibly sustain the pretence of being an impartial arbiter between them. While this problem was sometimes present in the countries of predominantly Protestant North-West Europe, it was much more endemic in the countries of predominantly Catholic South-West Europe. Here, the clash between the intransigent assertion of a would-be absolute state power, allied to the dominant classes and elites, and the discontented underprivileged groups or classes that seek to impede the decisions they are impotent to prevent, leads to outbursts of more or less violent direct action. 'To provoke a crisis is to compel the attention of excessively remote and deaf public authorities. As it is a way — almost the only one — to communicate, every Frenchman is a potential rioter.' These sentiments of the right-wing French Minister of Education in May 1968 could be extended, even if in a diluted form, to other European countries. As he goes on:

Social violence has lost the blind and almost desperate brutality that it had under the Old Régime. It has virtually been incorporated into ordinary social life. There is hardly a single achievement of the workers — wages, paid holidays, social security, length of workweek and tempo of workrate — that has not been torn from their private or state employers at the end of a serious crisis. How could workers not be tempted to join trade unions committed to confrontation rather than concertation?[20]

These unpredictable outbreaks bypass the formal channels that may exist for the expression of grievance. Such reactions tend initially to be spontaneous explosions of unorganised popular resentment, but in the advanced industrial societies they often quite quickly assume an organised form when they are not brutally repressed. Confronted by such opposition from particular segments of society, some of those who control the state are inclined to consider it simply as a problem of order, a matter of enforcing the law. However, this involves a double difficulty. The law is proving an increasingly ill-adapted regulatory instrument to deal with the ever-extending spheres of human conduct and socio-economic activity it endeavours to embrace. Furthermore, it is often very difficult to enforce the law against the determined opposition or the non-co-operation of even small minorities, much less the resistance of strategically well-placed producer groups who exercise a stranglehold over the supply of indispensable public or private services. Attempts to invoke the democratic basis of state authority in order to deny legitimacy to such assertions of selfish group interest generally prove fruitless unless the public authorities consider that they can utilise their coercive power to enforce their will, at least as a last resort. However, it is precisely to avoid such dramatic confrontations that recourse is had to the resources of consultation and co-operation.

To obtain the prior consent of the interested parties has become a prime consideration of public decision-makers, to the point where the traditional distinction between 'advice' and 'decision' has been blurred, even if it has seldom been blotted out. This has led to the proliferation of (literally) innumerable consultative bodies of a formal and informal kind at the national, regional and local levels, created by government 'to improve communication within the administration and to avoid or smooth over conflicts with the administered, once they are well enough organised to conquer or to be groomed into the status of consultative partners of government.'[21] The numbers of such consultative bodies in any case are bound to be misleading because they vary a great deal in their effectiveness. To abolish the inactive or uninfluential bodies would give offence to the groups represented on them, so they are seldom scrapped even when they no longer meet. In addition, a particular consultative committee will fluctuate in importance as circumstances change, so that any attempt at evaluation is liable to be out of date almost as soon as it is made. At times of crisis, even the most suspicious official opponent of the encroachment by private interests upon state prerogatives will be ready to welcome the assistance of co-operative interest groups, especially if they are capable of entering into binding commitments on behalf of their members. However, at all times the public authorities try to control the composition of these bodies, to ensure that they receive the kind of advice they would welcome. If state control becomes too obvious and state influence too unilateral, such bodies loose their virtue of discouraging interests from taking the law into their own hands. While the leaders who are nominated to sit on these bodies may be so flattered that they do not press demands vigorously, their members will become restive unless concessions are forthcoming. The implicit bargaining between segments of the state and segments of society that may be respectably shrouded in what purports to be an exchange of information, thus represents a vital link in the interpenetration — predicated on reciprocal influence — of state and society.

The institutionalisation of the interdependence between the public authorities and the interest groups may, in certain spheres, develop to the extent of the partial and informal 'incorporation' of groups into the machinery of government. The degree of involvement by interest-group leaders in public decision-making and policy implementation, their willingness to subordinate their sectional interest to what they accept as the public interest, may be such that they cease to be genuinely independent of the state. Such an arrangement has great advantages for the state, as it does not need to create an unwieldy bureaucracy to achieve the mobilisation of support for public policies but can operate in a functionally decentralised fashion. However, only those groups that have something to offer the state are candidates for such virtual 'incorporation'. Those that are simply making demands upon it, the pure pressure groups, are *persona non grata.* As far as the interest groups are concerned, their official and intimate association with the public authorities allows them more readily to present their particularistic demands as consonant with the public interest than would be the case if they remained 'unincorporated'. The position of the leaders of such groups is bound to be ambiguous and even equivocal. To retain their credibility with their members, they must obtain benefits from this sacrifice of part of their freedom of action; while to maintain their credibility with the public authorities, they must be able to guarantee the good conduct of their members. When the interest groups are themselves centralised, with power concentrated in the hands of peak organisation leaders, it is possible for the latter to become de facto agents of public policy. For this reason, governments have frequently fostered such organisations and done their best to build up the standing of their leaders as recognised spokesmen for particular policies. However, should the de facto 'incorporation' of group leaders into the state apparatus lead to loss of support from the rank and file, the discredited interest-group organisations will cease to function as consensual mediators between society and state, with a consequent recourse by disgruntled groups to direct action.

SATISFYING AND CURBING PUBLIC EXPECTATIONS

The apparently irresistible pressure of social demand upon the state has been reflected in the endemic problem of inflation in most liberal—democratic countries of Europe and the escalation of public expenditure as governments seek to satisfy these ever-growing needs. The volume and variety of human wants, which are converted into political demands by the interest groups and political parties, have led to the phenomenon of 'demand input overload', with which governments seem increasingly incapable of dealing. Instead of Herbert Spencer's ideal of the limited-liability company, some contemporary states have become 'a sort of unlimited-liability insurance company, in the business of insuring all persons at all times against every conceivable risk'; with the consequence that 'To be held responsible for everything is to feel compelled to intervene in everything'.[22] To exacerbate the problem further, this increase in public expectations has coincided with some spectacular vindications of Jeremy Bentham's presumption of the incompetence of government. So we have an inherently unstable situation in which the supply of public goods is not capable of keeping pace with the demand for them. In particular, states like Italy and Britain ineffectively face 'coercive groups' making 'non-negotiable demands for more than a country's whole output'.[23] A 'social contract', when it can be achieved, proves all too ephemeral, except in the highly corporatised polities of Scandinavia, Austria and the Netherlands. As voters, many of those who enthusiastically make exorbitant demands upon government convert their resentment against increased taxation into hostile votes against the parties in office. However, they appear to be far more sensitive to the visibility of taxation than to its overall level or even its rate of increase. Voter backlash has been most evident in countries like Britain and the Scandinavian countries where a high proportion of taxes take the visible and direct form of personal income and property taxes, rather than countries like France and Italy where the indirect form of sales and value added taxes, corporate income, profit and payroll taxes, predominate.[24]

If the performance of government cannot be improved through the type of economic and social planning developed by France in the postwar period, alternative ways of reducing public expectations may be expected to emerge. Recourse to the market involves an attempt to reassert the separation between state and societal remedies for economic and political problems, transferring many of these problems back from the state to society. Recourse to an informal 'neo-corporatism', by contrast, seeks to accentuate the solidarity between state and society, strengthening the links between 'public' and 'private' institutions, so that they can ideally settle the major policy issues before they become contentious problems. The resurgence of monetarist economic policies into fashion is one symptom of this response to the predicament of the state's incapacity to fulfil society's expectations. What the state has not succeeded in doing is simply left to the market, with no particular individuals being held responsible for the consequences because it is no one's responsibility to ensure that, for example, there is full employment.

An alternative response assumes the form of a non-fascist 'corporatism' (with Sweden rather than interwar Italy as a model) as a way of preventing 'demand input overload' by attaining the consensus about the allocation of resources that the pluralist approach has failed to achieve. As one of the analysts of this phenomenon has put the contrast:

> both pluralists and corporatists recognise, accept and attempt to cope with the growing structural differentiation and interest diversity of the modern polity, but they offer opposing political remedies and divergent images of the institutional form that such a modern system of interest representation will take. The former suggest spontaneous formation, numerical proliferation, horizontal extension and competitive interaction; the latter advocate controlled emergence, quantitative limitation, vertical stratification and complementary interdependence. Pluralists place their faith in the shifting balance of mechanically intersecting forces; corporatists appeal to the functional adjustment of an organically interdependent whole.[25]

An assessment of this recourse to revised versions of old remedies is, for the present, premature and has implications well beyond the demands by interest groups upon the state.

NOTES AND REFERENCES

1. Robert R. Alford, 'Paradigms of Relations between State and Society' in Léon Lindberg et al., Stress and Contradiction in Modern Capitalism, Lexington, Mass., Lexington Books, 1975, p. 155.
2. ibid, p. 150.
3. ibid, p. 147.
4. Isaac D. Balbus, 'The Concept of Interest in Pluralist and Marxist Analysis', Politics and Society, Vol. I, February 1971, p. 168.

5. See the English translations of the major works by Nicos Poulantzas, *Political Power and Social Classes*, London, New Left Books, 1973; *Fascism and Dictatorship*, London, New Left Books, 1974; and *Classes in Contemporary Capitalism*, London, New Left Books, 1975. See also Nicos Poulantzas (ed.), *La Crise de l'Etat*, Paris, Presses Universitaires de France, 1976.
6. Consult in particular Samuel H. Beer, *Modern British Politics. A Study of Parties and Pressure Groups*, London, Faber and Faber, 1965, and Graham Wootton, *Pressure Groups in Britain, 1720-1970*, London, Allen Lane, 1975.
7. See Peter Self and Herbert J. Storing, *The State and the Farmer*, London, Allen and Unwin, 1962, and Gordon Wright, *Rural Revolution in France. The Peasantry in the Twentieth Century*, London, Oxford University Press, 1964.
8. V.O. Key, Jr, *Politics, Parties and Pressure Groups*, New York, Crowell, 1947, p. 53.
9. Jack Hayward, 'Employer Associations and the State in France and Britain' in Steven J. Warnecke and Ezra N. Suleiman (eds), *Industrial Policies in Western Europe*, New York, Praeger, 1975, pp. 131-3. See also studies of some peak organisations: Wyn Grant and David Marsh, *The CBI*, London, Hodder and Stoughton, 1977; Henry W. Ehrmann, *Organized Business in France*, Princeton, N.J., Princeton University Press, 1957; Gerard Braunthal, *The Federation of German Industry in Politics*, Ithaca, N.Y., Cornell University Press, 1965; Joseph LaPalombara, *Interest Groups in Italian Politics*, Princeton, N.J., Princeton University Press, 1964, especially Chapter 8.
10. See Richard Kimber and Jeremy J. Richardson (eds), *Campaigning for the Environment*, London, Routledge and Kegan Paul, 1974.
11. Henry W. Ehrmann, 'French Bureaucracy and Organized Interests', *Administrative Science Quarterly*, Vol. V, no. 4, 1961, p. 548.
12. Source: adapted from Tables 11 and 12 of Samuel Eldersveld *et al.*, 'Elite perceptions of the political process in the Netherlands, looked at in comparative perspective' in Mattei Dogan (ed.), *The Mandarins of Western Europe. The Political Role of Top Civil Servants*, New York, Halstead Press, 1975, pp. 149-50.
13. *ibid.*, Tables 9 and 10, pp. 144, 147.
14. Ezra N. Suleiman, *Politics, Power and Bureaucracy in France. The Administrative Elite*, Princeton, N.J., Princeton University Press, 1974, pp. 324-8.
15. *ibid.*, pp. 337-59.
16. LaPalombara, *op. cit.*, pp. 266-300.
17. Jack Hayward, *Private Interests and Public Policy. The Experience of the French Economic and Social Council*, London, Longmans, 1966.
18. Jeremy Bentham, *An Introduction to the Principles of Morals and Legislation*, (1789) in *The Collected Works of Jeremy Bentham*, ed. Burns and Hart, London, The Athlone Press, 1970, p. 290.
19. Herbert Spencer, *The Man versus the State* (1884) Harmondsworth, Pelican, 1969.
20. Alain Peyrefitte, *Le Mal Français*, Paris, Plon, 1976, p. 376.
21. Jack Hayward, *The One and Indivisible French Republic*, London, Weidenfeld and Nicolson, 1973, p. 52. For a detailed study of the situation, particularly in France but also in some of the major European states, see Georges Langrod (ed.), *La Consultation dans l'Administration Contemporaine*, Paris, Cujas, 1972. On France, see Suleiman, *op. cit.*, pp. 330-6; on Norway, see J. Higley *et al* in Dogan, *op. cit.*, pp. 261-4.
22. Anthony King, 'Overload: problems of governing in the 1970s', *Political Studies*, Vol. XXXIII, nos 2-3, June—September 1975, pp. 286-7.
23. Samuel Brittan, 'The Economic Contradictions of Democracy', *The British Journal of Political Science*, Vol V, no. 2, April 1975, p. 145; cf. pp. 129, 142-5. For a more profound analysis of this problem, see Fred Hirsch, *Social Limits to Growth*, London, Routledge and Kegan Paul, 1977.
24. Harold L. Wilensky, *The 'New Corporatism', Centralization and the Welfare State*, London, Beverly Hills, Sage Professional Papers, 06-020, Vol. 2, 1976, pp. 14-21.
25. Philippe C. Schmitter, 'Still the Century of Corporatism?' in F.B. Pike and T. Stritch (eds), *The New Corporatism. Social-Political Structures in the Iberian World*, London, University of Notre Dame Press, 1974, p. 97. See also Wilensky, *op. cit.*, p. 21-3 and J.T.

Winkler, 'Corporatism', *Archives Européennes de Sociologie,* Vol. XVII, 1976, pp. 100-36.

SELECT BIBLIOGRAPHY

Comparative Political Studies, Vol. X, No. 1, April 1977, special issue on 'Corporatism and Policy-Making in Contemporary Western Europe'.

Griffiths, R.T., *Government, Business and Labour in European Capitalism,* London, Europotentials Press, 1977.

Lindberg, Léon *et al., Stress and Contradiction in Modern Capitalism,* Lexington, Mass., Lexington Books, 1975.

Meynaud, Jean, *Nouvelles Etudes sur les Groupes de Pression en France,* Paris, A. Colin, 1962.

Rose, Richard and Peters, B. Guy, *Can Government go Bankrupt? The Challenge to Public Policy,* New York, Basic Books, 1978.

Vernon, Raymond (ed.), *Big Business and the State, Changing Relations in Western Europe,* Cambridge, Mass., Harvard University Press, 1974.

Warnecke, Steven J. and Suleiman, Ezra N. (eds), *Industrial Policies in Western Europe,* New York, Praeger, 1975.

CHAPTER 2

Political Parties and Government Decision-Making

M. A. Wheaton

'Of all the instruments designed by man for the attainment of his political aims perhaps none has proved so enduring as a political party.'[1] Political scientists and sociologists have written a great deal about the role of political parties in modern societies. Political parties are seen as representatives of particular economic or sectional interests, as aggregators of group demands, as socialising agencies, or as a source of recruitment for political leadership.[2] The political parties of Western Europe perform these functions in a variety of ways and with differing degrees of success. They encompass a wide variety of traditions rooted in particular historical and cultural experiences and although there are many variations on a theme it is possible to identify certain common causes of party development and certain common party types. Those parties now dominating the politics of Western Europe have shown a remarkable resilience, one of the most important features of European party systems being how little their election fortunes have actually changed.[3] Viewed in the context of the last thirty years this is perhaps true, for continuity of existence remains the order of the day, although over relatively short periods of time particular parties' fortunes may vary considerably, which will have a crucial effect upon government formation and decision-making in the political system. Following some general observations on the role of political parties, attention will be concentrated — although not exclusively — on the Benelux countries, Italy, France and West Germany.

FORMATIVE INFLUENCES ON PARTY SYSTEMS

What are the common factors that have helped to create certain party types in Western Europe? Firstly, we may consider the impact of religion on politics, for religious commitment is still an important influence in determining party patterns. This does not necessarily mean, of course, that religious issues are of importance in particular systems, although they certainly were in the past, but rather that an individual's religious commitment is an important factor in determining his reaction to political issues. The pattern of impact of religion upon politics very much depends on the balance of Catholicism and Protestantism, for the former has been much more active in the political arena than the latter. The Catholic Church, as represented by the Vatican, has been concerned in recent times to advance certain social doctrines into the political arena[4] and to combat the forces of communism and socialism. The interest of the Church in politics often set up strong anti-clerical tendencies and created parties identified with or fundamentally against Church interests, notably in Austria. In almost wholly Catholic Italy, the Church's eventual blessing of the Popular Party and later the Christian Democratic Party created a close identification between Church and party interests, with the might of the Church being thrown behind the political party during election periods. This certainly had the effect of bringing Church identification to the fore, and gaining much working-class support for the Christian Democrats. In France, however, where religious conflicts have run deep, the Catholic Church has failed to sustain a party clearly identified with it, as the failure of the Mouvement Républicain Populaire (MRP) has shown. Nonetheless, French Catholicism, traditionally identified with conservatism, still provides much support for the parties of the Right and Centre, although this has tended to decline in the 1970s, since the creation of the new Socialist Party.

In other European states, such as Germany and the Netherlands, Catholicism and Protestantism exist side by side. In Germany, Christian Democracy is an alliance between these two churches, and the direct influence of the Church on politics is much more limited than in the Italian case. Nonetheless, the Catholic Church did provide an important base for Christian Democracy, although this influence has undoubtedly lessened. In the Netherlands, where Catholics and Protestants exist in almost equal numbers, religious affiliation has had an important influence on party development in the postwar period, and a large Catholic party and two smaller Protestant parties have continued a successful existence. The Netherlands perhaps provides one of the few examples in Western Europe of a long and active involvement by the Protestant churches in politics.[5] Even here, however, the religious factor has been on the decline and the Catholic and Protestant parties were finally, out of self-preservation, forced to merge into a Christian Democratic Alliance in 1976. In countries that are almost wholly Protestant, there has been little close identification between the Church and specific parties, partly because the goals of Protestantism were never so all-embracing as Catholicism, and partly because powerful anti-clerical traditions did not arise.

Secondly, we may consider the importance of rural and urban development, for in Western Europe the continued existence of large rural populations has had an important influence on the development and operation of party systems. The difference in the economic status of the rural communities of the North East of Italy and the Central Region goes a long way in explaining why the former is a strongly Christian Democratic area while the latter is an area of Communist Party domination. Equally, in France, the poorer peasantry have often given their support to the communist or socialist parties as a protest against central government's policies. In other European societies, particularly those of Scandinavia, rural/urban contrasts have been great and there remained a deep cleavage between the two. This has historically given rise to many agrarian-type parties, often of a conservative kind, which defend their particular interests. Latterly however, Scandinavia has witnessed the growth of a number of Centre parties which have succeeded in creating a new image of rural conservatism.

Thirdly, as we may have considerable division between urban and rural societies, so we may have considerable linguistic or cultural differences within a particular state's boundaries. For the most part, European state boundaries encompass monolinguistic societies, yet within a number of states there exist language or cultural minorities. In the Basque region of Spain, Brittany in France and the German-speaking area of the Italian South Tyrol, groups have from time to time used violent means of advocating their rights, although for the most part linguistic minorities have sought to advance their demands by more conventional means. In Switzerland linguistic differences have largely been catered for by the highly decentralised cantonal system and there are no important linguistic parties.[6] Modern Belgium is the most obvious example of a state where linguistic and cultural issues have had an important bearing on the modern party system, where both the Flemish *Volksunie* and the French-speaking *Rassemblement Wallon* have achieved considerable success. But the appearance of these linguistic parties is not necessarily an indication of the importance of linguistic division, in that the issue is closely related to the historic social and economic deprivation of the Flemish provinces.[7]

Finally, we may consider the influence of social class on politics, for class politics lies at the basis of many of the modern European political parties. Most European social democratic parties began life as parties with a restricted appeal to working-class interests, although their appeal in modern times is to a much broader range of the electorate. The German Social Democratic Party formally recognised its changed role in adopting the Bad Godesberg Programme of 1959, when it declared itself to be the 'party of the whole people' and no longer a party of the working class. Other European socialist parties have trod a similar path towards broadening their appeal, yet still the basis of their following lies in a solid core of working-class support. The various conservative parties of Europe have a clear identification with the middle and upper classes, although this is often reinforced by a religious attraction in the case of christian democracy, which helps to secure support for those parties beyond the confines of a narrow class appeal. Voting patterns still show a surprising degree of class identification and while in no European society can political parties be regarded as simply vehicles for particular class values, nonetheless class perceptions underpin many of the modern party systems. Although in Scandinavia, Holland and Germany class conflict has largely ceased as a major input into the system, in such countries as France, Italy and Great Britain class conflict is still a major contributory factor to political perceptions and goes beyond mere party rhetoric.

All these factors operate together in a variety of complex ways to produce the modern party systems. How these factors affect each society varies with the relative importance of particular issues, the degree to which differences may be accommodated into a relatively homogenous society, or the degree to which these factors have helped to produce internal divisions of a sectional kind.

Apart from what we may describe as the societal factors outlined above, it is important to mention that specific constitutional provisions may themselves have an important influence on the nature of party systems. The importance of electoral systems and in particular the effect of proportional representation in helping to create multi-party systems are a familiar theme of Duverger's classic, *Political Parties*. While the relationship between PR systems and multi-party systems may not be so automatic as Duverger suggested, nonetheless such systems allow smaller political parties a much greater chance of success. In Germany, the particular electoral provision requiring a 5 per cent national vote in order to secure representation has had an important effect in eliminating many small or regional parties, while the provisions of the Basic Law specifically attempted to outlaw parties of the political extremes.[8]

Modern European party systems are largely rooted in developments in the late nineteenth century, when the main cleavage lines were between a conservative and a liberal/progressive tradition. Added to this were the complexities of regional variations and Church involvement in politics with a subsequent strong anti-clerical tradition in many societies. The extension of the franchise in the late nineteenth and early twentieth centuries gave added impetus to the already growing working-class involvement in politics. The appearance of a number of large working-class parties created a realignment of the party system and the eventual creation of mass parties. But this was largely a movement to restructure not to destroy the party system. Social democracy, originating in Germany in the 1860s, rapidly established itself as a major political force by the turn of the century. Although later divisions were to lead to splits in the movement and the creation of separate communist parties, social democracy was to survive in various forms and to emerge from the Second World War strengthened. Indeed social democratic parties emerged as major governing parties in most of the West European states in the immediate postwar period.

The challenge of a united working-class party was often met by parties of the Right on a piecemeal basis. Liberal or radical parties frequently allied themselves with a variety of political groups to retain power, including the new emerging Catholic parties. After the Second World War, one of the most significant features of the development of the party system has been the creation of mass parties of the moderate Right. In most European states this has taken the form of christian democracy, based on the earlier Belgian experience. These were loose groupings based on broad Christian principles and not, except in the case of Italy, closely linked to the Catholic hierarchy. This is not to say that the Church does not exercise an influence, for in many European states the Church continued to exhort the faithful to vote for the party of Christian principles. In France the failure of the MRP did not lead to the formation of a party of the Right of a similar kind; instead, from the climactic events of 1958, a broad coalition of the Right was to appear in the form of Gaullism. With this exception, it was these broad christian democratic parties that were to concentrate their efforts on an appeal to a wider electorate and have been referred to as 'catch-all' parties.[9] In order to compete, many social democratic parties have moved in a similar direction. Modern European party systems are thus largely centered on the activities of christian democratic/social democratic parties, often with the added injection of a liberal strand occupying a position on the Centre—Right. Finally, due to a series of cultural and regional factors outlined earlier, many European states still have a number of small parties within their systems.

PARTY SYSTEMS, GOVERNMENTS AND OPPOSITIONS

A number of similar party types exist in Western European democracies, although the reasons for their existence are often rooted in a particular series of national, social and historical characteristics. It is not enough simply to itemise a series of similar party groupings; we should attempt some classification of party systems. Numerous attempts have been made to deal with the problem of classifying European party systems. Often, such attempts at broad classification become no more than an exercise in numerical ordering in which authors reveal that certain systems are two-party, multi-party and so on.[10] What is required however is a system that goes beyond mere arithmetic and tells us something about the nature of parties in a given system and what possibilities exist in those systems for parties to attain power or to be confined to virtually permanent opposition. What concerns us, then, is not simply the number of parties. Arising from a series of internal factors, what combination of parties can form a government?

Perhaps the most useful distinction that can be drawn is between systems that can be described as imbalanced, balanced or diffused.[11] This threefold classification does at least relate party systems to government formation and tells us something about the power structure in a particular society. An imbalanced system would be one in which a single party either governs alone or is an essential element in any governing coalition over long periods of time. Single-party government of the British type is the exception rather than the rule in most West European countries, but there are many examples of parties that can be described as essential governing parties. Often such parties' electoral position changes very little between one election and the next and often electoral contests become concerned not so much with attaining power or being excluded from it, but rather with the actual number of government posts a particular party will secure. LaPalombara and Weiner refer to such parties and systems as 'hegemonic'.[12] Such hegemonic or pivotal political parties may often be far ahead of other parties in the system in terms of electoral support or may occupy such a central position that no government can really be formed without their participation. There are a number of parties of this type. The most obvious example of an imbalanced system is that of the Italian Christian Democratic Party, which has had an unbroken period of office since the Second World War and provided all the Italian prime ministers. Government coalitions without Christian Democratic participation are virtually impossible and despite numerous predictions of its imminent demise, the party has continued to occupy a hegemonic position. The Social Democratic Party of Sweden occupied a similar position in that country for over forty years prior to its 1976 electoral defeat.[13] The Christian Democratic Party (CDU) of Germany, particularly during the period of Adenauer's leadership, occupied a dominating position in that society. As a corollary to this, such systems inevitably contain within them parties that may have no experience of power and may be confined to almost permanent opposition.

In contrast, a diffused party system is one in which there is no obvious polarisation and a number of political parties gain a similar percentage of the vote. No 'governing' party as such exists. France during the Fourth Republic is an example of this system, in which a number of governing coalitions were possible and changes of government were very frequent. The relation between election performance and type of government became increasingly divorced and coalition combinations changed between elections. In contemporary Western Europe, this type of system has its most obvious manifestations in Belgium and Holland. Since the late 1960s the appearance and success of a number of linguistic based parties have served to undermine the position of the more traditional parties and made government formation extremely complex. While diffusion in Belgium is of more recent origin, the Netherlands can be said to have existed in a diffused state for almost all its postwar history.[14] There, five separate political parties have dominated the system and government coalitions have usually been drawn from three of them. We shall return to the role of parties in the Netherlands later, for in many ways the Dutch system has peculiar characteristics. Diffusion, of course, need not necessarily be associated with government instability, for while the French Fourth Republic was associated with short-lived governments, Dutch governments, despite the complexity of formation, have tended to last for their full term of office.

Our third category is that of a balanced system in which there is a clear polarisation of forces but neither of these forces is predominant for long periods. We would naturally associate a balanced system with a two-party state although to do so would have a limiting effect on this categorisation. As Sartori reminds us, what is important is not simply the number of parties but around how many poles the parties are clustered.[15] For example, we may have a system of competition between three or four parties but those are centred on only two broad poles and changes in government combination may take place on a regular basis. Sartori describes this as a system of 'moderate pluralism', another way of describing our balanced category. Western Germany may now be classified as a balanced system, while Belgium before the cultural disputes operated a similar system of party competition.

Such a classification does have the advantage of relating parties to government formation and gives some indication of the likely government coalitions. Clearly such a classification has its faults and, of course, political systems may move from one categorisation to another with the passage of time. Indeed, postwar Western Europe has seen many countries begin their political lives in an imbalanced state and move towards a more balanced existence, while others have become more diffused. West Germany can be said to have moved from an imbalanced system to a balanced one. Throughout the 1950s, under Adenauer's leadership, the CDU was clearly the largest party and dominated political life. It far outstripped other parties and was a governing party par excellence. Over time however, as West German society became more integrated, many of the smaller regional and sectional parties disappeared, while at the same time the Social Democratic Party, owing to certain internal policy changes, began gradually to increase its support, finally overtaking the CDU in 1972. West Germany therefore now has a balanced party system with two major parties competing for power. In Scandinavia, both Norway and Sweden have moved from a position of one-party dominance by the Labour and Social Democratic parties respectively, at least for the time being, to a more balanced system. The Netherlands' diffused party system appeared, from the late 1960s onwards, to be moving towards greater diffusion. New political parties appeared, with the expressed intention of creating a more balanced system. At the same time, support for the three religious parties began to decline rapidly. This diffused trend was confirmed by the elections of 1971 and 1972, but it forced parties that had once operated as separate entities to seek election alliances. These alliances may mark the possibility of a major realignment in Dutch politics, for from them was created a new unified Christian Democratic Alliance in 1976. While many political parties continue to exist in the Netherlands, the 1977 elections saw for the first time competition between a progressive and a conservative/religious bloc. This may herald a polarising trend in Dutch politics and a more normal Christian Democrat/Labour Party battle, with the creation of a more balanced party system.[16]

In all the above categories, coalition governments are the norm, and the British one-party executive is the clear exception. Coalition types in Western Europe are very variable, and may be formed on the basis of one major partner in coalition with smaller parties or may be a coalition of a number of parties of equal strength. Where no one party has an absolute majority in an assembly, smaller parties, often of the centre, become essential to successful government formation. While in Britain failure to win a majority of seats by whatever margin may exclude a party from power for a number of years, in many European states smaller parties have played a significant part in government out of all proportion to their electoral strength. In West Germany, for example, the Free Democratic Party has been a member of most postwar governments. These smaller parties have often been able to elicit concessions from their major coalition partners as a price for their participation in government. Exceptionally, Europe has witnessed governments of the 'Grand Coalition' type, where the two major parties may join together. Both Germany and Austria have experienced such forms of government.

The relationship between political parties and government is as variable as the coalition possibilities. Where government is by one party, or one party is the major coalition partner, the political party machine may have a limited influence on government deliberation. The executive, through its distribution of government posts, may exercise considerable control over the party. In situations, however, where coalitions are unstable or are made up of a number of parties of similar strength, the relationship between the personnel of government and the political parties concerned may be very close. Here, the party plays an important role not only in determining the basis for possible participation in government, but also in nominating individuals to occupy particular government posts. In some coalition negotiations, individual parties and not the prime minister have been given the right of nomination. In such situations the relationship between aspiring political leaders and their parties becomes much more significant than in systems such as Britain, where the patronage power of a prime minister at the head of a single party is all-important. In multi-party or unstable coalition situations regular party consultation by ministers becomes the order of the day. In the unstable Italian political system, the Christian Democratic Party machine has played a decisive role in government formation and in determining the personnel of government. Here the party has often exercised more power than the formal state apparatus.

From the foregoing discussion it can be seen that Europe has a variety of party systems some of which provide almost unbroken government for some parties and periods of power and opposition for others. A further category of parties, often of the extreme Left or Right anti-system type, may be excluded from power almost indefinitely. It is important to consider the question of how parties fare in opposition. Does this mean their effective exclusion from the decision-making process or are there means by which opposition parties may exercise an influence over policy formulation? Whether or not an opposition party can play an important role or not is dependent on a number of factors and has been most clearly analysed by Dahl.[17] He identifies three general characteristics of systems that will determine the opposition's role: the site of decisive encounters, the degree of party competition, and the cohesion of the opposition.

The decisive site for encounters would normally be an election, though in some European systems it is not just the election that is important but the coalition-building negotiations that precede or follow it. In systems where coalition negotiation may be protracted, opportunities exist for parties that themselves may not eventually emerge as a government partner to have an important influence on the course of action pursued by the government. Opposition parties have often agreed to support a governing coalition in return for certain concessions, without participating in that government itself. Within the formal political structure, the precise role performed by the legislature will be an important factor in determining opposition patterns.

In some European societies, opposition facing a strong government may not be confined to total obscurity, for the legislative process may give them an important role to play. In political systems where legislative committees are of significance, opposition parties can often modify a government's programme or delay its passage. Such systems provide the opposition with considerable quantities of information and challenging the government's programme becomes easier. In Sweden, for example, the conservative opposition parties always had an important influence prior to 1976, as the Swedish tradition continues to place great emphasis on legislative deliberation. The role that the opposition can play is to an extent determined by the traditions operable in a particular society in that, whatever legislative devices may exist, the competitiveness of the party system will be decisive. Where highly disciplined parties exist, the ability of the opposition to influence the assembly's deliberations may be severely limited. Here, opposition parties may seek to play a role not by concentrating their activities on the assembly but by attempting to influence the bureaucracy or to harness interest-group demands. Where, as in Britain, the opposition is faced not only with a low level of legislative deliberation but also a highly disciplined governing party, the opposition parties' influence on decision-making is severely limited. Here, individual members of parties may expect to play a role in decision-making only when they are recruited to the executive.

Finally, the cohesion of the opposition is important, in that in a multi-party system a government party may have the ability to play off one party against another, and is not faced with a united opposition as it is in a two-party system.

These three factors ultimately create the conditions in which opposition parties can operate, but perhaps ultimately the role that opposition parties play depends upon the goals they pursue. Most European opposition parties have been committed to a change in the personnel of government as well as certain government policies. Kirchheimer has pointed to the fact that the decline in ideologically based parties has led to the appearance of opposition parties who have limited objectives of political change.[18] They are no longer committed to a fundamental restructuring of the political and social order, but place their emphasis on providing an acceptable 'alternative government'. The case studies in Dahl's *Opposition in Western Democracies* reveal a low level of opposition objection to government policies in many countries, and perhaps add weight to Kirchheimer's analysis that the traditional opposition function in the British sense has ceased to operate. But because 'oppositions' adopting a centrist stance may be the order of the day, and total objections to government programmes a thing of the past, this should not lead one to conclude that opposition parties have a limited function. Because of particular political circumstances, or because of the role performed by certain political institutions, opposition parties have been able to exercise an influence on government. Equally, it would be a mistake to judge the role of opposition parties purely on the basis of their performance at national level. In many European states local or regional government is of some significance, and political parties that are not in power at the national level may exercise considerable influence on local politics. In a federal political system such as Germany, national opposition parties may control state governments, and through the workings of that system may have considerable influence on the course of national politics. Indeed, in Germany, some party politicians seek to make their careers at the state level and do not enter the national parliament. In both France and Italy, local politics are of great significance; party politicians often launch and sustain their national careers from a local political base. In these two countries, the socialist and communist parties have controlled large parts of local and regional administration. This not only allows them a decisive role in local decision-making, it provides an opportunity for them to be viewed by the electorate as efficient and responsible alternative government parties.[19]

THE CONSOCIATIONAL MODEL

While in most European societies it is possible to identify a governing or opposition role for political parties, in some the picture is diffused. In both the Netherlands and Switzerland it is not possible to consider the interplay of party politics purely on the basis of government and opposition, for here systems have been created that have sought to accommodate all the many varied interests in these societies. The role of political parties is very different from that operating in the majority of European states. The Dutch and Swiss party systems have been described as 'consociational' democracies. By this we understand a system of élite accommodation in that, despite shifting government coalitions, there is a general acceptance throughout the political system that the basic interests of the major groups in society will not be challenged.[20] It is a system in which deliberate compromises by élites are carefully circumscribed and limit the extent to which political power can be wielded by one centre. While the Netherlands will be the focus of our attention, we should note that the Swiss system, operating a peculiar form of consensus in the Federal Council, has created an almost ossified party system in which the party share of government posts has not changed for twenty years and system development became almost impossible.[21]

Like most European societies, the basic pattern and division between the various political groupings was established in the latter half of the nineteenth century. In the Netherlands party divisions were broadly determined by conflicts over three specific issues: education, the franchise and social divisions. The education issue was a particularly important one and gave encouragement to both Catholic and Protestant populations to organise themselves into political groupings to secure religious freedom and the right to run religious-based schools. To represent these religious interests therefore, there emerged in this period the Roman Catholic People's Party and two Protestant parties, the Christian Historical Union and the Anti-Revolutionary Party. The proposed extension of suffrage by the Liberal cabinet of 1894 led to a split, which had the effect of pushing the majority of the Liberal party to the conservative Right. At the same time the movement towards industrialisation in the Netherlands saw the beginnings of Dutch socialism which, although it was at first of a revolutionary kind, soon adopted a social democratic centrist stance. So emerged the basic party divisions in the Netherlands, along secular/religious and progressive/conservative lines. The conflicts between these groups threatened to make Dutch politics highly unstable. In 1917, however, in order to end the conflict, a Commission comprising all the political parties met and recommended both freedom to organise religious schools and universal suffrage with proportional representation. Its recommendations were accepted and these two divisive issues settled, giving rise to a system that Arendt Lijphart has called the politics of accommodation. Each group in Dutch society, whether religious or economic, was allowed to develop in mutual isolation and there was a recognition by the succeeding government coalition that certain vital interests could not be interfered with. Thus, for example, a system of exclusively Catholic and Protestant education was allowed to develop. Equally, through a proportional representation system, all political groups were given an opportunity to gain parliamentary representation. By this system of accommodation or consensus, Dutch politics developed a stable system of government.

This system of operation very much depended upon the stability of support for the major parties in Dutch society. When this system began to break down in the late 1960s the whole system of accommodation was threatened. The Netherlands appears to be entering a period of polarisation, which in turn may lead for the first time in the modern period to large groups being excluded from areas of decision-making. But at least this polarisation may lead to a more dynamic policy approach by political parties, for the consociational system produced middle-of-the-road cabinets, failure to deal with long-term issues, and the devolution of policy-making out of the political arena and into a series of advisory bodies and expert committees.[22] In other words, political parties were unable to deal with contentious issues.

PARTY–INTEREST GROUP RELATIONSHIPS

How interest groups operate in relation to political parties will depend partly on the nature of society and its degree of homogeneity, and partly on the structure of governments themselves. Discussion of the nature of party systems is in itself an indication of the power positions in a given society and so the activities of interest groups will vary depending on particular government combinations. Clearly, where a party is dominant for long periods, interest-group activity differs from a system where a more balanced state exists. Political parties themselves are inevitably coalitions of interests and certain groups may have a formal link with a particular political party. The relationship between the trade union movement and many European social democratic parties is a case in point, as is equally that between many industrial groupings and conservative or christian democratic parties.

What is the degree to which interest groups use political parties to transmit their demands and do they use other means of securing access to policy-making? The pattern is perhaps as variable as are the states in Western Europe. In Sweden, interest groups are particularly powerful and play a vitally important role in the political system, often superior to that of the parties themselves. In such a system, interest groups do not necessarily have to penetrate political parties to gain influence but are recognised as bargaining agents in their own right and are regularly consulted. Parties and interest groups are two elements in the legislative process, though the existence of such powerful groups is not seen as undermining the existence of political parties. Interest groups are recognised by the government as having a virtually separate existence from political parties and performing a complementary role to them. In Germany, interest-group activity is equally important and groups may operate at a variety of levels, although contacts with government departments are not on the same recognised basis as they are in Sweden. About one-third of the members of the Bundestag are spokesmen for particular interests and the legislative procedure of the West German parliament, concentrating as it does on the work of committees, allows ample opportunity for interest groups to influence policy-making. Interest-group activity is less overt than it is in Sweden and there is a general tendency not to recognise the influence of interest groups in German society. Sontheimer refers to this as 'underdeveloped pluralism'.[23] Political parties are important channels for interest groups in Germany but only one area of access. In France, the transfer of power from the legislature to the executive with the formation of the Fifth Republic has resulted in less pressure by interest groups on political parties and a concentration at the executive/bureaucratic levels where policy is decided.

Perhaps the most striking example of closeness in the relationship between interest groups and political parties is to be found in Italy. Italian Christian Democracy, being itself a loose coalition of a number of competing groups as well as being the dominant political force in Italy in the postwar period, has attracted the activities of a number of interest groups. LaPalombara has analysed this relationship in terms of *parentela* (i.e. dealing only with those groups associated with the governing party, the Christian Democrats) or *clientela* (i.e. accepting only certain groups as spokesmen for particular interests).[24] An almost neo-feudal relationship exists between the Christian Democrats and a variety of groups. The various groups operating within the Christian Democratic Party, particularly the Church organisations and Confindustria, have exercised an important influence over the party's development. Each group has been keen to advance its own interests and ensure that its nominees secure positions of power within the Italian state. Colonisation of the bureaucracy has taken place to such an extent that it can be seen almost as an extension of Christian Democratic interests. Italian Christian Democracy is an example of extreme interest-group penetration, the distinction between the party and groups often becoming blurred and the two mutually reinforcing their position.

These varied patterns of interest group to party relationships are only to be expected in systems where parties represent broad coalitions of interests. Nonetheless, despite the consequences of economic development and increasing social integration of societies, there still exist a number of parties that operate almost in an interest-group role. While in many societies farming and rural interests are encompassed in conservative parties of various kinds, both in the Netherlands and in Finland rural parties continue to exist. Likewise, despite the growth of christian democracy, small religious parties continue, as do parties representing a particular cultural or language minority.

We have mentioned the general tendency of both christian and social democratic parties to move towards a position devoid of any real ideological identification and to move into the 'catch-all' party category. In becoming parties of this type the importance of membership declines and the preoccupation becomes one of securing the maximum amount of support from all sections of society. In expanding his notion of the 'catch-all' party, Kirchheimer argued that a party attempting to secure maximum support must steer a course so as not to antagonise particular interests. There is therefore a great danger that large voter-oriented parties will fail ultimately to represent any identifiable view, will cease to perform a role of aggregating interest-group demands and will become mere collectors of interest-group claims. Party competition in many European societies is already mere competition 'between two attractively packaged brands of nearly identical merchandise.'[25]

Conclusion

The party systems of Western Europe continue to remain an essential ingredient in most political systems, still providing the major source of recruitment to the executive and the major source of support for governments. The general pattern is one of polarisation and the movement towards more balanced systems. In future, such countries as the Netherlands could move to a German-type system in which government formation becomes more straightforward and decision-making concentrated in the hands of fewer parties. Coalition-building inevitably produces bargains often struck on the basis of the lowest common denominator of interests and the government's ability to pursue controversial issues becomes lessened. A polarised system, however, is often one in which 'catch-all' parties exist and here the fear of antagonising major group interests may equally prevent action on controversial issues. This should not be taken to mean that the 'end of ideology' has created parties that are simply the mirror image of each other, for clearly christian and social democrats, liberals and conservatives all view issues from distinctive standpoints. However, whether these party standpoints can be translated into action during the exercise of power, when parties are faced with the increasingly powerful role of bureaucracy and the intervention of interest groups, has become a matter of some doubt.

NOTES AND REFERENCES

1. R.H. Merelman 'Foreword' to M. Duverger, *Parties and Pressure Groups*, London, Nelson, 1971.
2. R.C. Macridis, *Political Parties*, New York, Harper and Row, 1967, pp. 17-18.
3. R. Rose and D. Urwin, 'Persistence and Change in Western Party Systems since 1945', *Political Studies*, vol. 18, September 1970, pp. 287-319.
4. E.E.Y. Hales, *The Catholic Church in the Modern World*, New York, Doubleday, 1960.
5. H. Daalder, 'Parties and Politics in the Netherlands', *Political Studies*, vol. 3, February 1955, pp. 1-16.
6. C. Hughes, 'Switzerland', in S. Henig and J. Pinder (eds), *European Political Parties*, London, Allen and Unwin, 1969.
7. K. Hill, 'Belgium — Political Change in a Segmented Society' in R. Rose (ed.), *Electoral Behaviour*, London, Collier-Macmillan, 1974.
8. A. Burkett, *Parties and Elections in West Germany*, London, C. Hurst, 1975.
9. O. Kirchheimer, 'The Transformation of Western European Party Systems' in J. LaPalombara and M. Weiner (eds), *Political Parties and Political Development*, Princeton N.J., Princeton University Press, 1966. On the application of this concept to France, see J. Charlot, *The Gaullist Phenomenon*, London, Allen and Unwin, 1971.
10. For example, J. Blondel, 'Party Systems and Patterns of Government', *Canadian Journal of Political Science*, June 1968, pp. 180-203.
11. G. Smith, 'What is a Party System?' *Parliamentary Affairs*, vol. 19, Summer 1966, pp. 351-62.

12. J. LaPalombara and M. Weiner, 'The Origins and Development of Political Parties' in *Political Parties and Political Development, op. cit.,* p. 35.
13. See N. Elder, 'The Swedish General Election of 1976', *Parliamentary Affairs,* vol. XXX, no. 21, Spring 1977, pp. 193-208.
14. G.L. Weil, *The Benelux Nations,* New York, Holt, Rinehart and Winston, 1970.
15. G. Sartori, 'European Political Parties — the Case of Polarised Pluralism' in R. Dahl and D. E. Neubauer (eds), *Readings in Modern Political Analysis,* Englewood Cliffs, N.J., Prentice-Hall, 1968.
16. M.A. Wheaton, 'Holland! Polarisation of Political Forces', *World Today,* July 1977, pp. 5-8.
17. R.A. Dahl (ed.), *Opposition in Western Democracies.* New Haven, Conn., Yale University Press, 1966.
18. O. Kirchheimer, 'The Waning of Opposition' in R.C. Macridis and B. Brown, *Comparative Politics,* Homewood, Illinois, The Dorsey Press, 1964.
19. S. Tarrow, *Between Center and Periphery. Grassroots Politicians in Italy and France,* New Haven, Conn., Yale University Press, 1977; P.A. Allum, *Italy — Republic Without Government,* London, Weidenfeld and Nicolson, 1975, pp. 85-88; and Jack Hayward, *The One and Indivisible French Republic,* London, Weidenfeld and Nicolson, 1973, pp. 25-47.
20. A. Lijphart, *The Politics of Accommodation,* Berkeley, University of California Press, 1968, p. 76. See also Hans Daalder, 'On Building Consociational Nations. The Cases of the Netherlands and Switzerland', *International Social Science Journal,* vol. 23, no. 3, 1971, pp. 355-70.
21. G.A. Codding, *The Federal Government of Switzerland,* London, Allen and Unwin, 1961.
22. J.F. Van Loon, 'Democracy in the Netherlands', *Acta Politica,* vol. III, 1968.
23. K. Sontheimer, *The Government and Politics of West Germany,* London, Hutchinson, 1972, p. 121.
24. J. LaPalombara, *Interest Groups in Italian Politics,* Princeton, N.J., Princeton University Press, 1964.
25. O. Kirchheimer, 'The Transformation of Western European Party Systems', *op. cit.,* p. 195.

SELECT BIBLIOGRAPHY

Duverger, M., *Political Parties,* London, Methuen, 1954.
Epstein, L., *Political Parties in Western Democracies,* London, Pall Mall, 1967.
Ionescu, G. and de Madariaga, I., *Opposition,* London, Watts, 1968.
Kolinsky, M. and Patterson, W.E., (eds), *Social Movements and Political Forces in Western Europe,* London, Croom Helm, 1976.
Lipset, S.M. and Rokkan, S., *Party Systems and Voter Alignments,* London, Collier-Macmillan, 1967.
Macridis, R.C., *Political Parties,* New York, Harper and Row, 1967.
Neumann, S., (ed.), *Modern Political Parties,* Chicago, University Press, 1965.
Sartori, G., *Parties and Party Systems,* volume I, London, Cambridge University Press, 1976.

CHAPTER 3

The Functions of the Modern State

Neil Elder

The scope of this topic is panoramic and the individual strokes must be broadly drawn. A number of development studies have appeared in the last two decades or so, using quantitative analysis in an attempt to disentangle the relative importance of the factors underlying the massive increases that have occurred in public expenditure in advanced Western societies in the last century to a century and a half.[1] In particular, they have sought to sift out the interrelationships between social, economic and political influences on the course of modernisation. Some brief general observations may first be made by way of commentary: the twin process of industrialisation and urbanisation created the *need* for state intervention of the modern type; economic factors have related primarily to the *capacity* of the state to intervene; and political factors have related, though in a more complex way than is sometimes supposed, to the *will* of the state to intervene. Again, state activity is often wider than statistics reveal: to take a random example, the credit market can be manipulated by restrictions placed upon commercial banks. The value of a reform, moreover, may bear little relation to its cost. Early measures of factory reform, for example, may be regarded as valuable but not costly; the recent reforms of local government structures in Britain may be regarded as costly but not valuable. These remarks are not intended as an aspersion upon development studies of the type referred to; it is suggested, however, that their value is heightened by close historical interpretation.

The proposition that industrialisation and urbanisation created the need for a rapid expansion of state functions hardly requires elaboration. Both processes were later strongly reinforced by the impact of war and of economic depression. The fulfilment of the need for increased intervention has had to wait to some extent, though, upon the growth of scientific and technical knowledge. States could do little to combat cholera outbreaks, except call for national days of prayer, while it was still believed that such outbreaks were caused by the bad air enveloping congested centres of human habitation. The belief that unemployment was never involuntary helped to create the harshnesses of the Victorian work-house. More generally, the belief that *any* state regulation of economic affairs could only be counter-productive helps to account for varying rates of national response to need. In some parts of Europe — Scandinavia, for example — the laissez-faire philosophy scarcely affected the course of public policy; and in a longer historical perspective it may be regarded as an aberration, having regard to the mercantilism of an earlier era. To the extent that it has been influential, however, it is probably best regarded as a political factor.

The proposition that economic factors relate primarily to the capacity of the state to intervene has particular relevance to the provision of the expensive services that in combination reflect the welfare policy of the state. Education and health care come into this category, as well as pensions schemes, unemployment benefits, child allowances and other varieties of financial support for specific welfare purposes. Expenditure under these heads has increased at a much faster rate than public expenditure as a whole in the course of modernisation. Another extremely expensive item has been defence, whose costs have soared as weaponry has become more sophisticated.

Economic growth may have provided the indispensable basis for the emergence of the modern state, but the time span between the take-off points for economic growth and the first appearance of welfare programmes of a modern type has varied widely from one country to another. The first major wave of industrialisation in France can be dated either to the July Monarchy or to the Second Empire, i.e. just before or just after the mid-nineteenth century; in Germany it was certainly no earlier. Yet it was imperial Germany that created the prototype of the new welfare state, whereas France had to wait until the Radicals laid the first foundations in the years between 1902 and the outbreak of the First World War. Similarly, Britain was the first country to industrialise; yet by 1914, and despite her pioneering venture in the field of unemployment insurance, she had been outdistanced in the matter of welfare provisions by Sweden, whose own industrial revolution did not begin in earnest until the last quarter of the nineteenth century.

The explanation of these variations is to be sought in political factors and is more complex than is sometimes supposed. The arrival of mass politics, for example, was not always the trigger for reform: manhood suffrage came early in France but state activity remained sluggish long thereafter. Voting for parties of the Left was, it may be argued, more important. Are then Third Republic Radicals to be regarded as a party of the Left? Certainly not in the same clear sense as the German social democrats of the Bismarckian era, who exercised a powerful but indirect influence in the direction of expanding the functions of the state. At the same time it is relevant to consider comparative political cultures. Periodic invocations of the national revolutionary tradition by the working class in France both disposed and consigned them to a long period of political impotence. In the case of Germany, state recognition of the need for extensive intervention was assisted by the survival of Prussian traditions of state paternalism and by the fact that the recent unification of the country on a wave of nationalist fervour provided a ready soil for the reception by Bismarck of Disraelian ideas about conservative values.

All the major modern ideologies — conservatism, liberalism, socialism — have indeed had a hand in the expansion of state activity. The extent to which the first two were impelled to this by the rising strength of the third is a nice historical point that it would be out of place to pursue at length in the present context. What can be confidently asserted is that conservative and liberal contributions cannot be exhaustively explained from this perspective. The perception of needs, and of reform as a by-product of the necessity to preserve law and order, were pertinent considerations. Or again, the creation of the relatively small public sector of the Swedish economy, for example, stems overwhelmingly from non-socialist regimes acting on pragmatic grounds, such as a shortage of private capital or a desire to increase state revenues by the foundation of state monopolies.

The circumstance that the level of public expenditure has already passed 50 per cent of the GNP in Italy, Sweden and Britain is indication enough that the expansion in the functions of the modern state bears no one-to-one relationship with ideological orientations. In the Italian case the roots of the extensive public sector can be traced back to the depression years of the 1930s when, for example, Istituto per la Ricostruzione Industriale (IRI), the sizeable state holding company, was set up. Since the war, conservatism, in the shape of the Christian Democratic Party — admittedly an amalgam of many tendencies but essentially conservative for all that — has presided over large extensions of the public sector. The nationalisation of electric power after the 'opening to the Left' in the early 1960s is an exception to the general rule that state activity has been expanded for matter-of-fact reasons. Those reasons include attempting to grapple with the problems of underdevelopment in the South; providing financial assistance to private firms in difficulties that it is hoped will be temporary, an activity that has come into increasing prominence in the past decade, as the creation of the Gestioni e Partecipazione Industriale (GEPI) agency in 1971 bears witness; creating public enterprises in order to break private monopolies, as in the cement industry; and protecting companies from foreign competition. All this has entailed a frequent blurring of the lines between the private and the public sectors. This trend is observable throughout Western Europe in the postwar period but it has probably gone further in Italy than elsewhere. For in Italy structural interlocking between the sectors has occurred to a peculiar degree, and it has been reinforced by clientelistic relationships and the frequency of selective interventions by the state.

In Sweden a generation and a half of virtually uninterrupted Social Democratic rule came to an end at the elections of September 1976, to be superseded by a three-party non-socialist coalition under Centre Party leadership. The style of state activity during the long Social Democratic ascendancy makes an interesting study in itself. Briefly, little attempt was made to expand the boundaries of the public or nationalised sector of the economy. A commission of inquiry was set up in 1920 by the minority Social Democratic government of the day to investigate the question of nationalisation; it was wound up fourteen years later (when the party was in power, as distinct from just in office) barren of result. Instead, the regime concentrated in the main on encouraging private industry to lay the golden eggs, and then on trying to ensure an equitable distribution of the product. In pursuance of this latter aim, public expenditure rose to a higher percentage of the GNP than anywhere else in Western Europe and welfare programmes were developed to a considerable degree of sophistication. A number of important reforms, for example, stemmed from the work of the Social Services Commission (1938-51), particularly in the areas of unemployment and health insurance. Then, in 1959, came the introduction of a pioneering scheme for supplementary pensions, essentially guaranteeing workers of all descriptions incomes at the rate of roughly two-thirds of their earnings during the best fifteen years of their working life. The size of the funds accumulated under this scheme, it may be added, brought the state an enormous access of strength on the capital market.

Looking at the postwar era as a whole, both Sweden and Britain provide illustrations of the tendency of parties of the Left to tax more heavily than those of the Right, to spend more freely, to redistribute wealth more evenly, and to be readier to expand state functions generally, in one direction if not in another. Governments of this complexion also tend to strive to keep down defence expenditures more than their opponents. This holds true in the Swedish case, despite the unusually heavy defence commitments imposed by a policy of armed neutrality, and also in Britain — as has frequently been seen since the mid-1960s — despite the sudden earlier escalation under Attlee in the wake of the Korean War, which exacerbated tensions within the Labour Party in the 1950s. No doubt, on the wider front, the debate in Britain in the late 1970s between Labour and the Conservatives on how best to spend North Sea oil revenues clearly illustrates again the traditional differences of priority setting between them.

When Western economies prospered — which, in the main, they did for a decade and a half after 1950 — states were able to accommodate themselves reasonably comfortably to the increased expectations of their peoples. It was during this halcyon period that the notion of 'the end of ideology' made its appearance and that concepts of the 'post-industrial society' began to be formulated. The latter reflected in part an increasing preoccupation with the qualitative rather than the quantitative aspects of growth. These new emphases included the expansion and democratisation of educational systems and, linked with this, the provision of skilled manpower able to develop advanced technologies, and the spreading of civilised values capable of enriching the leisure that automation was expected to bring in its wake. The advent of harsher economic times in the 1970s has contributed to making some of this seem dated and some seem premature. Yet recession, inflation, 'stagflation', balance of payments difficulties and the like — varying in severity from one country to another, but universally compounded by the oil price rises of 1973 — have led to further expansions of state activity, whatever the prevailing ideology of the regime in power. Thus the Centre—Right Fälldin government in Sweden was compelled by force of circumstances to expand state control over, and state aid to, the hard-pressed shipbuilding industry in 1977. Thus, the Conservative Heath administration of 1970-74 was forced into policy reversals over Cammell Lairds, Upper Clyde Shipyards and Rolls-Royce. In both cases selective interventions have been disliked in principle but necessarily pursued in practice. Is there, then, something inexorable about the extension of state functions? More specifically, is it to be regarded as an exponential process, leading inevitably towards something in the nature of a command economy? This question will be considered later.

Meanwhile, some attention must now be paid to the instrumentalities through which the modern state exercises its functions. The principal instruments of state action are the bureaucratic apparatus and the local government machine. The civil service structures best equipped initially to meet the challenge of modernisation were in general those with a high degree of professionalisation, and these were to be found in countries where the transcendentalist principle was historically strong in relation to the instrumentalist principle: France, Prussia (then Germany), early industrial Sweden, Denmark. The historic strength of the *dirigiste* principle in France is reflected in the fact that even in the early sixteenth century the number of royal officials in that country was estimated at 86,000, greater than in industrialised England in the nineteenth century.[2] Technical expertise was, and is, transmitted through the *grands corps*. The process was reinforced through the foundation of the Ecole Polytechnique in 1794. Through this institution penetrated Saint-Simonian ideas about the practicability of achieving an era of plenty through the application of science and technology. Admittedly, in the original doctrine this did not occur through the agency of the state, but in time the state came to be viewed as a natural vehicle for promoting progress.[3] In short, France entered the modern era with a strong technocracy able to take on the running of an extensive public sector of the economy, in a sense with a highly skilled and centralised direct labour department. Moreover, she developed an administrative system that was inexpensive as well as efficient, at least at the higher levels, by virtue of the fact that one official could combine legal, financial and technical expertise in his person as the result of extensive as well as intensive professional training. This professionalism was strengthened by the establishment of the Ecole Nationale d'Administration in 1946, with its social science emphasis. The ENA has sent out successive waves of self-confident and mutually acquainted peer-groups to ramify throughout the entire administrative system and also to provide a powerful contingent for the EEC organisation at Brussels.

A high degree of professionalism has also long characterised the German administration, building ultimately upon Prussian tradition. The precursors of modern civil service training everywhere were the courses in cameralistics established by Frederick William I of Prussia towards the end of the eighteenth century, with their grounding in financial law, administrative law and agricultural economics. These were, perhaps, as much a training in estate management as in state management. Yet it would be a mistake to regard the German administrative tradition as essentially pre-industrial, legalistic and anti-development, as a number of English-speaking commentators have done. For one thing, German states were taking over industrial functions at an early date; some in accordance with the older French pattern (e.g. the Meissen porcelain factory and breweries in Munich), some of a more modern character (part of the railway network, mining concerns). For another, although legal studies remain the gateway to an administrative career in Germany, the law courses are far more broadly based than is sometimes supposed in Britain, and they include economics, social insurance law, public finance and labour law. The same holds true of the curricula of the Higher School of Administrative Studies, founded at Speyer in 1947 to train German officials in a wide range of subjects, though in this case the courses are relatively short. Economic expertise has become, in Germany as in France, a significant qualification for success in the higher echelons of the public service.

If Prussia represented the Spartan tradition in early industrial Europe, then Britain, from the professional administrator's viewpoint, could be described as Boeotia — the rustic state — despite the fact that she was the homeland of the industrial revolution. It may be something of an exaggeration to say that 'in British political mythology, the State is in some sense sinful'.[4] But it could certainly be argued that Britain was the most minimalist of states until well into the industrial era, concentrating on the traditional state functions of the maintenance of law and order on the domestic front and, for the rest, on the defence and security of the realm and the conduct of relations with foreign powers. Even within these traditional functions she was minimalist. 'In 1797, when Britain was fighting for survival and the French fleet massed off the coast of Normandy, there were fifty-eight civil servants at the War Office and twice that number at the Lotteries Office.'[5] Part of the explanation for British administrative retardation was paradoxically the very fact that it was in Britain that the industrial revolution began. Economic circumstances and in particular initial competitive advantage, help account for the strength of the classical laissez-faire doctrine. These combined with the fact that the administrative tradition represented a development from the aristocratic to the gentleman amateur; and this in turn stemmed, at least in part, from the impact of liberalism upon Crown powers and entitlements, checking the emergence of an *étatist* tradition.

The most difficult of the Western European states to classify in this general perspective is Italy. A Roman law country strongly influenced by the Napoleonic code, her original bureaucratic apparatus was statist in temper and remains so. However, this machine has proved less well adapted to perform the functions of the modern state than either of the two other systems in the same tradition mentioned earlier. One reason has been the low pay that prevailed until the reform of 1973; low pay encouraged venality and caused officials to take on outside work in addition to their ordinary duties in order to make ends meet. Secondly, and partly as a result of low pay, the Italian public service has recruited disproportionately strongly from the southern region of the country. This has contributed towards giving something of a pre-industrial flavour to the operations of the bureaucracy. Thirdly, the accusations of narrow legalism and conservatism that have been inaccurately levelled at the German system apply with some force to the Italian. Training facilities for officials in modern disciplines have generally lagged behind those provided by the other major industrial powers of Western Europe, witness, for example, the tardy establishment at Caserta of a Higher School of Public Administration. Fourthly, despite the creation of a junior ministerial post in charge of civil service reform by the Centre—Left government of 1963, both the industrial and non-industrial sectors of the public service continue to consist of a chaos of agencies of varying legal status, often poorly co-ordinated. Thus the public health function, as Allum records, is dealt with by no fewer than eleven ministries and public agencies.[6] In the light of all this it is hardly surprising that there should be frequent complaints of formalism and legalistic restrictiveness causing delays and blockage in the execution of policy or that public dissatisfaction should find expression in the sardonic proverb, '*il pesce puzza alla testa*' (the fish rots from the head). To be fair, though, there is a bright side to the picture. Administrative bodies in the industrial sector such as IRI and ENI have shown great enterprise and initiative on occasion; the Banca d'Italia enjoys a high reputation; and 1970s' pay and regional government reforms can be expected to improve matters. A further instalment of administrative modernisation has also been canvassed.

These broad-ranging observations on the major Western European national administrative systems may now be briefly concluded. In France, the continuing strength of the *étatist* tradition has meant that the government and its servants — especially under the conditions of the Fifth Republic — still readily see themselves as the sole guardians of a public interest or common good distinct from and superior to fragmented and partial interests. The inclination is to decide rather than to mediate. In Germany this same tradition has been historically important and traces of it still survive, but it has been greatly weakened since the foundation of the Federal Republic. What remains from earlier times, apart from the abiding importance of the legal tradition — or, perhaps more accurately, as a facet of that tradition — is a liking for comprehensive codified solutions to political problems whenever these can be achieved. In both France and Germany the degree of administrative professionalism remains great, in France at any rate at the higher levels and in the technical administrations, in Germany more generally. Status is reflected accordingly. In Italy, political circumstances, including the strength of factions, have made administrative reform difficult. In Britain, the old practice of recruiting the educated amateur to government service persists and the Fulton Committee did not wish to recommend stopping the inflow of those with 'irrelevant' subjects.[7] The general climate, however, has been changing in the direction of greater professionalism since the Plowden Report of 1961.[8] Increased post-entry training was the preferred route, first through the provision of courses in quantitative techniques and cost-benefit analysis and then through a whole range of courses in economics, social administration, statistics, etc., at the Civil Service College. The number of professional economists recruited to the governmental machine has expanded rapidly. At the same time, in a broader perspective, the British administration tends to see its role as one of mediation rather than decision, reflecting the comparatively low-key attitudes of most British governments towards their own role in conflict resolution. Higher civil servants, in all developed Western countries, generally recognise the necessity and desirability of close practical contacts with relevant outside groups, as is shown elsewhere in this volume. What is at issue here are *styles* of government.

To refer to the bureaucratic apparatus of a state as an 'instrumentality' of state action is in a sense misleading, for it appears to imply that civil servants are excluded from the shaping of policy norms and are simply executants of programmes emanating from the party political platforms. Such is not the case. Indeed, it could be argued that the increasing complexity of the tasks falling to the modern state to perform has increased civil service influence at the upper levels of the hierarchy by giving them additional power to define the options available and to make policy recommendations. Central finance or budget ministries have thus generally come to play a crucial role in the determination of economic policy, including putting a brake sometimes on the activities of economic planners in other areas of the state or para-state administrative system. The small central departments in Sweden overhauled their organisation in 1965 in order to facilitate long-term planning and thereby, in effect, the steering of the extensive decentralised sector of the administrative apparatus. A similar preoccupation can be detected in the pages of the Fulton Report in Britain, with its recommendation for the creation of a Senior Policy Adviser or Advisers in 'most, if not all, departments' in charge of a Planning Unit, 'to ensure that day-to-day policy decisions are taken with a full recognition of likely future developments' and to 'determine, after consultation with the Permanent Secretary but subject only to the approval of the Minister, what problems his Planning Unit should tackle'.[9] At the same time, more sophisticated methods of co-ordination and monitoring policies, such as Programme Analysis Review techniques, have evolved and spread throughout Western administrative systems. In the British case, for example, this type of approach is built upon by the Treasury-based Public Expenditure Survey Committee (PESC). Finally, the increasing complexity of business has enhanced the co-ordinating influence of such agencies as the Elysée Office (given the key position of the Presidency under the Fifth Republic), the Federal Chancellor's Office and, more modestly, the British Cabinet Office.

The belief that civil service influence over policy has increased, is increasing, and ought to be diminished has led to growing pressure in some quarters for sympathetic expertise to be imported from outside the regular administrative system in order to buttress the position of the political decision-makers and to devise fresh sets of policy options. Such a demand is beside the point in many West European states, such as Sweden and France, where provision has long been made for injections of this kind. In Sweden it has been customary for the government of the day to appoint a sprinkling of qualified party men to posts in the central departments (under the Social Democrats they were nicknamed *politruker,* by joking analogy with the Soviet Union). In France there are the ministerial *cabinets,* though here it might well be objected that the net effect has been actually to increase civil service influence because of the extent to which recruitment is made from the members of the *grands corps.* However, in Britain both parties have felt the need for more or less cautious importations into, and supplementation of, the regular administration. Thus successive governments have brought in their own special economic advisers; there have been outside secondments to particular ministries and, perhaps the most spectacular initiative of all, there was the creation of the 'think tank', the Central Policy Review Staff, located in the Cabinet Office, by the Heath administration in 1970. This last-mentioned device certainly contained civil servants, but not exclusively, and its *raison d'être* was, in the words of its first head, to give 'advice independent of government departments (but not of their knowledge and information — that would be impossible), and of particular political beliefs. The accent was to be on multi- or trans-departmental issues and not on problems requiring immediate attention'.[10] Much of the work of the CPRS could be viewed as an attempt to stimulate civil service creativity, partly by acting as an irritant to the oyster.

The local government machine, as was mentioned earlier, is the second major instrumentality for the performance of the functions of the modern state. The degree of autonomy actually enjoyed in policy-making varies widely for local government authorities from one country to another. It is, for example, by long tradition relatively low in France, thanks to the power of the *tutelle administrative*, and relatively great in the Scandinavian countries, where it has been underpinned by the power vested in local authorities to levy their own income taxes within generous limits. Some comparative tax figures (see Table 3.1) will help to illustrate the point, though they do not take account of e.g. licence revenues, which make the French authorities' position rather stronger than appears. (Central government figures are given first, total state revenues in brackets after them.)

TABLE 3.1   *Fiscal revenues in France and Sweden, 1965—1974*

	France[11] (billion francs*)		Sweden[12] (million Kronor*)	
	Indirect taxes	Direct taxes	Indirect taxes	Direct taxes
1965			12.718 (13.179)	11.242 (20.236)
1970	111.24 (124.30)	47.25 (51.34)	20.067 (21.160)	17.521 (39.378)
1974	168.32 (184.10)	90.73 (94.81)	32.150 (33.549)	23.864 (52.609)

* At current prices

These figures reflect shifts in the overall tax balance between direct and indirect taxes in both France and Sweden. In France, where postwar tax policy has strongly favoured the latter type, and where VAT was invented, a trend is discernible towards increased reliance on direct taxes — 'visible' taxes, in Wilensky's terminology.[13] In Sweden, where the balance was more even as between the two categories, a perceptible movement is apparent towards the indirect or 'less visible' type of tax. These variations in pattern can have highly significant implications for tax-welfare backlash.

A relative freedom to raise money in their own right does not guarantee local authorities a proportionate autonomy under modern conditions. For one thing, there has been a secular trend towards forced amalgamations of such authorities in the hope of providing more efficient services at lower cost both in Britain and Sweden. This, it may be objected, should be a safeguard against the whittling away of local autonomy. But at the same time there has been an equally strong tendency towards increased local government activity combined with diminished local government responsibility, often justified in terms of the necessity for interdependence and co-operation between state authorities at the two levels. This in turn has contributed to swelling the chorus calling for a reversal of modern centralising trends and for the increase of 'participatory democracy'.

This latter cry, so frequently used in a sense so vague and/or idealistic as to be meaningless, can yet have precise connotations in particular national contexts when the central-local government relationship is at issue. Thus the preferred policy of the Social Democratic governments of Sweden during the 1960s and 1970s was to press on with local authority amalgamations and to discount criticisms that local government was becoming more remote from the people, while simultaneously making provision for increased participation in government at the national level. This last was principally promoted by increasing 'lay' — usually interest-group — membership of the central boards, which frequently powerfully influence policy in the particular fields for which they have administrative responsibility. Many of these boards have branches at regional and sometimes local level, and they regulate, for example, the labour market, protect the environment, look after consumer interests, etc. The preferred policy of the non-socialist Swedish coalition voted into power in 1976 is to decentralise functions wherever possible. So, for example, it seeks to promote direct democracy at the local level by championing the use of referenda on particular issues. A desire to head off the sudden spate of ecological defence parties in the local elections of the 1970s can be discerned behind this proposal. More significantly, the coalition seeks, for example, to transfer a measure of power over community planning from the branches of the governments, each under its Provincial Governor, to elected representatives of the people at the same stratum of government. The Centre Party, the dominant partner in the tripartite grouping, is particularly keen on decentralising decision-making, with the Liberals not far behind. The difficulty is how to reconcile this with the equally firmly held objective of equalising living standards throughout the various regions of the country.

The degree of freedom from central control enjoyed by the *Länder* within the German federal system is naturally much greater than that of local government authorities within a unitary state, but even in this case the same tendencies are apparent towards greater central involvement in the affairs of the parts. It is true that the *Länder* jealously guard their administrative autonomy, and that Germany in consequence has a number of separate bureaucracies alongside that of the federation as a whole. But in Germany (as in the USA) 'co-operative federalism' has become the order of the day. Education is one of the few subjects constitutionally falling within the exclusive competence of the *Länder*. But while educational expenditure in Germany rose from 16.8 billion DM in 1965 to 38.7 billion DM in 1972, federal involvement has been growing in parallel. Increased demand for the service has quite simply overstretched the financial resources of the individual states. So we find university building projects as one of a list of matters subject to conditional federal grants-in-aid, as is the case with hospital developments and urban renewal programmes. Such grants-in-aid were legitimised by a constitutional amendment in 1969, but this merely recognised a practice brought about earlier by force of circumstance. Similarly, federal funds assist the financing of the Honnef Plan for providing financial aid to deserving students. Increasing interlocking has brought with it the growth of new cross-level authorities, such as the Council of Arts, Sciences and Research, set up in the educational sector in 1957, or the joint planning commissions created under the terms of a 1969 constitutional amendment. The fact that different parties are often in power at the two levels complicates the task of obtaining vertical co-ordination within the federal system. The pace of change is thereby slowed, and the manner of change is necessarily incrementalist. At the same time, the system ensures that the central authorities remain sensitive to *Länder* (and to local) interests and susceptibilities.

Regional policy has become an increasingly important preoccupation of most Western European governments in the past two decades. The primary reason has been a desire to iron out severe discrepancies in economic development between different areas within the state and to promote industrial growth and employment in the backward regions. The most intractable problem of all in this respect remains that of the Italian South. Successive Christian Democratic dominated coalitions have sought to use public sector resources and to earmark percentages of investment for development here, using the Cassa per il Mezzogiorno as their main agency for channelling aid from government funds. But it has remained difficult to attract labour-intensive industries to the region, and the more alluring earning prospects in the North have continued to act as a magnet to southern labour. The riots in Reggio Calabria in 1970-71 when it was decided to site the local provincial capital at Catanzaro provide a melancholy commentary on regional depression as well as on local pride.

Economic pressures underlying regional policy may also be reinforced by the pressure to decentralise decision-making and widen participation in government. The final establishment of twenty regional governments in Italy in 1970 came about principally in reponse to this latter kind of influence. Modest though the functions of the Italian regions are, at least they include housing and education. Similar pressures to decentralise have materialised, as has been mentioned, in Sweden, and also, *inter alia,* in Britain and France. In both these latter states, however, they have run counter to the unitary grain of state policy and have taken a distinctly subordinate place to economic considerations. Thus in Britain the setting up of the Regional Economic Boards and Regional Economic Councils in 1965 came about chiefly as a part of the national economic planning machinery and has not been linked to the creation of corresponding structures within the framework of local government. The official view on devolution in the latter sense has remained reticent. Neither, it might be added, have effective measures been taken to co-ordinate the work of the regional agencies either at their own or at the national level. In France a fine flurry of activity in the matter of regional reform began in 1955, significantly again in the context of a National Plan, with the establishment of twenty-one planning regions. Subsequent instalments of reform in 1964, 1969 and 1972 have created new agencies at regional level but have effectively limited increased participation to purely consultative bodies. The *dirigiste* tradition has proved too strong to allow of significant modification, and the new breed of regional prefects continues to embody it. In Germany, finally, regional economic planning is subsumed under the head of a joint federal/*Land* planning function with the appropriate joint commission in charge and with the same restrictions on central action as with other designated joint tasks.

This brief review of regional policies can serve as one illustration of the fact that the modern state has become steadily more enmeshed in the business of general economic management whatever the size of the nationalised sector of the economy. It is not surprising, therefore, that as Self put it economists are increasingly called on to achieve by their art what the market once did by nature.[14] Immediate postwar preoccupations were with reconstruction, which gave rise, for example, to the first French Plan, and with the maintenance of full employment, a consideration that helped to bring the Attlee government to power in Britain in 1945. Keynesian measures to counter cyclical fluctuations — first resorted to in Sweden at the time of the depression through the influence of Wicksell and the Stockholm school of economists — became a powerful influence on French and British policy in the postwar era and were subsequently adopted by Germany at a time of the Grand Coalition (1965-69). More recently, inflationary tendencies and balance of payments problems have both immensely complicated the tasks of social management facing modern governments by tending to make collective bargaining an integral part of macroeconomic policy. National reactions have varied widely, largely in some sort of accord with the national political culture. Thus France has been much readier than Britain, for example, to impose price freezes and to let the market accommodate itself to them. Germany, following her traditional postwar neo-liberal line, has pursued price stability through normal fiscal policies. Equally characteristically, and in harmony with her preference for the comprehensive codification of policy, she passed in 1967 a Law to Promote Stability and Growth in the Economy in which price stability, high employment, external equilibrium and steady economic growth were declared to be *equal* objectives of the state. A Trade Cycle Council was set up in pursuance of these aims. In Britain, after several stormy passages, aggravated by an unusually high comparative rate of inflation, the reality has been borne in upon successive governments that an incomes policy has to have at least a large voluntary component, hence the 1974-77 'Social Contract'. In Denmark, the first act of a minority Social Democratic government on taking office in 1975 was to impose a wage settlement limiting increases for two years ahead to 2 per cent a year. In order to placate the unions, changes were made to the cost of living adjustment in an egalitarian direction so that the standard of living of the higher paid was adversely affected. Even in

Sweden, where collective bargaining has been traditionally conducted by straight negotiations between the two sides of industry, at least since the Saltsjöbaden Agreement of 1936, the framework for the discussions is now inevitably set by governmental fiscal policy.

The heyday of economic planning on the grand national scale would appear to be over in Western European states; there would therefore seem to be little point in surveying planning techniques and planning machinery. In France, where this type of activity was most fully developed outside the communist world, there is certainly still planning of this kind, but expectations have become more modest as awareness of the uncertainties has increased. One factor in the situation has been the growing importance of international trade, largely in consequence of the development of the European Economic Community. This has complicated target-setting. Another contributory cause has been the hostility of the Finance Ministry's budget division and of the spending ministries, which have refused to be bound by Plan investment programmes. Significantly, the centre of gravity appears to rest more securely than ever with the Finance Ministry, at least until further notice, through the adoption of the planning, programming, budgeting system (PPBS).[15] In Britain also, which followed France in a more modest attempt at extensive indicative/incrementalist planning in the 1960s, the Treasury has reasserted its traditional dominance while the Department of Economic Affairs has long since passed away. In Italy the Ministry of the Budget was put in charge of national economic planning in 1965-67, along with an inter-ministerial committee; but three departments continued to share economic affairs (Treasury and Finance being the others), and monetary and credit policy was shaped by an inter-ministerial committee on which the Bank of Italy had representation. The economic adversities of the 1970s have tended towards the same end of diminishing the hopes of accurate forecasting as the factors mentioned in the preceding cases.

Germany, of all the major industrial powers of Western Europe, has been the keenest to keep economic planning to a minimum. She has the least need of it anyway: she has had the best growth rate in Western Europe since 1950 (5.7 per cent per annum on average to 1974; Italy and France next, both over 5 per cent; Britain last, 2.8 per cent). The explanation for the aversion to planning lies in the Erhard-Eucken doctrine of the 'social market economy', essentially requiring the state to ensure fair conditions for the forces of competition. Supporting this approach, at least in part, was a reaction from the centralism of the Third Reich and a dislike for the regimented economic system of East Germany. Its corollary was the provision of compensation on a considerable scale for those categories of people most hard-hit by the operation of a free market, e.g. via housing subsidies and an extensive system of social security. It was embodied in a whole series of enactments such as the 1957 Law against Restraints on Competition, which among other things set up the Cartel Office for the purpose one might infer from the title. From the mid-1960s on, there has been a marginal shift in emphasis towards what has been styled the 'enlightened market economy'.[16] This has implied a reinterpretation of the conditions for fair competition and an increased need for state regulation on social and economic grounds. Thus the law on cartels was relaxed to make it easier for firms to merge and enjoy economies of scale, and subsidies were given, for example, to enterprises in the coal, computer and aeronautics industries. At the same time, special assistance continued to be granted to small and medium-sized businesses through the activities of a special division within the Ministry of Finance.

An attempt was made by the Social Democrat-Free Democrat coalition after 1969 to strengthen government planning by expanding the planning staff in the Chancellor's Office and putting it under a minister rather than a secretary of state. Although this was not an economic planning reform, it was designed in part to diminish the influence of the finance authorities and to quicken the pace of social change promised at the polls. Ambitious plans were also drawn up for long-term priority setting in the light of departmental projects. But friction arose when the central planning division came out with a short-list of top priority schemes without consulting the planners in the ministries, and in 1973 the scale of operations was much reduced.

The transition of Germany from 'social' to 'enlightened' market economy is symbolic of the fact that the modern state is increasingly engaged in detailed as well as general interventions in economic life, whatever the attitude taken towards economic planning. The process may have gone less far in Germany than elsewhere but it is still clearly visible. Mergers are encouraged in order to increase domestic strength against foreign and/or multinational company competition. States increasingly seek to generate wealth as well as to redistribute it. The activities of the British National Oil Corporation or Norwegian Statoil provide the most recent example of this tendency; but the same motive can be detected behind the grant of money for research and development programmes and for high technology projects (sometimes initiated by the state, as with Concorde). Prestige considerations, and again the desire to provide protection against competition from abroad, also play a part in these latter ventures. Special agencies are created, such as the IDI in France, the IRC and later the National Enterprise Board in Britain, to channel resources to priority sectors in industry. Assistance is given to ailing areas of the economy, sometimes merely as a form of social security, to avert unemployment, sometimes to tide them over until better times.

In conclusion, is the extension of state activity in contemporary Western Europe to be regarded as an exponential process, leading inevitably towards something in the nature of a command economy? A number of arguments can be presented to make this appear anything but a fanciful speculation.

One set can be grouped under the heading of 'overload' theories. Rising expectations of government outputs; the emergence of the concept of 'relative poverty' and the widening of individual reference groups, chiefly as a result of the growth of the mass media; the interests of the 'spending' ministries; the circumstance that each generation feels no debt of gratitude to the past and is apt to take its standard of living for granted, whatever the state of the national economy; the 'relative price effect' in respect of the tertiary sector: all these put the modern state under pressure to expand its activity. It admittedly does not necessarily follow that a command economy is the only way out, but it is certainly one possible way out. The greater the inflationary pressures, the more attractive is this particular solution likely to appear.

Again, ideology, contrary to some expectations, is far from ended. The natural dynamic of even social democratic parties is, one might well argue, hostile to private enterprise: can mixed economies therefore be expected to survive in the longer term? Even in Sweden the TUC has championed a scheme for the gradual take-over of private enterprise through a centrally administered, union-controlled fund financed by earmarking a steadily accumulating share of the profits made by private firms.

Finally, there is the Heilbroner thesis that industrial growth itself is an exponential process, incapable of indefinite continuance. The difference of industrial growth from state activity in this regard lies in the terminal points: of industrial growth, ultimate stagnation; of state activity, the displacement of private economic decision-making by public authority. A transcendentalist outcome nevertheless seems unlikely, despite all these considerations, save in the event of some economic catastrophe. It would run counter to the Western *Zeitgeist*.

NOTES AND REFERENCES

1. See e.g. Guy Peters and David Klingman, 'Patterns of Expenditure Development in Sweden, Norway and Denmark', *British Journal of Political Science*, vol. 7, 1977, pp. 387-412 and bibliography.
2. Malcolm Anderson, *Government in France*, Oxford, Pergamon Press, 1970, p. 16.
3. John A. Armstrong, *The European Administrative Elite*. Princeton, N.J., Princeton University Press, 1973. Chapter 3.
4. Edmund Dell, *Political Responsibility and Industry*. London, Allen and Unwin, 1973, p. 29.
5. T. A. Critchley, *The Civil Service Today*, London, Gollancz, 1951, p. 27.
6. P. Allum, *Italy — Republic without Government*, New York, W.W. Norton, 1975, p. 146.
7. London, HMSO, Cmnd. 3638, vol. I, 1968, para 79.
8. See R.G.S. Brown, *The Administrative Process in Britain*, London, Methuen, 1971, pp. 27-30.
9. London, HMSO, Cmnd. 3638, vol. I, 1968, see 97 in List of Recommendations, p. 201.
10. Lord Rothschild, *The Times*, 5 September 1977
11. *OECD National Accounts*, vol. II, 1974, p. 132.
12. *ibid.*, pp. 280-1.
13. Harold L. Wilensky, *The 'New Corporatism'. Centralization and the Welfare State*,

London, Beverly Hills, Sage Professional Papers 06-020, vol. 2, 1976, pp. 14-21.
14. P.J.O. Self, 'Economic Ideas and Government Operations', *Political Studies*, vol. XXIII, nos. 2-3, June/September 1975, pp. 381-9. See also Self, *The Econocrats and the Policy Process*, London, Macmillan, 1976.
15. See J. Carassus, 'The Budget and the Plan in France' in Jack Hayward and Olga Narkiewicz (eds) *Planning in Europe*, London, Croom Helm, 1978, Chapter 2.
16. Georg H. Küster, 'Germany' in R. Vernon (ed), *Big Business and the State*, Cambridge, Mass., Harvard University Press, 1974, pp. 64-86.

SELECT BIBLIOGRAPHY

Armstrong, J. A., *The European Administrative Elite*, Princeton, N.J., Princeton University Press, 1973.
Dell, E., *Political Responsibility and Industry*, London, Allen and Unwin, 1973.
Heclo, H., *Modern Social Policies in Britain and Sweden*, New Haven, Conn., Yale University Press, 1974.
Heilbroner, R. L., *Business Civilization in Decline*, London, Marion Boyars, 1976.
Molin, B., Mansson, L. and Strömberg, L., *Offentlig förvaltring*, Stockholm, Bonniers, 1969.
Vernon, R. (ed.), *Big Business and the State*, Cambridge, Mass., Harvard University Press, 1974.
Wilensky, H. L., *The 'New Corporatism', Centralization, and the Welfare State*, London, Beverly Hills, Sage Professional Papers, 06-020, vol. 2, 1976.
Young, S., *Intervention in the Mixed Economy*, London, Croom Helm, 1974.

CHAPTER FOUR

Trade Unions in Western European Politics

M. S. Joseph

TRADE UNIONS IN WESTERN EUROPE

Trade unions can be examined from a number of perspectives. Because of their traditional links with socialist and, to a lesser extent, Christian Democratic movements, priority is often given to the influence of unions on party politics. However, unions throughout Western Europe have developed their own policy-making bodies and functional organisations, which, although often affiliated to parties, exist independently and in their own right. These organisations are constantly engaged in complicated relations with government and management. Functional union contacts with government and management may be influenced by the political identity of the party/parties in government but contacts are not abandoned when the party in government is not closely linked to the major union. Conversely, union-linked parties in government, while receptive to certain union demands, have numerous other administrative and economic pressures to respond to. Tensions between union-linked parties and unions has regularly coincided with the party's assumption of government responsibilities.[1]

Union-linked parties in government have been consistently accused of *embourgeoisement*. A number of writers have discussed the dilemma of parliamentary socialism and working-class interest in socialism.[2] Analysis of what is meant by 'working-class interest' is greatly complicated by the range of contemporary unionisation. Traditional industrial workers' unions are increasingly supplemented by white-collar and lower managerial unionism. A large number of trade unionists, particularly in the latter categories, accept the status quo; they see the role of the union in terms of professional representation only. One of the most rapidly expanding unions in Britain, NALGO, is unwilling to affiliate to the Labour Party. In Sweden and Germany there are large professional union confederations apart from the main industrial confederations. Furthermore, it would be a serious exaggeration automatically to equate traditional industrial unions with committed support for programmatic redistributions of wealth. The theme of this essay is the operational scope of unions in capitalist society.

TABLE 4.1 *Variables in union development*

Legal—Constitutional	Physical	Historical	Operational and Organisational
Constitutional position of the unions within the state.	Level of unionisation in national labour force.	Date of industrialisation. Product range after industrialisation.	Union(s) emphasis on representation of members' immediate economic interests and workplace conditions.
Freedom of association, rights of unions to recognition, rights of unions to 'closed shop'.	Unionisation levels among different areas of employment, i.e. agricultural, industrial, distributive, blue-collar and managerial.	National tradition of trade union activity.	Union(s) emphasis on political ends over short-term wages and conditions.
Legal standing of wage agreements between unions and employers.		Numerical presence of union confederations (single or multiple union confederations).	Level of centralisation/decentralisation of union structures at confederation level.
Constitutional and extra-constitutional integration of unions in government through corporate organs of consultation.		Affiliations of unions to political parties, religious, regional or linguistic groups.	Level of centralisation/decentralisation of union structures at individual union level.
Constitutional and extra-constitutional integration of unions in enterprise management on boards of industries in state, para-state and private sectors.		Relationship between national economy and international economy.	Financial status of union confederations.
			Financial status of individual unions.
Credible coercive potential (judicial or physical) of machinery of state over unions.			Research and executive facilities of union confederations.
			Research and executive facilities of individual unions.
			Credible coercive potential of union confederation.
			Credible coercive potential of individual unions.

THE DEVELOPMENT OF LABOUR ORGANISATION

I do not propose to discuss all the variables of union development; I have listed them in Table 4.1. Most of the variables are self-explanatory. The industrialisation date and product range variables require brief explanation. In a study of industrial conflict in Britain and Scandinavia,[4] Britain's early industrialisation, with a broad product range, is compared with Sweden's later and more compact industrialisation. The diversity in British production led to the formation of many entrenched craft unions, whereas in Sweden the relatively compact range of production limited the number of craft unions. Ingham points out that the compactness of production encouraged employers to co-operate on the wage front from an early stage. In the metal industry the employers rapidly formed a federation and by the early 1920s there was a coherent Swedish Employers Association. In Britain, employers resisted federation on sectoral and intersectoral lines, thus failing to provide unions with an incentive to organise as industrial unions. In contrast to Sweden's 44 employers' associations, the Donovan Report[5] noted that Britain had 1350 employers' organisations in the late 1960s, the majority outside the Confederation of British Industry. Employers' co-operation in Sweden obliged the unions to organise on an industrial basis; by 1950 only 10 per cent of members of the Swedish industrial workers' union (LO) organised on a craft union basis.

In Sweden the Social Democratic government, which came to office after serious labour disturbances in the 1930s, encouraged binding collective agreements between employers and unions. The government endorsed the findings of the Nothin Commission; this led to the acceptance of Basic Agreements, which were legally binding bargains between management and unions. In Britain, collective bargains were not legally binding; they were not underpinned by any peace clauses because neither labour nor management supported legally binding agreements.

Traditions in national patterns of industrial relations have restricted conscious reform. The only European example of a forced change was West Germany. However this change was largely due to the consequences of the Third Reich for post-1945 Germany. By the early 1950s it was clear that, compared with the Weimar period, there had been centralisation of party and union values. In the late 1940s the allies, particularly the Americans and the British, reorganised the labour movement into industrial unions. The change was only possible because of the disruption of the Nazi period for German society and the authority of the Zonal Control Commissions of the allies. Although French and Italian societies had been deeply affected by wartime occupation and non-parliamentary regimes, neither experienced the level of disruption of Germany or the supervised reconstruction of political, administrative and labour institutions.[6] In France, de Gaulle's government immediately assumed full responsibility for institutional reconstruction. In Italy, the Allied Control Commissions released such powers to the De Gasperi government in January 1946.

Trade Unions and Political Parties

Political parties of the Centre, the Centre-Left and the conventional Left were provided with finance, support cadres and collective membership by unions. What did unions receive for their support?

Britain. The trade unions and the Labour Party had close links dating to the turn of the century. The Labour Party was dependent on the unions for finance and organisational support. A large, although decreasing, proportion of the parliamentary Labour Party were drawn from the unions. They discussed policies through formal and informal links and were commonly assumed to share the same values. The Labour Party, particularly when out of office, has worked closely with the Trades Union Congress. Labour, while in opposition in the early 1970s, attempted to improve its strained relations with the unions (due to Labour's attempt to introduce an Industrial Relations Bill in 1969) by passing motions at their conferences and the Labour-TUC Liaison Committee that, in addition to committing the subsequent Labour government to scrapping the Conservative's Industrial Relations Act, placed considerable emphasis on state take-overs of leading banks, insurance companies and private enterprises.[7] After Labour's victories in 1974 there were extensions of state intervention, particularly in industries in financial difficulty. The expansion of the public sector fell considerably short of formal party and union demands. While many Labour politicians decried the leadership's lack of commitment to the scope of previous resolutions, the failure hardly concerned the mass of unionists. Although union leaders consistently called for more state intervention and co-ordinated planning, these ends were not their highest priority. Because government had responsibility for monetary policy and was the largest employer and contract distributor in the country, it was inevitable that unions had close contacts with government, but the essential functions of the British unions and the Labour government were different. For the unions the primary goals were collective bargaining and job protection. The primary responsibility of Labour governments was administration across broad ranges of economic and social demands. On particularly sensitive issues, Labour governments catered for union demands, putting state funds into areas of industry contrary to the advice of expert bodies. In 1977 the government, against the advice of the Central Policy Review Staff and against the wishes of the Central Electricity Generating Board, placed a job preserving order for power turbines. The approach of the Labour government to the British Leyland car company was also governed by political rather than economic factors. Previous Conservative governments had been almost as willing to resort to unco-ordinated investment. Labour, particularly after their experience of 1969, when the unions thwarted their White Paper on union reform, were generally receptive to union pressure on matters of legal regulation, but although unions were consulted on economic policy, Labour governments were far more dependent on the Treasury, professional economists and international bankers in policy-making.

Sweden. The Swedish Social Democrats (SAP) and the Swedish industrial workers' union (LO) had close relations, with substantial affiliated support of the party from the union. Joint commissions and party recruitment of SAP leaders from the LO institutionalised the relationship. In addition to consultations on broad social and economic policy, union representatives were placed by the party on influential public boards, including those determining the use of reserve funds to counter cyclical unemployment and reviewing proposed foreign investment by Swedish companies. Although the LO influenced SAP's social, industrial and tax policies, they had little direct responsibility in investment decisions in either the private or public sectors. Under LO pressure, Sweden adopted worker participation in formally unitary management boards. Evidence suggested limited union satisfaction with worker participation.[8] The majority of LO members supported continued links with SAP, rather than the independence of the two professional unions, the Tjänstemännens Centralorganisation (TCO) and Svenska Akademikers Centralorganisation (SACO), yet the relationship was considered less important in the 1970s. The LO had no particular difficulties co-operating with the Centre Party Coalition that disturbed the SAP hegemony in 1976.

During the 1970s Sweden experienced increasing unemployment and failed to resolve the problem of integrating foreign workers. The SAP had no magic formula to handle problems facing most European governments. The limits on the development of SAP-LO relations were set by the advanced social legislation universally accepted in Swedish society; there were no incentives for intensified LO support of the SAP.

Germany. The German industrial workers' union (DGB) had extensive links with the Social Democratic Party (SPD) and important, if less effective and less visible, links with the Christian Democrats (CDU). In the early 1950s the CDU Chancellor, Konrad Adenauer, was responsible for the introduction of parity-co-determination in the mining and steel industries, as well as establishing comprehensive welfare and educational systems. However, the labour wing of the CDU (*Sozialausschüsse*) were an intra-party minority and their influence hinged on their value to Adenauer in his particular method of managing CDU affairs.⁹ After 1963 the CDU/CSU shifted its internal balance in favour of its business elements.

The offices of the DGB's sixteen federations were the most common area of recruitment for SPD leaders. In 1972, ten of Herr Brandt's fifteen SPD ministers had been recruited through the DGB. The Bundestag's extensive committee system encouraged liaison between the DGB and union representatives in the party *Fraktions*. During the long period in opposition, it was possible for DGB-linked SPD parliamentarians to play a substantive role in legislative proceedings.¹⁰ The Bundestag's committees for labour and for social affairs (subsequently merged) were 'colonised' by parliamentarians with DGB backgrounds.

In 1969 the SPD became the senior partner in the governing coalition. One of the DGB's main demands on the new government was that it should extend 'co-determination'. During the CDU/CSU-SPD 'Grand Coalition' the SPD Economic Affairs Minister, Karl Schiller, had instituted the Concerted Action Group for improving government-management-union relations. However, DGB officials pressed for extended consultation at industrial plant levels. SPD leaders had mixed feelings on the extension of co-determination. Furthermore the SPD were bound by their coalition partner, the Free Democrats (FDP), who opposed extending the scope of the 1952 Works Constitution Act.

The DGB placed considerable emphasis on formal corporate representation. In view of the high level of professional staffing in the DGB, it was hardly surprising that the union pressed for equal dialogue with leading civil servants, ministers and managements. However, the formal Concerted Action Group did not meet expectations and was subsequently abandoned.

Italy and France. In France and Italy the union movements were divided on cultural and international lines. The largest of the unions in both countries, the French Confédération Générale du Travail (CGT) and the Italian Confederazione Generale Italiana del Lavoro (CGIL), were predominantly, although not exclusively, communist in their leadership. In France and Italy the labour movements achieved a considerable degree of co-operation during the war but afterwards latent national tensions and international diplomatic and economic pressures re-divided the unions. In France, most of the members of the christian progressive Confédération Française des Travailleurs Chrétiens (CFTC) union, signalled their de-emphasis upon Catholicism by changing their name in 1964 to Confédération Française Démocratique du Travail (CFDT), committing themselves to a radical anti-capitalist position based upon the conception of democratic planning and workers control. The CGT-FO (Force Ouvrière) was a social democrat splinter from the CGT, not unlike the social democratic splinter from the Italian CGIL in 1947. The re-division of the Italian labour movement took place during the same time span as the re-division of the French labour movement. Under the combined pressure of the Church and Catholic union leaders, not to mention American intervention, the Confederazione Italiana dei Sindacati dei Lavoratori (CISL) was formed as a christian workers' union, which had close relations with the Christian Democratic Party. As in France, the collapse of postwar tripartism affected the division of union confederations.

Unions in France and Italy, although they had intervened dramatically in their political systems, traditionally had limited influence. Levels of unionisation were very low and the employers' confederations, the Conseil National du Patronat Français and the Confindustria, had greater influence upon government economic, fiscal and wage policies. The combinations of internal divisions and limited unionisation stunted the fulfilment of labour's potential in wage bargaining. The CGT and CGIL, in response to the isolation of the Parti Communiste Français (PCF) and Partito Comunista Italiano (PCI) from government, organised a number of major strikes in the late 1940s, which, in the face of determined opposition from the French and Italian governments and lack of unity in the labour movement, failed.

During the 1960s dramatic changes in the structure of French and Italian industry took place. Management in larger enterprises required stabilised industrial relations with more scope introduced into collective bargaining. The CGT and CGIL, although fulfilling certain 'economic functions', initially rejected collective bargaining as a form of wage control. Public sector wages in particular were used as instruments of incomes policy and there were a number of strikes in the public sector. However the government and leading employers, to restrain wage demands, were willing to enter into articulated bargaining covering a number of non-wage areas, including vacation allowances, worker consultation boards and pensions improvements.[11] Industrial relations were changing, if slowly, before the dramatic events of May-June 1968; the role of union-linked parties in these changes was minimal.

The changing position of labour in Italy was linked to the development of the economic system. The levels of wage demands in the late 1950s increasingly related to the profitability of the large exporting companies. All unions, including an increasing number of Catholic union leaders, were dissatisfied with the government. They placed increasing emphasis upon inter-confederal co-ordination of bargaining tactics.

Between 1960 and 1963 the Christian Democrats, to stabilise their parliamentary position and to retain control of local administrations, brought the Italian Socialist Party (PSI) into their coalition. The Centre-Left government, formally embarking on an ambitious reform programme, served to place a temporary curb upon union demands. Leading Christian Democrat progressives and Socialists were given important portfolios but the senior figures of the Christian Democratic Party retained the key regulatory positions, particularly the Treasury. Socialists rapidly lost confidence in the capacity of the government to introduce reform in a political structure entirely resistant to indicative planning, let alone the *dirigiste* planning discussed in the early 1960s.

The failure of the Centre-Left alliance and the continued ascendancy of short-term fiscal and monetary policies contributed to the frustration of the unions. As in France, the inability of the unions' representatives to act through the party system directed unions to plant-level questions. In the metal industry the unions co-operated in plant-level bargaining from the early 1960s.

In the 1970s the Italian labour federations continued to co-operate, although they did not become autonomous from the parties. Private corporations and public companies entered into broad ranging collective bargains. The increasing extent of state involvement in industry, combined with union concentration on social and economic questions, led to closer bargaining between senior ministers and union leaders. The government made a number of major concessions to unions on labour legislation and introduced price indexation into wage agreements, which incorporated automatic escalation clauses.

From 1973 to 1977 the Christian Democrats depended on PCI co-operation. The PCI took a responsible approach to its new status. There were many explanations for their support of weak DC governments, involving PCI leader Berlinguer's tactical guidance of the party. The Central Committee of the PCI had serious doubts on the consequences of union relations with the party and the CGIL Secretary, Luciano Lama, a PCI member, endorsed Berlinguer's line, although strong doubts were expressed within the CGIL.

Conclusions. Where labour-linked parties were frequently in office, a number of social and economic demands were met. However, while they were broadly consulted on economic questions, unions were not brought into central decision-making, even when ministers concerned had union links. Secondly, in all the states covered, even where the leading unions were communist-linked, government and corporate management had to accommodate union interests in some measure.

INTEGRATED AND NON-INTEGRATED SYSTEMS: BRITAIN AND GERMANY

Britain. British unionism is frequently compared unfavourably with German unionism. There has been a tendency to exaggerate the lack of industrial integration achieved by British unions. Even if one dismissed the National Economic Development Council as powerless and uninfluential and the Labour-TUC Liaison Committee as exclusive to a distinct phase of Labour-union relations, the portrait of non-integration was false. Unions provided representatives to sit on countless industrial, health and welfare tribunals.

Unions fulfilled countless advisory and representational roles for their members beyond their wage bargaining responsibilities.

In early 1977 the leader of Britain's largest union, the Transport and General Workers, was popularly believed to be more powerful than the prime minister; yet his motion on pay policy was rejected at his own trade union conference within months of his accolade in the public opinion polls. In certain respects the problem of union leaders in Britain was that, far from having too much power, they did not have enough power:

> After 100 years the power situation in the TUC in one respect has remained almost unchanged. Neither the General Council nor the Congress has the power to compel unions to take a particular course of action.[12]

To this one must add that the leaderships of individual unions were unable to make decisions that would bind their membership. The Social Contract between the Labour government and the unions (1974-77) indicated the capacity of union leaders, under great strain, to give their support to a policy of pay restraint in return for concessions on a wide range of public social and economic policies. However, union leadership did not have the power to commit intermediate branch structures to finite policies. The relative success of wage restraint in 1975-77, after the enormous settlements of 1974, probably owed more to high unemployment than to the considerable efforts of leading unionists.

In Britain, although unions had industry-wide bargaining, wages, bonuses, productivity arrangements and fringe benefits were largely determined at plant levels. Local union leaders were unprepared for such functions to be transferred to central level. Union interpretation of industrial practices were usually locally determined. Demarcation and restrictive practices were a particular problem for the conglomerate unions. The national leaders of the Transport and General Workers Union and the Amalgamated Union of Engineering Workers were both humiliated in their attempts to intervene in local but very harmful disputes. The British motor industry was particularly damaged by intra-union skills disputes disturbing whole assembly lines.

The central aim of the 1969 Labour government's White Paper *In Place of Strife* was to oblige central union leadership to involve itself in the mediation of intra-union disputes. The Conservative government's 1971 Industrial Relations Act, although broader in scope, had similar aims: to increase the responsibility of central unions in arbitration. In response to the Act, the unions, at the cost of a number of sequestrations, refused registration with the newly established Industrial Relations Court. The 1971 Act was introduced by a government that made some claim to assert its self-appointed role of curbing union power. The Act entirely soured union relations with government. It was based upon an unrealistic assessment of the distribution of power in British unions and was destined to fail. Power in British unions was regionalised. The majority of regional and local leaders depended on being able to support the maximum demands of their members. Local leaders did not feel responsibility for broad economic policy and had a different role from senior national union leaders.

The major industrial actions in the coal industry, which led to violent picketing and ultimately to a general election, although based on wage demands, were conditioned by union resistance to what they saw as a 'union bashing government'.

The problem of broadening the corporate identity of workers was examined by the Committee on Industrial Democracy, chaired by Lord Bullock.[13] The Report of January 1977 recommended setting up unitary management boards with parity of workers and management representatives. It pointed to the EEC Green Paper on worker participation and the increasing number of European variants of worker participation. The Report's recommendations for restructuring the composition of boards of firms with over 2000 employees advocated a greater level of co-determination than either the Swedish joint boards or the German two-tier boards prescribed in the 1976 Co-Determination Act. British management was able to console itself with the knowledge that legislation was unlikely because of Labour's marginal parliamentary foothold and an underlying lack of enthusiasm among Labour ministers. Furthermore the unions, in spite of the enthusiasm of the union leaders on the Committee, were far more concerned about future pay claims.

Germany. Members of the Hannover Provisional Zonal Executive of the German unions, meeting in 1945, formulated a centralised framework of union organisation. The Executive's policy was endorsed at the Bielefeld conference of the Northern Zone unions in 1946. The pattern adopted in the North was accepted by unions in the other zones. The DGB established its own formal constitutional structure, with a congress, council and management board. Later the DGB established its own economic research institute in Dusseldorf. DGB leaders supported the legal recognition of fixed-term collective agreements (*Tarifvertragsgesetze*) and favoured the establishment of the federal, *Land* and local labour courts. None of these constraints had to be imposed upon reluctant trade unions.

The DGB leaders saw their stewardship depending on their ability to constrain local determination of industrial action. All sixteen unions refused financial or organisational support to strikes that had not been authorised by the *Land* and federal offices of the union. Under federal law, strikes within the duration of agreements were actionable, as were failures on behalf of employers to meet conditions of an agreement. The DGB, to limit possible subversion, insisted that plant workforces should secretly ballot before resorting to industrial action. In 1954 the employers' association

(BDA) and the DGB agreed to establish joint conciliation offices. Although methods of recording strike activity can disguise the incidence of local disputes, between 1956 and 1971 there were only five major strikes. Advanced conciliation procedures, the federalisation of DGB unions and accepted legal practices in industrial relations were important in containing industrial unrest. It would be wrong, however, to attribute Germany's favourable industrial relations exclusively to legal factors. International economic factors and the high level of German technical and economic expertise were equally important. The DGB largely identified itself with the standards of German management. This is hardly surprising as the central union offices were filled by highly skilled professional staff with training similar to that of management.

The DGB had a Federal Wages Policy Department and the wage claims of all unions were based on sophisticated production forecasting techniques. The complications for unions, management and government of union claims designed to regain relativities with other workers (a constant problem in Britain) was largely avoided. In 1967 the Minister of Economic Affairs, attempting to stimulate internal demand, even asked that the DGB increase their recommended wage claim figure (*Sockelbetrag*) from 5.8 per cent to 6.5 per cent.[14]

The feature of German industrial relations with particular relevance to other European systems was co-determination (*Mitbestimmung*). Between 1951-52, when parity worker representation was introduced into the steel and coal industries' supervisory boards, and 1976, when parity representation was legislated for the supervisory boards of all companies with over 2000 employees, the DGB pressed for greater co-determination. However, it is important to appreciate that German co-determination has been set in the context of two-tier management boards. The workers were only represented on supervisory boards. The *Vorstand* (chairmanship) remained the exclusive preserve of the shareholders' representatives. Under a 1971 Act the workers were permitted to select a labour director to the *Vorstand*. In 1967, during the 'Grand Coalition', the Biedenkopf Commission, established under DGB pressure, examined the representation ratios applied in the existing works constitution legislation. The Commission, although willing to change the ratios on supervisory boards from 1:2 to 5:7, rejected parity composition.

The DGB continued pressing their case. After 1969 they demanded that the SPD reciprocate the support the unions had given in the election, even though there was no evidence that German workers were particularly concerned with their leaders' preoccupation with co-determination. The 1971 Act, which obliged all firms with over 100 employees to establish finance committees with worker representation to discuss commercial policy, did not introduce parity representation, but it did introduce works conciliation boards (*Einigungsstelle*) with equal employer and employee representation. Where reconciliation was impossible, cases could be transferred to the labour courts.

The 1970s, particularly after 1973, were marked by increasing unemployment, which was partially cushioned by the shedding of migrant labour. The DGB, although concerned about the economic situation and the increasing number of wild-cat strikes, responded with moderate wage demands. As a partial quid pro quo, Chancellor Schmidt formulated a new bill extending parity co-determination on all supervisory boards with more than 2000 employees working for the company. As a concession to management and the FDP, the workers' quota on the supervisory board had to contain representatives of senior white-collar employees (*Angestellte*) who were not members of the DGB.

The 1976 Works Constitution Act was introduced with a two-year transitional provision, but in July 1977 thirty of the 650 firms with over 2000 employees, including Hoechst and Bayer, appealed to the Constitutional Court. German management had profited from its sophisticated relations with the unions, but business and a number of CDU/CSU leaders complained of an emerging 'trade union state'. For the DGB leaders there were inherent dangers in their participation on boards of management. Firms operated in a competitive market situation. If unions became partially responsible for authorising financial policies they might be obliged to choose between the short- and long-term prospects of their company's workforce. The danger of advanced plant participation procedures was potentially serious for industrial unions because they threatened to fragment wage patterns and weaken central union federation power.[15]

TRADE UNIONS IN AN INTERNATIONAL PERSPECTIVE

International labour organisations had broad interests but limited capacity to intervene at international levels. National unions had used international labour organisations for certain national ends, but the organisations never achieved supra-national authority. European unions, including those with international affiliations, were organised on exclusively national lines. Their membership perceived their union roles primarily in economic terms. Wage bargaining, job security and industrial law were the priorities. Broader problems such as education, environmental questions and diplomatic and trading relations with unapproved regimes were secondary. This is not to argue that trade unions were unconcerned with such problems. They paid considerable attention to welfare, education, foreign policy, for instance, but their main aims concerned their short-term interests. The limited scope of international union co-operation was a natural extension from the limited priority commitments of unions at the national level.

Since 1945 the organisations of European union co-operation were divided. The European Regional Section of the International Confederation of Free Trade Unions (ICFTU) opposed the World Federation of Trade Unions (WFTU), the Moscow-based organisation to which the largest unions in France and Italy belonged. In the 1950s, the union organisation of the European Coal and Steel Community (ECSC) the Committee of 21, and its EEC successor the European Secretariat (established in Düsseldorf in 1958), were based on ICFTU membership. The ECSC and the EEC led to increasing consultative responsibilities for unions, and during the 1960s all European labour confederations established offices in Brussels. The CGT and the CGIL, both WFTU members, established the *Comité Permanent*. Neither the EEC Council of Ministers nor the Commission formally recognised the *Comité*. Functional integration of union confederations through EEC work should not be over-stated. Although the international federations, as well as individual national unions, established European offices, mainly in Brussels, the work of the EEC during its first decade hardly involved the unions. In 1969, after labour unrest throughout much of Europe, during which the Communist parties of Italy and France had exercised great restraint, the EEC Commission extended recognition to the *Comité Permanent*. French and Italian nominations to the EEC's Economic and Social Committee were made, but under the insistence of the DGB and French FO delegates the CGT nominees were excluded from meetings of union members of the Committee. The opposition of the DGB and FO were natural extensions of their domestic positions.[16] In the 1970s, inter-European union affairs were complicated by the enlargement of the EEC détente and 'Eurocommunism' which cannot be discussed here. Instead we must briefly consider the relationship between trade unions and multinational corporations (MNCs) in the developed states of Western Europe.

Government attitudes to multinationals have varied. Within EFTA and the EEC governments usually facilitated outward investment by home-based multinationals. Government attitudes to inward investment by foreign multinationals were more complicated. In Britain, Conservative and Labour governments were equally willing to accept investment from any source, while France, particularly during the Gaullist decade, was identified with a tough policy of economic nationalism. France's reputation was rather curious considering that in 1971-72 38 per cent of all intra-EEC foreign investments were located in France. Sweden and Switzerland, both outside the EEC, placed 36 per cent of their investments in France.[17]

Multinationals were endlessly debated at union conferences and party meetings. The 1973 joint ICFTU-WFTU-WCL (World Confederation of Labour) meeting in Chile was convened to discuss multinationals. Given the difficulties that multinationals posed to national systems of company law and the limited development of international union organisation, what countervailing powers did unions have? In the late 1960s there were transnational industrial actions. In 1968, French, German and Italian glass workers gave support to French employees of the French multinational corporation St-Gobain.[18] In 1971, there was an example of transnational union co-operation in the tyre manufacturing industry. However, affairs were more accurately portrayed by the bitterness of French unions in the Chrysler-Simca plant when in 1975 Chrysler, with extensive incentives from the British government, agreed to establish a production line of their Alpine model in Britain. German employees of the American Litton Industries were willing to take on assembly work previously undertaken by Litton's Imperial subsidiaries in Britain.

What were the differences between union relations with MNCs and uninationals? Unions within territorial boundaries were supposed to pressure for the geographical equalisation of wages within each industrial sector to prevent the shift of investment to low-wage areas. Examination of investment by the *large* MNCs in the European context did not suggest that the low-wage factor was of *primary* importance in investment policy. Wage differences within Europe were not dramatically great after the various transfer payment systems were accounted for. Large multinationals were more concerned with the internal market prospects of the state in which they located their subsidiaries than with trans-European wage differentials.

Did MNCs pose particular threats to unions by their right to withdraw investment? In practice, there have been few such cases of multinational withdrawal. In the motor industry, Ford and Chrysler threatened withdrawal from Britain, probably with the aim of intimidating both the government and the unions. The Dutch-German AKZO chemical company closed a number of plants, although these closures were not related to counter-union strategy. The same must be said for the closure of FIAT's German assembly plant and Leylands' Innocenti company in Italy. It may be noted that the motor industry was concerned in four of these examples. With the exception of Volvo's take-over of DAF, only American MNCs had a trans-European manufacturing capacity in the motor industry. Co-operation between European motor industries existed mainly at the levels of design and components purchase.[19]

The common characteristic of MNCs was their capital intensiveness. Firms undertook extensive negotiations with host governments as well as market research before they located plants. In the context of wage bargaining, threats of capital withdrawal by MNC managements were more theoretical than practical. Multinationals were, however, as prepared as uninationals to use the sanction of curbed future investment as a counter in bargaining.

The only country to experience an outflow of MNC capital was Italy, owing to the political situation in the mid-1970s, although Italian banks and firms were probably the major exporters of capital. However, it is important to note that there were a number of disincentives for foreign investment in Italy outside the petroleum industry. The extensive scope of IRI and ENI investment placed foreign subsidiaries at a disadvantage. Furthermore, the highly protected position of fully employed workers and the transfer payment system made Italian labour increasingly expensive without reciprocal industrial peace obligations underpinning collective bargains. Additionally, investigations of MNC activities in Italian politics discouraged the immediate broadening of investment.

European unions concerned with the relationship between job losses and international investment had more reason to be concerned about the behaviour of certain uninational firms than about foreign subsidiary plants. Over the last decade it was in the labour-intensive areas, where multinationals were least involved, that job losses were most serious. The European clothing market began to contract much of its work to low-wage areas such as Portugal, North Africa, India and Singapore. A number of uninationals moved their manufacturing to low-wage and often non-unionised locations. Some national firms contracted their labour-intensive work to Eastern European countries.

The relationship between job loss and foreign investment by home-based MNCs was highly emotive. Workers on the supervisory board of Volkswagen threatened industrial action if the firm established a large assembly plant in the United States,[20] while the Swedish unions have joined government officials on a joint board vetting outward Swedish investment.

The prospects of unions extending their national activities concerning wage structures at inter-sectoral or inter-enterprise levels are remote. Wage bargaining has been contained within nationally determined wage norms, whether these are stated explicitly or not. Multinational companies generally associated with the employers' federations of the host state and fitted into the wage convoy, although they were in the forefront of encouraging productivity bargains and were a source of wage-drift. Wage structures fitted into national bargaining cycles. International enterprise bargaining is unlikely because it is incompatible with national incomes policy and depends upon accounting data that is not generally available. Further obstacles have been the different transfer payment and taxation systems and the threat constituted by international agreements to national union federations.[21]

The most frequent complaint against MNCs concerned their elusiveness; their legal, administrative and financial affairs were too secretive. Host government departments have had extensive links with MNCs but they have not always been in a position to assess the MNCs' long-term policies. It was important for national unions to know about MNCs' pricing policies, about inflow and outflow of profit, about multiple sourcing of products and about compliance with local taxation. Many of the legitimate concerns of unions with MNCs related to the limited capacity of the nation-state to codify its relations with MNCs. Unions, concerned with the preservation of jobs, could only press for the protection of sensitive areas of national production by tariffs and selective state investment on the basis of data made available by law. Unions had no substantial international counter to MNCs, although the EEC had a data bank on company activity. The prospects for making MNCs more accountable to their employees depended largely on the unions, on the basis of their own information and research, being able to press their case on national governments. For the unions to adapt themselves to this role, new systems of worker representation were essential, as well as a high calibre of union staffing.

Conclusion

Since the Second World War, profound changes in the structure of European economies occurred, deeply affecting the composition and role interpretation of trade unions. The growth of disposable incomes and welfarism encouraged unions to make broad-ranging but politically limited demands. The unions largely accepted the norms of the mixed economy.

The economic recession of the 1970s placed union leaders in an exposed position. Governments recruited union leaders to the cause of wage restraint, although the same governments found it difficult to reduce unemployment, stabilise prices, or introduce sustained selective import control. Unemployment, in contrast to the immediate postwar decades, had become once again a fact of life. Unions for their part discussed voluntary maximum working weeks, but such proposals were largely irrelevant to the underlying problem of depression in the world market for the products of many of Europe's leading companies. While the revenues of oil states were predominantly invested in Europe and the United States, the structure of international production was changing quickly. Far Eastern exporters were a particular threat to Western labour. It was increasingly clear that unless European labour organisations and political parties supported long-term investment in industry in preference to short-term economic goals, then whole new sectors of employment would be at risk.

NOTES AND REFERENCES
1. David Coates, *The Labour Party and the Struggle for Socialism,* London, Cambridge University Press, 1975.
2. For the social democrat view, see A. Crosland, *The Future of Socialism,* London, Jonathan Cape, 1958. For a Marxist view, Coates, *op. cit,* and Ralph Miliband, *The State in Capitalist Society,* London, Weidenfeld and Nicolson, 1969. Also Paul Foot, 'How the Labour Government has led socialists down another blind alley', *The Times,* 14 August 1975, p. 14.
3. *NALGO:* National Association of Local Government Officers.

4. Geoffrey K. Ingham, *Strikes and Industrial Conflict: Britain and Scandinavia,* London, Macmillan paperback, 1972.
5. *The Royal Commission on Trade Unions and Employers Associations 1965-1968,* London, HMSO, Cmnd. 3623, 1968, p. 7.
6. R. Dahrendorf, *Society and Democracy in Germany,* London, Weidenfeld and Nicolson, 1967, pp. 387-8. David Schoenbaum, *Hitler's Social Revolution: Class and Status in Nazi Germany 1933-1939,* London, Weidenfeld and Nicolson, 1966, p. 298. S. Verba, 'Germany: The Remaking of Political Culture' in L. Pye and S. Verba (eds) *Political Culture and Political Development,* Princeton, N.J., Princeton University Press, 1965, pp. 131-54. G. Loewenberg, 'The Remaking of the German Party System' in M. Dogan and R. Rose (eds) *European Politics: A Reader,* London, Macmillan, 1971, pp. 259-80.
7. For a full discussion of this topic, Stuart Holland, *The Socialist Challenge,* London, Quartet Books, 1975, Chs. 5, 6, 7 and 8. For the earlier period, Jacques Leruez, *Economic Planning and Politics in Britain,* London, Martin Robertson, 1975, pp. 37-77, 129-223.
8. See comments on Sweden and Germany in the *Report of the Committee of Inquiry on Industrial Democracy,* London, HMSO, Cmnd. 6706, 1977, p. 94.
9. Peter Merkl, 'Equilibrium, Structure of Interests and Leadership: Adenauer's Survival as Chancellor', *American Political Science Review,* vol. LVI, no. 3, 1962, pp. 634-50.
10. Gerhard Loewenberg, *Parliament in the German Political System,* Ithaca, Cornell University Press, 1967.
11. J.-J. Cechslin, 'The Role of Employers Organisations in France', *International Labour Review,* vol. 106, 1972, p. 391. J.-M. Verdier, 'Labour Relations in the Public Sector in France', *International Labour Review,* vol. 109, 1974.
12. 'A Centenary of the British Trade Union Congress (1868-1968)' J. Saville and R. Miliband (eds), *Socialist Register,* London, Merlin Press, 1968; cited in Ingham, *Strikes, op. cit.,* see also G.A. Dorfman, *Wage Politics in Britain,* Ames, Iowa State University Press, 1973.
13. *Report of Committee of Inquiry on Industrial Democracy,* London, HMSO, Cmnd. 6706, 1977.
14. E.C.M. Cullingford, *Trade Unions in West Germany,* London, Wilton House, 1976, p. 97-8.
15. T. Kirkwood and H. Mewes, 'The Limits of Trade Union Power in the Capitalist Order', *British Journal of Industrial Relations,* vol. XIV, no. 3, November 1976, pp. 295-305.
16. B.C. Roberts, and B. Liebhaberg, 'The European Union Confederation: Influence of Regionalism, Detente, and Multinationals', *British Journal of Industrial Relations,* vol. XIV, no. 3, November 1976, pp. 261-72.
17. Lawrence G. Franko, *The European Multinationals,* London, Harper and Row, 1976, Chapter I. More generally, see below, chapter 12.
18. *ibid,* p. 233.
19. L.T. Wells, Jr, 'Automobiles' in R. Vernon (ed.) *Big Business and the State: Changing Relations in Western Europe,* Cambridge, Mass., Harvard University Press, 1974.
20. Lawrence G. Franko, *The European Multinationals, op. cit.,* p. 231.
21. L. Ulman, 'Multinational Unionism: Incentives, Barriers, and Alternatives', *Industrial Relations,* vol. XIV, no. 1, February 1975, pp. 1-31.

SELECT BIBLIOGRAPHY

Crouch, C. and Pizzorno, A. (eds), *The Resurgence of Class Conflict in Western Europe,* 2 vols., London, Macmillan, 1978.
Franko, L.G., *The European Multinationals,* London, Harper and Row, 1976.
Jacobs, E., *European Trade Unionism,* London, Croom Helm, 1973.
Kendall, W., *The Labour Movement in Europe,* London, Allen Lane, 1975.
Kirchner, E.J., *Trade Unions as a pressure group in the European Community.* Westmead, Saxon House, 1977.
Vernon, R. (ed), *Big Business and the State,* Cambridge, Mass., Harvard University Press, 1974.

PART II

State and Society in Eastern Europe

CHAPTER 5

Party, State and Groups in Eastern Europe

Georg Brunner and Hannes Kaschkat

Since the death of Stalin a process of political differentiation has developed in the Soviet Union and Eastern Europe. This process has followed a different course in individual countries and has by no means been linear. The limited scope of the present study makes it impossible to give a detailed account of this development in all countries.[1] Thus attention will be focused on the basic characteristics concerning the sphere of Soviet hegemony, whilst a special chapter of this book (chapter 8) is devoted to the most significant exception in Eastern Europe, namely Yugoslavia.

THE SEAT OF POLITICAL POWER

From the purely formal point of view, the political system of Communist-ruled countries is divided into three subsystems: the party, the state and the social organisations. Whilst both the party and the state represent unified subsystems in the sense that they are organised along uniform and centralised lines under the direction of their supreme organs, the subsystem of the social organisations is composed of several organisational units, which, whilst being in themselves structured in a centralised way, do not have any governing organs in common. The formal tripartite division of the political system only partially takes account of the political subsystems that, on the face of it, fall within the sphere of the state, namely the security organs and the army. But these exercise so much weight of their own within the state that they can be regarded as relatively independent subsystems.

The correlation of the political subsystems

The theoretical model according to which the three subsystems are to be integrated to form the whole political system is derived from the basic ideological propositions of Soviet Marxism-Leninism, which is the binding ideology in all Communist-ruled countries. According to this ideology, the subsystem that lends cohesion to the whole is the party. It is superior to all the other subsystems and uses the latter as instruments with differing functions to accomplish its political goals. The thesis of the leading role of the party stems from Lenin, whose élitist party doctrine attributed to the Communist Party an absolute monopoly of insight and leadership on the grounds that it incorporated the most progressive social consciousness.[2] Despite a few modifications, the political ideology has adhered to this doctrine and, following the hardening of ideological attitudes that set in at the end of the 1960s, it is now proclaimed with increased emphasis. The party's monopoly of leadership is regarded as an inviolable principle of Communist rule and, in keeping with the Brezhnev Doctrine developed in 1968, the Soviet Union claims the right of intervention if it should be violated by a country belonging to the 'Socialist Commonwealth'.

The 'leading role of the party' applies both to fundamental political decisions and to the general direction and control of the other subsystems. The formulation and execution of political guide-lines is to be left to the state and the social organisations; the party should not interfere in day-to-day administrative work. The deeper significance of this division of functions is the support it gives to the party's claim to political leadership whilst relieving it of all political responsibility. When things go wrong, only an organ that is an immediate acting agent can be held responsible and, in view of the division of functions envisaged, this can never be a party organ. For the party to be responsible in such an event would be incompatible with its claim to infallibility and would thus impinge upon the communist doctrine of legitimacy at its roots.

Whether and in what way the abstract, theoretical model of a party dictatorship as outlined above is translated into reality can only be established by analysing the facts. In undertaking this, it is advisable to draw a distinction between its historical, functional and institutional aspects.

Viewed *historically,* a dictatorship of the party proper was first developed in the Soviet Union in the 1920s. During the Stalinist period this system underwent fundamental changes. Of the individual political subsystems, the social organisations were fully developed in the 1930s, the state apparatus was strengthened vis à vis the party and the security service was transformed into a power factor of great significance. Between the institutions of the political subsystems there existed an unsteady and variable balance, which Stalin manipulated according to the principle of divide and rule. Stalin's one-man dictatorship was based on the rivalry between the individual bureaucracies, the latter being periodically purged and played off against one another with the help of Stalin's private office, headed by Poskrebyshev. This system was gradually introduced into Eastern Europe after the Communist take-over. As a consequence, the dictator usually combined the offices of party leader and head of government in his own person, as Stalin had done since 1941. With the death of Stalin the personal basis of one-man dictatorship disappeared and the ensuing struggle for succession that went on under the guise of collective leadership inevitably grew into a dispute between the individual bureaucracies. Thus it followed that the personal defeat of one of these contenders necessarily brought about a loss of power on the part of the political subsystem represented by him. The liquidation of Beria, the head of the MVD, in 1953, led to a weakening of the security service; the sacking of Malenkov, the head of government, in 1955, reduced the influence of the state; and the fall of Marshal Zhukov, the Minister of Defence, in 1957, reversed the rising political influence of the army, which, it must be added, never at any time cherished Bonapartist ambitions. Since Khrushchev gained his victories from his position as party leader, it was obvious that the party should simultaneously gain a dominant position over the other political subsystems. The superior position of the party, corresponding as it did to ideological requirements, was also maintained after Khrushchev had taken over the office of head of government in 1958 and the whole system had begun to take on an increasingly personal character. It proved impossible for a one-man dictatorship of the Stalinist type to develop, since tendencies in this direction were checked by the alliance of the political subsystems. The re-establishment of collective leadership after Khrushchev's fall in 1964 brought about a readjustment of the power of the individual subsystems. There arose an astonishingly robust power system, structured along oligarchic lines, in which the party enjoys, it is true, a certain superiority, but in which the party leadership has to endeavour to promote a balance of interests and the integration of all the subsystems. In the Eastern European countries, developments since the death of Stalin have varied but, in general, tyrannical one-man dictatorship has been replaced by an oligarchic party dictatorship, in which the superior position of the party leader and the influence of the individual subsystems are developed to differing degrees.

As far as *functional* aspects are concerned, the assertion that fundamental political decisions are taken by the party and are carried out by the state together with the social organisations needs some qualification according to the subject areas involved. There are areas that the party attends to with particular energy and where it leaves the implementing organs hardly any freedom of action. These include the production of ideology, agitation and propaganda, as well as foreign, military and security policies. In contrast, the state has relatively wide freedom in the field of economic policy where an extensive bureaucracy is necessary for the preparation of decisions. But even here distinctions must be made. Thus the Communist Party of the Soviet Union (CPSU) frequently devotes attention to specific questions in the field of agriculture, whereas this seldom occurs in the industrial sphere, although a notable exception is the armaments industry. The Communist parties of the individual countries use their powers to establish general guide-lines to varying degrees. In Hungary these powers are used with far more reserve than in the Soviet Union or East Germany. Since the Hungarian economic reforms of 1968, responsibility for a number of decisions concerning production has even been transferred from the state to the industrial plants themselves, which in this respect are only under state supervision. Such far-reaching economic reforms were never envisaged in East Germany and the Soviet Union and here even the far more modest reform initiatives of 1963 and 1965 respectively have gradually petered out.[3] The functions of the social organisations are determined by their own specific character. They devote their main energies to the field of political socialisation, in particular agitation and propaganda and the administration of cultural activities. Special mention should be made of the trade unions, which exercise important implementing functions in the spheres of production propaganda, social administration and labour law.

This outline of the system of functions has to be further refined by taking into account *institutional* aspects. The individual political subsystems consist of numerous institutions that do not as a whole exercise the functions of the subsystem. In accordance with the general organisational principle of democratic centralism, there is a relative concentration of power at the top of the individual subsystems. At the level of the general system only the Politburo, the party leader and the Secretariat of the Central Committee from among the party organs can be regarded as real power-wielding agents inasmuch as they can make independent fundamental decisions on their own or, at least, can influence the decision-making process decisively.[4] The Central Committee, which according to the party statutes should run the party between Party Congresses, and the Central Auditing and/or Control Commission only have secondary importance since they are concerned primarily with the areas of consultation, information and integration.

When we turn our attention to the state, things are somewhat more complicated. The most important organ here is undoubtedly the Council of Ministers, but in the majority of countries it is far too large a body to be able to take fundamental political decisions.[5] Only the leading group consisting of the chairman and his deputies can be regarded as genuine power-wielding agents, a group that has crystallised in all countries, but that has not been institutionalised everywhere as a Presidium. In contrast, the presidential organ of the highest representative body, i.e. of parliament, which is given various names in the individual countries, plays a secondary role and is comparable to the Central Committee from the power politics viewpoint.[6] This also applies to countries that have a State Council since it exclusively reflects the personal power of the party leader, who is also its chairman.[7] The subsystem of the social organisations does not have any central body comparable to the party and state organs.

The system of transmission

If the supremacy of the party is to be attained, there must be a guarantee that the will of its leading organs is imparted to the other political subsystems. To this end, a system of transmission has been developed, the most important elements of which are firstly, the binding nature of party resolutions. Party resolutions are binding not only on party members, but also on all state organs, social organisations and their functionaries. The priority they have over legal norms derives from the party's monopoly of leadership and the instrumental character of law. Secondly, the personal union between the party, state and social organisations is achieved by filling all the relatively important offices in the state and the social organisations by party members, who, in this capacity, are subject to party discipline. The integration of top state and social officials into the corresponding committees of the party has proved to be particularly effective, since such officials thereby participate in formulating the party resolutions that they have subsequently to carry out. In this field, Romania has taken the most far-reaching steps; since 1967 local party leaders have assumed the chairmanships of the corresponding people's councils ex officio.[8]

A third instrument of party control consists of the powers of the party regarding personnel. The control that the party has over the personnel of the political subsystems is exercised primarily by employing two methods: the nomenclature system and personnel policies. The term 'nomenclature' refers to a register of leading positions, over which personnel decisions can be made only with the agreement of the nomenclature office. The most important positions in the state, economy and society are included in the party's nomenclature. The nomenclature of the central party leadership usually comprises all ministers, top officials of the ministries and other central administrative authorities, the directors of large industrial enterprises, diplomats, higher military commanders and the top officials of the social organisations and the mass media.[9] The term 'cadre policy' refers basically to the right of the party to determine the guide-lines for the selection, training and employment of officials. The party establishes the criteria for personnel decisions and devises career patterns; these criteria vary according to the time and country. The most important cadre-policy decision is that of deciding the weight to be attached to the often conflicting selection criteria of political reliability and professional qualifications. Although the weight attached to professional qualifications has generally grown since Stalin's time and distinctions have to be drawn according to the sphere of activity, in cases of conflict the criterion of party reliability has been able to retain its priority in most countries, despite all fluctuations. In the case of East Germany, this development has been impressively traced in a recent study.[10] Hungary constitutes an interesting exception. There, in

December 1961, party leader Kádár proclaimed in an address to the National Council of the Patriotic People's Front the principle of 'whoever is not against us, is for us'.[11] With the exception of top political positions, the principle of cadre selection is that professional qualifications have priority.

Fourthly, there is the party's power of direction and control. This is exercised by the full-time party apparatus, the primary organisations in the workplaces and the party groups in the elective organs of state and the social organisations. However, considerable differences can be noted in the political practice of individual countries. A comparison of the provisions of the party statutes concerning the powers of the primary organisations bring these differences to light in a symptomatic way. Traditionally, a distinction is made between the primary organisations in production-oriented workplaces and those in the state administrative organs. The former have extensive rights of investigation and control over the management, whereas the latter possess only a limited authority to report deficiencies observed to higher party bodies. In the Soviet Union, the greater right of control was extended to the whole sector of culture and education in 1971. The East German Communist Socialist Unity Party followed the Soviet example in the same year and has subsequently gone far beyond it inasmuch as its new statute of 1976 gives the primary organisations a right of control over the state administrative organs. In contrast, the Hungarian Communists gave up the formulation of special control powers when a new party statute was passed in 1966 and contented themselves with a very generally worded definition of tasks.

Finally, there are organisational interconnections between the party and state bureaucracies. It occasionally happens that the duality of state and party is eliminated by an amalgamation of the two. This method was particularly favoured by Krushchev, in keeping with his efforts to establish party absolutism. It does, however, involve great dangers since the direct involvement of the party in administrative work also leads it at the same time into the danger area where it can be held responsible when things go wrong. With the setting up of a mixed agricultural administration of party-cum-state in 1962, Khrushchev went against the dictates of political good sense in a very critical area. Fate took up the challenge and presented the Soviet Union with a catastrophic harvest the following year. Thus, after Khrushchev's fall, all reforms aimed at establishing an institutional link between party and state were quickly rescinded. A parallel development also took place in the countries of Eastern Europe. At present, Romania is an exception since in July 1972 Ceausescu called for a unitary management of society.[12] The party's Central Committee translated this call into resolutions in November of the same year and since then the personal union and organisational amalgamation of party and state has been pushed forward energetically.[13]

THE NATURE OF POLITICAL POWER

The question of how to characterise the nature of such political power as we have localised above has been hotly debated among experts. After the Second World War, it became common practice to refer to both the communist and fascist systems as 'totalitarian'. Since the beginning of the 1960s, the concept of 'totalitarianism' has been subjected to increasing and, at times, severe criticism. This is not the place to go into these discussions in detail, nor to examine the individual arguments for and against.[14] We would merely like to state briefly the reasons why we consider that the communist political systems can still be adequately described by the concept of 'totalitarian dictatorship'.

'Totalitarian dictatorship'?

If one looks upon the political system as a power organisation in which decisions are made and carried out, three questions can be regarded as being important for the designation of political systems. Who wields power (makes the decisions)? How wide is the scope of such power (decisions)? By what means is such power exercised (are the decisions carried out)? Or to put it another way: the three most important aspects are the power structure, the scope of power and the exercise of power. Since these are not simple questions requiring yes/no answers, the answers to them involve manifold nuances and differentiations. The difficulties in this undertaking need not be dealt with in detail here, since it is clear that the totalitarian dictatorship should be situated at one end of the scale of possible answers and combinations of answers. As political reality hardly corresponds with ideal types, no political system on earth can be expected to answer our questions with mathematical accuracy. Bearing this in mind, a political system to be qualified as totalitarian dictatorship is 'total' in the sense that the power to make political decisions of nation-wide importance is concentrated at the centre of the power system and that the scope of power and the means open to it are virtually absolute. All these three characteristics apply to the communist systems of the present day, notwithstanding undeniable changes that have taken place during the last two decades.

Monistic power structure. We have noted that three bodies are entrusted with the making of supreme political decisions: the Politburo, the Secretariat of the Central Committee and the Presidium of the Council of Ministers. However, the relationship between them is not characterised by the principle of the separation of powers, but rather is so constituted that they represent a power centre in the politico-sociological sense. First of all, a hierarchy exists between them: the Politburo is meant to be the supreme decision-making organ, the Secretariat of the Central Committee its executive organ and, in accordance with the thesis of the leading role of the party, the Presidium of the Council of Ministers is the executive organ of both party bodies. A binding delineation of their respective responsibilities does not exist; rather, the pragmatic principle of the division of labour is adhered to, whereby the power to decide who should do what is placed in the hands of the Politburo. As far as their personnel is concerned, the three bodies are closely linked to one another inasmuch as the Secretariat of the Central Committee and the Presidium of the Council of Ministers are largely integrated into the Politburo. We are thus concerned with a relatively closed, oligarchic group of individuals, which constitutes the sociological substratum of the institutions. The extent to which the institutions are integrated from the point of view of personnel differs in the individual countries. To cite three examples: on 1 August 1977, the governing bodies of the Soviet Union comprised 45 positions, which were filled by 37 individuals; the corresponding figures for East Germany were 52 positions and 35 individuals; for Hungary, 28 positions and 21 individuals. The details of the personnel interconnections are shown in Table 5.1. From this table it can be seen that the integration of the Secretariat of the Central Committee into the Politburo is total in East Germany, whilst in the Soviet Union and Hungary it is only just over half. In East Germany and Hungary, approximately half of the members of the Presidium of the Council of Ministers have a seat in the Politburo, whilst in the Soviet Union the personnel integration is surprisingly confined to the top positions. Further details of this integration will be discussed later in another connection. Here, it is merely intended to serve as an illustration of the monistic power structure.

TABLE 5.1 *Interrelationship between composition of some communist governing bodies*

Country	Politburo	Secretariat of the Central Committee	Members also in the Politburo	Presidium of the Council of Ministers	Members also in the Politburo
Soviet Union	20 (14 + 6*)	11	6	14	2
East Germany	28 (19 + 9*)	12	12	12	5
Hungary	15	7	4	6	3

* Full members plus candidate members.

The scope of power is virtually total. The actual decision-making power of the power centre is at least latently absolute as far as its subject matter is concerned. The fact that its scope is total is safeguarded by the ideology of the system, which lays claim to exclusiveness, accords the top ranks of the party a monopoly of insight and leadership and maintains at least the potential socio-political relevance of each and every matter. It is true that this range of power is not achieved everywhere and at all times to the same degree. Fluctuations and differences can be observed. Thus, the Khrushchev era witnessed a general extension of the field of ideologically neutral issues, i.e. of those that the individual was free to decide about for himself. This state of affairs has changed in the meantime. Since the events of 1968 in Czechoslovakia, and even more as a result of Western attempts to bring about détente, the scope of personal freedom has once again been increasingly reduced, though not to the same degree in every country. Without doubt the range of such power as practised today in Hungary is considerably smaller than in all the other countries within the sphere of Soviet hegemony. With all these developments, one thing is decisive in the long run, namely that the power centre remains willing and able to determine autonomously the scope of power.

The exercise of total power. In principle, the power centre can mobilise every conceivable means to carry out its decision. Of course, fluctuations and differences can be observed here as well. The systematic mass terror of the Stalinist era is no longer practised anywhere today. However, the selective use of terror against political dissenters is still used quite frequently. Thus in Romania, for example, such practices based on terror can look back on a relatively unbroken tradition. In other countries, terror has recently been revived after a phase of relative leniency, as, for example, has been the case with the persecution of dissidents in the Soviet Union and the human rights movement in Czechoslovakia. Once again, the decisive point is that there are no effective checks on the total disposition of the means of exercising power, since the legal protection of the individual is deficient and the law, moreover, is subordinated to politics on account of its instrumental character.

The totalitarian nature of communist dictatorships can be and occasionally is called into question on two accounts. The first concerns the participation of the people in the political decision-making process, the second, that of the social groups. If it is true that democratic or pluralistic elements have developed in communist countries to such an extent that the monistic power structure described above no longer corresponds to reality, then the question can in fact be asked whether such countries have changed in the course of time from totalitarian into authoritarian dictatorships.

'Socialist democracy'?

The existence of a 'socialist democracy' is expressly affirmed in the self-evaluation of the communist systems and has even been given increased emphasis in the ideological and constitutional writings of recent years. At the same time, however, it is maintained that 'socialist democracy' in Eastern Europe is identical with the 'dictatorship of the proletariat', although this does not apply to the Soviet Union where developments are claimed to have already progressed further. The theoretical contradiction between the sovereignty of the people and the supremacy of the party is resolved ideologically by asserting that sovereignty is not ascribed simply to the people, but to the working people. The people are not seen as an unorganised, egalitarian unit but rather as a class-structured entity. 'Developed socialist society' is still meant to be a class society. Consequently, the individual classes are endowed with varying degrees of legitimation. The greatest degree of legitimation is attributed to the most conscious and progressive elements, which are united in the party. Thus, the way leads from the 'sovereignty of the working people' to the 'leading role of the party', justified as it is by the latter's élitist monopoly of insight.

Relevant literature and also some constitutions[15] mention various forms of participation, by means of which 'socialist democracy' is to be realised and the people are to exercise their power. There are four ways in which these possibilities of participation are put into practice.

Elections. In all Communist-ruled countries, the people's representatives are elected at all levels of the territorial administration and, in theory, these should be the most important holders of state power. However, these elections are not expected to be elections in the sense that a choice between several political alternatives is possible. They are primarily propagandistic events designed to mobilise the people for particular purposes (usually the fulfilment of plans) and to demonstrate the assumed political unity of the community. 'Thus the holding of elections becomes an occasion on which the state consciousness of millions of citizens manifests itself.'[16] To what extent, in addition to their main propagandistic functions, elections may tentatively allow the electorate to participate by giving expression to its will, depends on the electoral practice and the franchise of the individual countries.

The electors have practically no influence on the nomination of candidates. This is normally undertaken by the Communist Party via the National Front, or a similar organisation, whilst the electors' assemblies, at which the candidates are presented, have no decisional importance. The only exception to this is Hungary where the monopolistic right of the Patriotic People's Front to nominate candidates was broken by Electoral Law No. III/1970. Now, in addition to the Patriotic People's Front, electors' assemblies can also nominate candidates from their own ranks, but this very rarely occurs in practice.

In the election process itself, electors can indicate their rejection of the official candidate by abstaining or by voting against such candidates. Such behaviour on the part of the electors has no effect as a rule since the election is so organised that both the turnout and the number of votes-for cast tend to amount to well over 99 per cent. Anglo-American research into the 'missing one per cent' has not come up with any results worthy of note.[17] The results of electoral behaviour depend first and foremost on the electoral system. In this respect, a distinction has to be drawn between two groups of countries. In the Soviet Union, Albania, Bulgaria, Romania, Czechoslovakia and Hungary since 1966, individual candidates stand in single-member constituencies and are elected according to the absolute majority principle, while in East Germany and Poland candidates are elected from a single list in multi-member constituencies.

In the case of single-member constituencies, whether the will of the electors exercises any influence depends on whether only one or several candidates are put forward for election. With the exception of Hungary (since 1967) and Romania (since 1975), only one official candidate has been, and still is, nominated. Thus the will of the electors can only attain practical relevance if a candidate is rejected by more than 50 per cent of the electorate. This has never occurred at the national level and even at local elections this is a very rare exception. For example, the statistical probability of this happening at elections for the local Soviets in the USSR is 1 in 13,000.[18] In Hungary and, more recently, in Romania, the elector can occasionally exercise a personal choice since he can decide between several (usually two) candidates, who are all committed to the same political programme. Thus in the Hungarian parliamentary elections of 1967, two candidates were nominated in 9 of the 349 constituencies, whilst in 1971 this was the case in 49, and in 1975 in 34, of the 352 constituencies.[19] In several cases this produced a considerable split in the votes cast, a fact that allows one to conclude that this constituted a genuine election. By way of contrast, in the Romanian parliamentary elections of 1975, where two candidates were put up in 139 of the 349 constituencies, there were few indications that the electorate made a genuine decision.[20]

In those systems where candidates are elected from lists, the will of the people can play a role if the elector is able to alter the position of candidates on the list by crossing out the names of individual candidates, provided that the list contains more names than the number of seats. In theory, these requirements are met in both East Germany and Poland today. In practice, the possibility of changing the order of the candidates in the list is excluded in East Germany since, according to the 1976 Electoral Law, the order of candidates can be changed only if individual candidates are struck off the list by more than 50 per cent of the electors. How remote this possibility is from reality is revealed by the fact that, as a rule, official candidates receive over 99.9 per cent of the votes cast. In Poland, the situation is different. There is no comparable restrictive regulation and it is claimed that 15 per cent of the electors make use of their right to strike candidates off the list.[21] This small percentage is admittedly not enough to defeat official candidates, but it is sufficient to change the order in which candidates are elected in the end. In this respect, the Polish Sejm elections can be seen as a limited test of popularity.[22]

Accountability. This sometimes takes place by members of the people's assemblies and occasionally by other state officials prior to their election. Such rare cases of accountability amount to propaganda events. The right of the electors to recall their representatives is similarly without significance. Whilst there are isolated accounts of such occurrences at the local level, they usually involve cases of crass criminality and drunkenness so that the people's representative has become a downright embarrassment to the party. Moreover, the right to recall representatives is so arranged from the legal angle that the electors can scarcely recall a representative on their own. In East Germany and Romania, electors' assemblies are only accorded the right to make suggestions, not a genuine right of recall.

Activity in social organisations. The social organisations exercise in the main an agitational and propagandistic function. This constitutes the sole task of the various propaganda associations and the main task of the youth organisations. The professional associations of writers, artists, architects, etc., play a central role in the administration of cultural affairs and, in particular, provide privileges to favoured groups in the cultural intelligentsia. To a certain degree they also represent the interests of their members. The trade unions are the agents of production propaganda and carry out important administrative and supervisory tasks in the spheres of labour and social law (such as work and health protection or social insurance). On the other hand, they rarely come to the fore as representatives of the interests of the employees; only in Hungary do they play an appreciable role in this capacity. Finally, the social organisations also include the sports associations and the paramilitary organisations, which are responsible for the pre-conscription training of young people and the supervision of post-conscription military readiness. In some countries (East Germany, Poland, Czechoslovakia, Bulgaria), there are also other parties in addition to the Communist Party. They have unconditionally recognised the leading role of the Communist Party and regard their main task as being that of transmitting the will of the Communist Party to a particular group of the population. Consequently, the social organisations have very few opportunities to influence the political process. But even these limited possibilities can hardly be used in a democratic way, since the activities of the organisations are, in accordance with the principle of democratic centralism, directed by a full-time group of officials and the influence of rank and file members is reduced to a minimum.

Grassroots participation in the executive and control processes of the state. The effective forms of participation were extended in the Khrushchev era with considerable publicity but have, in the meantime, been partly withdrawn. Assisting the police, honorary participation in the committees of local representative organs, working as people's controller of the apparatus, which under various names (worker-and-peasant inspection, people's control, state control) exercises considerable economic control, all such activities fall into this category. In this connection, mention should also be made of the honorary work done by lay justices in the courts. Finally, citizens have the right to file petitions, informing the authorities of the complaints and wishes of the population. All in all, these possibilities of participation are very limited. They are really relevant only at the local level of the state administration, where relatively close social contact exists, but even here they serve only to channel advice, suggestions and information.

To sum up, the practical consequences of 'socialist democracy' do not affect the monistic power structure of communist systems of government and are scarcely conducive to bringing about direct influence by society on the decision-making process. In purely formal terms, the Politburo and the Secretariat are elected by the Central Committee and the Presidium of the Council of Ministers is elected by parliament. In these elections, however, the nomenclature system has overriding authority with the result that the Politburo selects new members by co-opting them itself and decides on the composition of the two other bodies. The limited possibilities of participation open to the population are confined to the lowest levels of the executive and control processes. These possibilities are not without importance in the field of local government affairs for the citizens concerned, but their significance as a whole must be termed minimal. The population has no influence at all on the appointment of the agents of the supreme power.

'Socialist pluralism'?

While the direct influence of society on the political process within the framework of 'socialist democracy' is admitted by communist ideology, the possibility of indirect influence via social groups together with the notion of 'socialist pluralism' is strictly rejected and is decried as capitalist defamation. The party alone is accorded the right to lay down which social interests constitute the public interest. That special, divergent interests should have the right to exist is totally repudiated. The unsolicited setting up of interest associations is illegal and is punished by the criminal law. This basic ideological conception, together with the arsenal of repressive measures at its disposal are, of course, not able to eliminate the sociological fact that groups of individuals with differing interests also exist in 'socialist societies'. However, such interests cannot operate freely, but only within the framework of existing institutions. In recent years, Western research has devoted increased attention to the phenomenon of group interests[23] and has sometimes prompted very far-reaching hopes about a change in the system. As early as the mid-1960s, it was claimed that the GDR had already escaped from the bonds of totalitarianism and had changed into a 'consultative authoritarianism'[24], while an 'institutional-pluralistic model' has been applied to the Soviet Union.[25]

The individual interest groups. Any attempt to define the individual interest groups gives rise to considerable difficulties since they are not organised into associations of their own and cannot appear in public. Nevertheless, four aspects would seem to be of importance regarding the constitution of interest groups, namely, functional, territorial, national and personnel considerations. Of course, the actual weight attached to each of these depends on the particular conditions in each country.

From the point of view of *functional* considerations, a distinction can first of all be drawn between the two large groups of the power élite and the intelligentsia, based upon the different relationship they have to political power. The members of the party élite occupy positions of power and can exercise direct influence on the political process. The intelligentsia does not occupy any positions of power and thus its opportunities of exercising influence are smaller. Its relative strength lies in the expert knowledge and prestige of its members, which the power élite can do without only to a certain degree. The power élite is divided up along the lines of the political subsystems into party officials, state officials, members of the military establishment and security officials. Between them there exist interconnections of varying intensity. The party officials constitute the most important interest group, but it is by no means homogeneous. Probably the most important subgroups are those of the party ideologists and party organisers. The former, who are to be found primarily in the agitprop apparatus, hold the most conservative views and their main interest is aimed at preserving the old, petrified power structures. The party organisers, on the other hand, usually occupy general co-ordinating or special administrative posts in party management and tend to be more pragmatic and willing to accept changes furthering efficiency. The differences, however, must not be over-emphasised. The state officials form a far more specialised and disparate group. Their main areas of activity are those concerned with the economy, the provision of social and cultural services, the foreign service and the judiciary. Because of their deeper involvement in the everyday affairs of policy implementation and administration, state officials are likely to have a more realistic outlook on problems created by socio-economic development. In comparison, the military establishment constitutes a relatively closed group sharing common career patterns and vested interests, although the difference between professional officers and political officers is not inconsiderable. On the whole, they are interested in increasing military expenditures and, in the Soviet case, in a foreign policy on imperialistic lines. Officials of the security apparatus stick together as well, but there are some personnel exchanges between them and the party apparatus. Many of them are staunch supporters of neo-Stalinist tendencies, opposing any kind of reform. The intelligentsia is divided up into the technical-economic intelligentsia and the scientific-cultural intelligentsia. Since there are many industrial branches and many types of leading positions, the technical-economic intelligentsia displays pronounced differences, that between the production-oriented engineer and the manager trained in economics being the most striking. The technical-economic intelligentsia scarcely has any associations of its own in the subsystem of social organisations so that it is dependent on its contacts with the state economic bureaucracy in order to assert its interests. Finally, the scientific-cultural intelligentsia is the most heterogeneous group, with fewest possibilities of exercising influence. From the organisational point of view, the scientists are accommodated by the academies of sciences, whilst the cultural intelligentsia is distributed among the various professional associations (such as writers, artists, architects). Whether the leading bodies of these professional associations are prepared to give expression to group interests to any extent or whether they see their task to be exclusively that of transmitting the will of the party to their members is a question that has to be answered differently from association to association and from country to country.

The same problem exists for the social organisations, but is not so acute since, in most cases, an attachment to one of the groups of officials can be discerned. The youth organisations and the numerous propaganda associations are generally attached to the party officials. The paramilitary organisation, which is to be found in all countries, is closely connected to the army. The various economically oriented co-operative associations and the sports associations probably often have the same interests as the state officials responsible for them. The most complicated problem is posed by the trade unions, which are closely connected to both the party (propaganda) and the state apparatus (labour and social administration). Whether, in addition to this, they also represent the interests of employees to any extent — which according to ideological precept should be the case — and thus allow us to speak of trade union officials as a special interest group, is a question to which there is no general answer. An answer can only be given by analysing the actual activities of trade unions. At present, the unions come closest to assuming the role of an interest group in Hungary, where, since the economic reforms of 1968, this function has been emphatically promoted by the party and state leadership.[26] The reason for this fairly liberal attitude towards the workers' interests in Hungary is presumably the Kádár régime's intention to fill the gap traditionally separating the toiling masses from their Communist rulers as well as to counteract the socially negative effects of an economic reform that appeals to the profit motive.

From the *territorial* viewpoint, a distinction has to be made between central, regional and local interest groups according to the level of administration. On the one hand, each territorial unit has to be regarded as a relatively autonomous political subsystem with its own group of officials, who are interested in promoting their own special interests within their sphere of influence. On the other hand, each territorial unit is part of a hierarchy, being connected to a higher and a lower territorial unit, and this fact can give rise to opposing interests, which, in turn, can produce a feeling of solidarity among its groups of functionaries. To what extent the territorial group interests take precedence over the group interests of its officials is dependent on many factors. Generally speaking, one can say that the weight attached to territorial group interests increases in proportion to the size of the country. Thus, in the Soviet Union, they play a very prominent role: the regions of Moscow, Leningrad, Kiev, Kharkov, Minsk, the Donets basin or the industrial areas in the Urals and around Novosibirsk have a considerable influence on the national political decision-making process.

National interests are conducive to the formation of groups in those countries in which the problem of nationality plays a role, as in states comprising several peoples (the Soviet Union), states with large national minorities (Romania) or states comprising two peoples (Czechoslovakia) (see chapter 6).

Finally, particular significance must be attached to the clan-like *groups of personal followers* that, generally speaking, derive their cohesion from the fact that their members have gone through an important stage of their lives together. Thus, in the Soviet Union, a large section of the strong Brezhnev group comes from around Dnepropetrovsk in the Ukraine where the General Secretary grew up, completed his training as an engineer and from 1935 to 1941 and 1947 to 1950 occupied leading positions. The hard core of members originating from those periods was later joined by followers who came into close contact with Brezhnev when he was a political officer (1941-46, 1953-54) or party boss of Moldavia (1952-53) and of Kazakhstan (1954-56). Additional groups of this kind are the 'White Russian partisans' around Politburo member Mazurov, whose feeling of attachment dates back to commonly shared experiences in the Second World War; the 'Kharkov group' around the ousted Podgorny, who made his career in the Ukrainian party apparatus; and the followers of the deposed Shelepin — since dispersed — whose shared characteristic was that they had served in the Komsomol or in the secret service.

Clashes between three groups of personal followers characterised the period of communist take-over in Eastern Europe, and had their roots in the personal experience of their members before and during the war. There were the 'Muscovites' who returned home beneath the shield of the Red Army after having emigrated to the Soviet Union; the 'illegals' who had remained in their homeland, had been persecuted and had worked in the underground movement; and those who had emigrated to the West. Today, these groupings are scarcely of importance any more. Now, the personal groups of followers date in the main from the postwar period. An example of this is the group around Honecker in East Germany, whose members began their political careers in the youth organisation in which the party leader held the position of First Secretary from 1946 to 1955.

Methods of exercising group influence. Within the framework of the institutional system described above, interest groups have various possibilities at their disposal for influencing the political decision-making process. In particular, special significance may be attached to four methods, namely, contacts with the power-wielding agents, public expression of opinion, advisory roles and representative activity in the power-wielding bodies.

Contacts with the power-wielding agents can be either of a formal, institutional character or of a personal, informal kind. Since the members of the power élite hold positions of power, they have institutional access to the power-wielding agents. The top organs of the party (Politburo, Secretariat of the Central Committee) and of the state (Presidium of the Council of Ministers) are themselves primary power-wielding agents. The top-most military and security officials have immediate access to them. The intelligentsia has access to the power-wielding agents via the appropriate ministries, the departments of the Central Committee, the professional associations and the academies of sciences, but in each of these cases such contact is only indirect. In addition to this, informal contacts based on personal acquaintance play a most important role.

Public expression of opinion represents an indirect form of access to the power-wielding agents. Since freedom of speech does not exist in Communist-ruled countries and the mass media are controlled by the agitprop apparatus of the party, this form of group influence has limited effect. The possibility of expressing one's opinion in public first of all presupposes that one has access to the mass media. In this respect, the position of individual interest groups differs. The party and state officials enjoy the most favourable position since they have a wide range of mass media at their disposal, which even partly take into account differences within the group. The position of the trade unions is also quite favourable since they at least publish a daily newspaper with a large circulation. The army also has its own press organ, but only in the Soviet Union does the Ministry of Defence publish its own daily paper (*Krasnaia Zvezda*). The security organs generally do not possess their own mass media. The technical-economic intelligentsia is dependent on the party and government media and on technical journals, while the professional associations and other groups within the scientific-cultural intelligentsia have a widely ramified press of their own.

To what degree group interests are articulated in the mass media depends on the particular conditions in the individual countries. The mass media of East Germany have always been dominated by uniform propaganda and thus variations in stress and nuance are hardly noticeable. In the Soviet

Union, though, differing opinions on individual problems are sometimes expressed. This is especially the case when particular subjects are specifically opened to public discussion, as happened with the education reforms of 1958, the economic reforms of 1965, and the passing of the Kolkhoz Model Statutes of 1969. In this way, the alliance of educationists, cultural officials from the state apparatus and party officials finally succeeded in 1958 in frustrating Khrushchev's plan — supported as it was by industrial managers and labour administration officials — to replace the general education of the secondary schools by vocational training and instead pushed through the introduction of polytechnic education.[27] Group interests are given the strongest expression in the relatively loosely controlled mass media of Hungary. Here it is mainly the trade unions that give public expression to the interests of the employees up to a certain point and occasionally even criticise government measures. On 10 February 1971, for example, the trade union daily newspaper *Népszava* severely rebuked the First Deputy Minister of Light Industry for replying incorrectly to complaints about the technical backwardness, unsatisfactory wage situation and lack of apprentices in the printing industry.

The exercise of influence by giving *advice* is particularly characteristic of the trade unions and the scientific intelligentsia, since in this way their knowledge is used by the party and state leadership.[28] To this end, Khrushchev arranged enlarged plenums of the Central Committee on particular problems and numerous experts were summoned. This practice was also imitated in other countries, particularly in the GDR, but with the end of the Khrushchev era it fell into disuse in the late 1960s. Today, advice is mainly given to the party and state bureaucracies via specialist committees, which are partly ad hoc bodies, partly institutionalised ones, and which do not operate in public. Thus, in their preparatory work before making decisions, the party leaders rely on the work of various commissions, workgroups and occasionally that of permanent bodies such as the Central Institute for the Management of the Socialist Economy, attached to the Central Committee of the Sozialistische Einheitspartei Deutschlands (SED). In addition to the ministries, a variety of advisory organs are also involved, to which scientists, specialists and representatives of the social organisations belong. The main task of all these consultative bodies is to improve the quality of the decision-making process, but, of course, there is more than a remote possibility that group interests also become involved in the process of making decisions in addition to providing expert knowledge.

Representation in the power-wielding bodies is probably the most effective method of exercising group influence since it guarantees direct participation in the process of arriving at decisions. Thus, an analysis of group representation in the leading political bodies provides valuable information about the weight of the individual interest groups in the various countries.

The most important examples of such leading bodies in which an integration of group interests takes place are first of all the Politburo, the supreme power-wielding agent, and then the Central Committee and the Central Auditing and/or Control Commission, which represent together the most important consultative and information bodies of a general character.

The power-wielding bodies are controlled everywhere by party and state officials, with the former having the upper hand. Apart from this general feature, however, these bodies display considerable differences in detail. The dominant role of the party officials is most obvious in East Germany where, since the beginning of the 1960s, they have even strengthened their position, whilst that of the state officials has remained very much the same. In the Central Committee and the Central Auditing Commission of the CPSU, on the other hand, the difference in the proportion of party and state officials was reduced from 12.1 per cent to 4.7 per cent between 1961 and 1976. In the Politburo, though, the number of party officials has constantly remained double that of state officials, as in the GDR. This differing development may be attributable to the increase in the importance of the state apparatus coupled with the expansion of the dominant position of party leader Brezhnev which has existed since the party absolutism of Khrushchev. Here, in the 1960s, a state of equilibrium developed and this has only changed in favour of the party officials since 1971. One is probably not wrong in assuming that this shift is linked with developments in Eastern Europe and the Soviet Union since the events of 1968 in Czechoslovakia, which made it appear advisable to give the party bureaucracy's monopoly of leadership some visible expression. In the Soviet Union, members from the foreign service form a prominent group among the state officials (about 5 per cent in the Central Committee and the Central Auditing Commission), having first gained a representative in the Politburo when Foreign Minister Gromyko was admitted in 1973. This special feature can be explained by reference to the Soviet Union's imperialist position in the world and the increase in its foreign political activity. The army's large quota of representatives can also be explained in the same way. Although a slight decline can be observed, the army's share of representatives totals 7.8 per cent in the Central Committee and the Central Auditing Commission (Hungary, GDR: 2-3.5 per cent), and since April 1973 the Minister of Defence has also been a member of the Politburo. This example was followed by the SED in October 1973, whereas the Hungarian Minister of Defence had to give up his candidate's seat in the Politburo in 1970 following the abolition of candidate status. At present, the proportion of security officials in the Central Committee and the Central Auditing Commission is of the order of 2 per cent in all three countries, a surprisingly low figure. It is however noticeable that this proportion has been on the decrease in Hungary for some time now, whilst in the Soviet Union it has risen since 1971. Of considerably greater significance than these rather marginal changes is the representation of the security organs in the Politburo. For the first time since Beria's liquidation in 1953, the head of the *KGB* was given a candidate's seat in the Politburo in 1967 and became a full member in 1973. Here, too, the GDR followed the Soviet example: State Security Minister Mielke was admitted to the Politburo as a candidate in 1971 and was raised to the rank of full member in 1976. In contrast to the growing influence of the security organs in these two countries as well as in some other Eastern European countries,[29] in Hungary — where there are no special state security authorities, all police duties being concentrated in the Ministry of the Interior — the security officials have been denied access to the Politburo.

In the case of the other interest groups of officials, the picture is very varied. The trade unions are most strongly represented in Hungary, a fact that reflects their real significance. They have a long-established claim to a seat in the Politburo and only lost their second seat when the Politburo was reduced in size in 1966. Their share of members in the Central Committee and the Central Control Commission remains over 7 per cent. In contrast, the Soviet trade unions are represented at the very most by a candidate in the Politburo and their representation in the large leading bodies is around 2 per cent. In East Germany, the trade unions assume an intermediate position: they are guaranteed one full member's seat in the Politburo but otherwise their representation quota is approximately 4 per cent. The intelligentsia is undoubtedly represented most strongly in East Germany. Here the technical-economic intelligentsia has even had one representative, albeit only a candidate, in the Politburo since 1963, in the person of the chairman of an agricultural co-operative. In the Central Committee and the Central Auditing Commission, it regularly supplies over 10 per cent of the members. Against this, the scientific-cultural intelligentsia shows a declining trend, but its 8 per cent of representatives is still remarkably high. In Hungary, the representation of the intelligentsia varies considerably from one Party Congress to the next. Viewed as a whole, it has risen since 1966, with the technical-economic intelligentsia gaining a slight advantage over the scientific-cultural intelligentsia. The representation of the intelligentsia in the Soviet Union is much lower by far: the representation of the technical-economic intelligentsia amounts consistently to 2 per cent whilst that of the scientific-cultural intelligentsia has risen from 3 to 4 per cent during the period observed. Finally, the percentage of workers' representatives has constantly risen in recent times, particularly in the Soviet Union (1976: 7 per cent), but also in Hungary (1975: 4 per cent). In East Germany (1976: 3 per cent) a parallel development is absent. However, one can only attribute a propagandistic significance to this state of affairs since no signs can be detected that the representatives of the workers, collective farmers and employees are particularly active in the Central Committee.

What conclusions can be drawn from these remarks concerning the relationship between state and society in communist countries? Can one dare to assert that the political process running from the top to the bottom is complemented by a process rising from the bottom to the top? We believe that this question cannot be answered in the affirmative, although an unqualified negative answer would also be inappropriate. Of course one cannot speak of a pluralism in the Western sense of the word, since the group interests present in society are not able to form together freely and are therefore not in a position to exercise any influence worth mentioning on the political process. But there is a pluralism in the sense that the existing political institutions offer some interest groups a basis on which to build and exercise influence. One can perhaps refer to this pluralism as an 'apparatus-pluralism', since the points at which the interest groups crystallise are those sections of the political subsystems that manifest themselves as power apparatuses: the party apparatus, the state apparatus, the army, the security apparatus and possibly the trade union apparatus. The interests of the technical-economic intelligentsia and the scientific-cultural intelligentsia in fact lie outside these apparatuses, but they can only become effective through them. Access to the power apparatuses is the privilege of particular groups, whilst the major part of society is denied any influence on the political process. The paths leading from society to political power are narrow, tortuous and only accessible to the initiated.

NOTES AND REFERENCES

1. For detailed studies of this kind, see the following earlier works: Z.K. Brzezinski, *The Soviet Bloc* (1960), Cambridge, Mass., Harvard University Press, 2nd ed., 1967; W.E. Griffith (ed.), *Communism in Europe*, 2 vols., Cambridge, Mass., MIT Press, 1964/66; J.F. Brown, *The New Eastern Europe*, New York, Praeger, 1966; G. Ionescu, *The Politics of the European Communist States*, London, Weidenfeld and Nicolson, 1967.
2. See A.G. Meyer, *Leninism*, Cambridge, Mass., Harvard University Press, 1957, pp. 19ff.; W. Leonhard, *Sowjetideologie heute*, vol. 2, *Die politischen Lehren*, Frankfurt a.M., Fischer, 1962, pp. 33ff; R.T. De George, *Patterns of Soviet Thought*, Ann Arbor, Mich., University of Michigan Press, 1966, pp. 128ff.
3. See H.-H. Höhmann, M.C. Kaser and K.C. Thalheim (eds), *The New Economic Systems of Eastern Europe*, London, C. Hurst, 1975.
4. Little is known about the Politburos and the Secretariats of the Central Committees since their work takes place in secret. For this reason, there are only a few publications about them and these only deal with a few aspects. The following may be numbered among the most important studies on the Soviet Politburo: G.K. Schueller, *The Politburo*, Stanford, Cal., Stanford University Press, 1951; M. Fainsod, *How Russia is Ruled* (1953), Cambridge, Mass., Harvard University Press, rev. ed. 1963, Chapter 10; D.N. Jacobs, 'The Politburo in the First and Fifth Decades of Soviet Power' in K. London (ed.), *The Soviet Union*, Baltimore, Md., The Johns Hopkins Press, 1968, pp. 45ff.; T.H. Rigby, 'The Soviet Politburo', *Soviet Studies*, vol. XXIV, 1972, pp. 3ff. A certain amount of information on the Soviet Secretariat of the Central Committee is to be found in A. Avtorkhanov, *The Communist Party Apparatus*, Cleveland, Ohio, Henry Regnery and Co., 1966.

5. Whereas the Soviet Council of Ministers consists of over 100 individuals, that of Albania comprises only 20 members. Between these two extremes, the strength of the Council of Ministers varies from over 50 (East Germany and Romania) to 30–40 (Poland and Bulgaria) to 20–30 (Czechoslovakia and Hungary). On this aspect there is very little literature. Recently a comprehensive Dutch dissertation was published on the development of the Soviet Council of Ministers: G.P. van den Berg, *De regering van Rusland en de Sovjet-Unie*, Leiden, Elve, 1977. For information on the East German Council of Ministers see E. Richert, *Macht ohne Mandat* (1958), Cologne, Westdeutscher Verlag, 2nd ed. 1963, pp. 79ff.; U. Hoffman, *Die Veränderungen in der Sozialstruktur des Ministerrates der DDR 1949-1969*, Düsseldorf, Droste, 1971. The party organ *Népszabadság* of 25 December 1976 published interesting details on the work of the Hungarian Council of Ministers.
6. In the Soviet Union it is called the Presidium of the Supreme Soviet; in Albania, the Presidium of the People's Assembly. In Poland, East Germany, Romania and Bulgaria, it bears the title of State Council. In Czechoslovakia, we find the peculiarity that the presidial powers are divided up between the State President and the Presidium of the Federal Assembly.
7. Such a situation exists in East Germany (Ulbricht 1960-71; Honecker since 1976), Romania (Gheorghiu-Dej 1961-65; Ceausescu since 1967, who has also been State President since 1974) and Bulgaria (Zhivkov since 1972). There were indications that Brezhnev also had nursed such plans at least for a time. See V.G. Beljaeva and O.E. Lejst, 'Soedinenie zakonodatel'stvovaniia i upravleniia v predstavitel'nykh organakh vlasti Sovetskogo gosudarstva' *Sovetskoe Gosudarstvo i Pravo*, no. 9, 1973, p. 21; cf. pp. 17ff. In June 1977 Brezhnev achieved this aim, partly at least, by ousting Podgorny and taking over the chairmanship of the Presidium of the Supreme Soviet.
8. In Poland, a similar but not so far-reaching personal union between the offices of local party leaders and the presidiums of the national councils was introduced in the course of the administrative reforms of November 1973.
9. The Soviet nomenclature system has been thoroughly examined by Western experts. See, e.g., the studies of B. Harasymiw, 'Nomenklatura: The Soviet Communist Party's Leadership Recruitment System', *Canadian Journal of Political Science*, 1969, pp. 493ff.; J.F. Hough, *The Soviet Prefects*, Cambridge, Mass., Harvard University Press, 1969, pp. 114ff., 149ff.
10. R. Schwarzenbach, *Die Kaderpolitik der SED in der Staatsverwaltung*, Cologne, Verlag Wissenschaft und Politik, 1976.
11. *Magyar Nemzet*, 10 December 1961.
12. *Scînteia*, 20 July 1972.
13. Thus, there are at the national level the following mixed party–state leading bodies: National Defence Council, Central Council of Workers' Control of Economic and Social Activities, Council on Problems of Social and Economic Organization, Council on Socio-economic Development. For details see M. Cismarescu, 'Die verfassungsrechtliche Entwicklung der Sozialistischen Republik Rumänien 1965-1975', *Jahrbuch des öffentlichen Rechts*, 1975 (New Series, vol. 24), p. 231ff. and 274ff.).
14. See: C.J. Friedrich, M. Curtis, B.R. Barber, *Totalitarianism in Perspective*, New York, Düncker and Humblot, 1969; M. Jänicke, *Totalitäre Herrschaft*, Berlin, Düncker and Humblot, 1971; T.H. Rigby, 'Totalitarianism and Change in Communist Systems', *Comparative Politics*, 1972, pp. 433ff.; L. Schapiro, *Totalitarianism*, London, Macmillan, 1972; P. Graf Kielmannsegg, 'Krise der Totalitarismustheorie?', *Zeitschrift für Politik*, 1974, pp. 311ff.; W. Schlange, *Die Totalitarismus-Theorie*, Stuttgart, W. Kohlhammer, 1976.
15. This is done particularly clearly in Article 21, section 2 of the GDR Constitution of April, 1968.
16. K. Sorgenicht, W. Weichelt, T. Riemann and H.-J. Semler (eds), *Verfassung der Deutschen Demokratischen Republik — Dokumente — Kommentar*, East Berlin, Staatsverlag der DDR, 1969, vol. 2, p. 55f.
17. P.B. Maggs, 'Negative Votes in Soviet Elections', *Res Baltica*, 1968, pp. 146ff.; J.M. Gilison, 'Soviet Elections as a Measure of Dissent', *American Political Science Review*, 1968, pp. 814ff., especially 819ff.; E.M. Jacobs, 'Soviet Local Elections', *Soviet Studies*, vol. XXII, 1970, pp. 61ff. and 70ff.

18. This figure is the mean average of the eight local elections held between 1957 and 1975. For the individual figures see G. Brunner, *Politische Soziologie der UdSSR,* Wiesbaden, Akademische Verlagsgesellschaft, 1977, vol. 2, p. 45f.
19. Source: *Népszábadság* of 22 March 1967, of 2 April 1971 and of 17 June 1975. For details of the Hungarian elections see W.F. Robinson, *The Pattern of Reform in Hungary,* New York, Praeger, 1973, pp. 206ff.; P.A. Toma and I. Völgyes, *Politics in Hungary,* San Francisco, W.H. Freeman, 1977, pp. 57ff.
20. Source: *Scînteia,* 17 March 1975.
21. V. Zabielski and A. Patrzalek, 'Der Sejm der Volksrepublik Polen (I)', *Zeitschrift für Parlamentsfragen,* pp. 412ff. especially p. 424.
22. Thus, for example, in the Sejm elections of 1972 three members of the Politburo who all headed their respective lists — the Secretary of the Central Committee and former Minister of the Interior Szlachic, the Secretary of the Central Committee responsible for cadre questions Babiuch and the trade union leader Kruczek — were all relegated from the first to the last place. See *Trybuna Ludu* of 21 March 1972.
23. See especially H.G. Skilling and F. Griffiths (eds), *Interest Groups in Soviet Politics,* Princeton, N.J., Princeton University Press, 1971, and B. Meissner and G. Brunner (eds), *Gruppeninteressen und Entscheidungsprozess in der Sowjetunion,* Cologne, Verlag Wissenschaft und Politik, 1975.
24. P. Ch. Ludz, *Parteielite im Wandel,* Cologne, Westdeutscher Verlag, 1968, pp. 35ff.
25. J.F. Hough, 'The Soviet Elite', *Problems of Communism,* January-February 1967, vol. XVI, no. 1, pp. 28-35 and J.F. Hough, 'The Man and the System', *Problems of Communism,* March-April 1976, vol. XXV, no. 2, p. 14; cf. 1-17.
26. See W.F. Robinson, *op. cit.,* pp. 238ff.; P.A. Toma and I. Völgyes, *op. cit.,* pp. 67ff.
27. On this point, see J.J. Schwartz and W.R. Keech, 'Group Influence and the Policy Process in the Soviet Union', *American Political Science Review,* 1968, pp. 840ff.; D.R. Kelley, 'Interest Groups in the USSR', *Journal of Politics,* 1972, pp. 860ff., especially pp. 864ff.
28. For details on the Soviet Union see T. Kirstein, *Die Konsultation von 'Aussenstehenden' durch den Partei — und Staats — apparat sowie den Obersten Sowjet der UdSSR,* Berlin, OHO Harrassowik, 1972.
29. Similar personnel developments have taken place in Albania and Poland. In Albania, the long-standing Minister of the Interior Haziu was made a full member in 1971, after having been a candidate for a considerable time. In Poland, Kowaczyk was made a candidate in 1973, shortly after his appointment as Minister of the Interior, and in 1975 was raised to the rank of full member.

SELECT BIBLIOGRAPHY

Beck, C. *et al., Comparative Communist Political Leadership,* New York, David McKay, 1973.
Brown, J.F., *The New Eastern Europe,* New York, Praeger, 1966.
Brunner, G., *Politische Soziologie der UdSSR,* 2 vols, Wiesbaden, Akademische Verlagsgesellschaft, 1977.
Fainsod, M., *How Russia Is Ruled* (1953), Cambridge, Mass., Harvard University Press, rev. ed. 1963.
Farrell, R.B., (ed.), *Political Leadership in Eastern Europe and the Soviet Union,* Chicago, Aldine Publishing Company, 1970.
Kanet, R.E., (ed.), *The Behavioural Revolution and Communist Studies,* New York, The Free Press, 1971.
Meissner, B. and Brunner, G. (eds), *Gruppeninteressen und Entscheidungsprozess in der Sowjetunion,* Cologne, Verlag Wissenschaft und Politik, 1975.
Skilling, H.G. and Griffiths, F. (eds), *Interest Groups in Soviet Politics,* Princeton, N.J., Princeton University Press, 1971.

CHAPTER 6

State and Nationality Under Communism

Terry McNeill

What are the objectives of communist régimes in the sphere of nationality policy? How do communist régimes cope with the problem of reconciling state unity with ethnic diversity? As communist internationalism metamorphoses into national communism, what consequences has this for relations between the state and the dominant nationality and what impact does it have on the treatment of the smaller minorities? Is minority nationalism a serious obstacle to the ideological objectives of the communist state? Do communist régimes follow a common line in their nationality policies, or are there crucial and significant differences between them?

These are some of the questions that suggest themselves and that we propose to answer in the context of an examination of the nationality policies of several multinational Communist states. The Soviet Union, Yugoslavia, Czechoslovakia and Romania have been chosen primarily because in the pre-communist period ethnic strife was a prominent feature of their internal politics, and also because they provide interesting contrasts in their patterns of ethnic differentiation and in other factors that might be conjectured to have a bearing on régime policy. We begin with the Soviet Union, partly on account of its lengthier experience of dealing with nationality issues, but principally because — at least for a time — it provided a model for the others to follow.

SOVIET UNION

Although insistently denied by its advocates, the USSR emerged as a result of the activities of the Red Army rather than through the common consent of its various peoples. Apart from a few unavoidable instances, and despite pledges to the contrary in their party programme, the Bolsheviks adamantly refused to accept the legitimacy of national self-determination. Nationalities that took advantage of the new government's initial weakness in order to secede were rapidly and ruthlessly reabsorbed. In spite of the ease with which this was accomplished, the Bolsheviks were nonetheless acutely aware that force by itself was unlikely to provide a very enduring base for their new state, or to keep separatist-inclined minorities in thrall for ever. So they cast around for some arrangement that, without conceding any point of principle, would nevertheless be sufficiently palatable to the minorities to make them endure incorporation in the Soviet state. The formula they hit upon was federalism, or rather a variant of it, which conferred upon the minorities semblances of self-government but left the essential unity and centralism of the state intact. In effect this meant that the nationalities were given considerable autonomy in secondary areas (language, cultural affairs, etc.) while all matters of real importance were reserved strictly to the central government. In its essentials this is the formula still in force today and has been retained in the 'Brezhnev Constitution'.

Soviet communists describe their state system as 'national in form and socialist in content'; a more accurate description would be 'federal in form, but unitary in content'. For while it is true that the fifteen largest nations making up the federation have their own (supposedly) sovereign republics and that these republics possess governments, legislatures and other panoply of independent states, in reality most of this is just window-dressing. The actual power of the republics is slight and extends only to matters of secondary importance. They have no financial independence and strict centralisation denies them effective control of the more important sectors of the local economy. The composition of their governments, although ostensibly decided by legislatures, is in fact decreed by central supervisory organs to whom they are fully accountable. In reality, republican leaders are simply servitors of the federal power and the republics they head little more than administrative sub-divisions within a highly centralised system.

The real power in the land is the Communist Party (CPSU), which operates under principles of centralism and subordination that effectively nullify the notional federalism of the state structure. The declared objective of this powerful organisation is the progressive obliteration of the more significant (and mutable) forms of ethnic differentiation within Soviet society and the reduction of the various peoples to a single identity. As projected, this identity eschews any particular ethnic associations and will manifest supra-national characteristics consistent with communism — characteristics conveyed by the concept 'soviet', as in 'soviet man', 'soviet people', and 'soviet patriot'. Integral to the realisation of this identity will be the gradual erosion of linguistic, cultural and other present supports of ethnic particularity, and the reduction of the republics to the status of regional administrative entities. Officially it is claimed that ethnic assimilation will proceed as an ineluctable consequence of 'the building of communism' and that no attempt is being made to hasten the process. In practice, however, the régime has used every means available to it, from the vilest brutality to the most insidious manipulations, to break the attachment of minorities to their 'bourgeois nationalist' historic identities. Also, it is abundantly apparent that under the guise of 'sovietisation' the non-Russian peoples of the USSR are in fact being subjected to a process of imposed Russification. Censorship and centralised media control, for example, curb the use and development of minority tongues. Likewise, the local languages are being steadily 'enriched' with Russian words and expressions. Their orthography, syntax and spelling have been altered to assimilate them to Russian models. Translation of foreign works into local languages is being curtailed, despite the fact that census returns show little change in the numbers using these languages. Cinema is largely in Russian, as is something like three-quarters of the radio and television programmes in the minority regions. It is stated that there is a free choice between attending an indigeneous or a Russian-language school, but the fact that the bulk of the texts is in Russian, added to the knowledge that career opportunities are greatly enhanced by an education through the master tongue, induced many parents to opt for the Russian schools.

A more telling indicator of the progress of Russification, however, is the altered demographic balance in the non-Russian republics. The turning-point came in the 1930s when, with the onset of forced economic development, large numbers of workers were transferred from the Russian heartland to provide the labour force of the new developing regions. At the same time squads of Russian and other cadres were drafted to take over organisation in the administrative networks of these regions, often in the process displacing local incumbents. Again, in the 1950s, the opening up of grain lands in Kazakhstan and the East brought further influxes of Russians and other Slavic nationals. Augmenting the historic process of Russian colonisation of the peripheral lands, the net effect of these population shifts has been a marked dilution of the national character of many non-Russian republics. Thus the Kirgiz are now a minority in Kirgizia, as are the Kazakhs in Kazakhstan. There has been a dramatic fall in the proportion of Tadzhiks in Tadzhikistan and in that of the indigeneous populations of Latvia and Estonia. Turkmenians and Usbeks show similar trends in their own republics. Even more striking has been the ethnic displacement within the smaller national territories of the interior where, in many cases, Russians now form majorities of the population. The urban centres of the Asiatic republics (Dushanbe and Tashkent for example) have been similarly Russified. As a further consequence of these demographic shifts, the ethnic composition of the local administrations has changed and all now include very significant numbers of non-indigenous functionaries.

Régime spokesmen attempt to explain this wholesale Russian penetration of the ethnic territories as an example of 'socialist internationalism', which requires that a stronger nation lend assistance to the less advanced. It seems, however, that this assistance is not sought nor always welcomed by its recipients. Instances have emerged, for example, of republican leaders deliberately forgoing industrial development projects for fear that they would open the door to yet further influxes of alien labour.[1] Still more common is the practice of trying to reserve the better jobs for members of the local nationality — an exclusiveness often directed not only at Russians but at any 'outsiders'.

However, it is not in the outlying ethnic territories that the disproportionate weight of Russian presence makes its greatest impact but in the leading bodies of state and party administration. The USSR government and its associated agencies, the CPSU Secretariat and the all-powerful Politburo, as well as the higher reaches of the armed forces, are almost exclusively Russian preserves. Few minority nationals nowadays find places at this level in the Soviet system; fewer still of those who do make it could be regarded as legitimate representatives of ethnic constituencies.

Despite the fact that leaders in the ethnic homelands are selected on grounds of proven loyalty to the régime and its objectives, they are still often regarded with distrust. Thus while it is accepted that the first secretaryship in a republican party may be held by a member of the indigeneous nationality (or, perhaps more accurately, the eponymous nationality), the second secretaryship is almost always occupied by a Russian. The former is the more prestigious position but it is the latter that has primary responsibility for the placement of local cadres and so in effect controls the entire republican party apparatus. It should also be noted that this 'watchdog' secretary has his own direct and independent lines of communication with Moscow. Furthermore, the Russians appointed to these watchdog positions tend not to come from the local Russian community, but are 'parachuted' in from the outside for a tour of duty that is deliberately kept short so as to preclude the growth of excess familiarity between them and their charges.[2] The institutionalised suspicion that these arrangements highlight would appear justified in Moscow's eyes by the number of ethnic leaders purged over the years for 'nationalist deviations'.

On the other hand, the suspicions that the régime obviously harbours about the political reliability of many minority nationals are now less acute than they were at times in the past. There has, for example, been no repetition of the mass deportations of nationalities such as Stalin carried out during the war. But a more telling indicator of the milder view that Moscow takes of its minorities is the increasing numbers of them now deemed acceptable for party membership. It is true of course that some of this increase may be explained in incidental terms — by changes in demographic factors, by the impact of urbanisation and development on the generally more backward minority regions, which bring increasing numbers of the minorities into the categories that the party primarily recruits from — but the increase goes beyond what may be adequately accounted for in these terms alone. It seems probable that the present leadership is deliberately stepping up recruitment among the minorities in order to strengthen party influence in areas where traditionally it has been weak. Expanded minority presence in the party, however, could well have a double-edged effect. For while it may draw the minorities into a closer identification with the objectives of the Soviet régime, it will at the same time provide them with better opportunities to defend their national bailiwicks from outside encroachment.

Aside from the issues already touched on, one of the most persistent sources of friction between the minorities and the régime lies in the realm of economic policy. The problem is that the Soviet economy is treated as a single entity with plans being shaped so as to secure (at least theoretically) maximum advantage to the country as a whole, and without necessarily taking account of the special preferences of particular localities. The strategy the planners follow favours regional specialisation within the all-Union economy, with the outcome that some regions have been developed in a rather lopsided way. Uzbekistan, for instance, has been turned into a one-crop economy and is now dependent on outside sources for the greater part of its food supplies. For a short time, under Khrushchev's limited experiment in economic decentralisation, opportunities for injecting localist perspectives into development plans increased, but they diminished with the decision in 1965 to return to traditional centralised administration. From 1973 the role of the republics in the planning process has been reduced still further by the decision of the authorities to impose a new system of regionalisation that largely ignores ethnic boundaries. This reorganisation was not accepted lightly, and at the time provoked a tense exchange in the Soviet press between 'states righters' defending the sanctity of existing Soviet interstate frontiers and various rationalisers who favoured abandoning ethnic considerations where they impeded economic efficiency.[3]

Economic nationalism such as was displayed in the reorganisation debate is a relatively common occurrence, certainly more common than overt political nationalism. Over the past decade republican leaderships have become noticeably outspoken in pressing the particular demands of their region upon the central authorities. Central Asian leaders would like to see their republics develop a more diversified economy and advance beyond the level of primary producers. Baltic spokesmen, on the other hand, have tried to stave off the kind of development likely to draw in excessive numbers of non-indigenous labour. They also manifest a strongly proprietorial attitude towards local natural resources — particularly shale oil — which they have tried to retain for the exclusive benefit of the local economy. The Ukraine habitually tries to capitalise on its status as the number two republic to exert disproportionate pressure on the all-Union exchequer for extra capital funding, at the expense of weaker and more needy republics. In general, the better-off republics attempt to defend their assets against equalitarian moves on the part of the central planners, whereas weaker republics persistently press for special treatment.

Overall, the policy of assimilation (or Russification) of minority nationals embarked on by the régime has had rather mixed fortunes. Greatest success has been attained among the smaller, territorially scattered peoples, several of whom have been almost entirely absorbed. The larger, more compact nations however have proved more resilient and strongly resist attempts to erode their particular identities. They manifest the highest degree of linguistic loyalty, and although it is true that the 1970 census showed that Russian had firmly established itself as the lingua franca of the USSR, with 76 per cent of the population able to communicate in it, it also revealed that 93.9 per cent of Soviet citizens continue to regard their respective languages as their native tongues.

Resistance to assimilation appears to be weakest among nations with strong historical or cultural ties with Russia (Belorussians, for example), and among groups that espoused orthodoxy. Generally, however, resistance appears to have stiffened in recent years, and if anything traditional ethnic allegiances are now stronger. The last decade, for example, has witnessed a renewed ferment among intellectual circles in the Ukraine, coupled with the appearance of Samizdat literature devoted to national protest. The highpoint of nationalist activity was reached under the former party boss, Shelest, whose eventual dismissal was at least in part occasioned by his softness towards the nationalists. Under his replacement the KGB have been given a much freer hand, with the result that many of the more prominent activists have since been neutralised.

Lithuania too has become a hotbed of nationalist protest, but unlike the Ukraine it is not confined to intellectual circles. The fact that the nationalists are also champions of religious freedom and are prepared to confront the authorities on these grounds has won them broad popular support. In the recent past there have been a number of large-scale public demonstrations on the religious issue, leading to self-immolations and on one occasion to a pitched street battle with KGB military units. The scale of the protest and the evident depth of feeling behind it seems to have non-plussed the authorities and led for a time to a noticeable softening of the official stance on religious matters.

Central Asia is another area with the potential for a combination of national and religious protests and shows signs of growing restlessness among sectors of the local intelligentsia, accompanied by what must be for the authorities a particularly worrying development: evidence of pan-Islamic aspirations.

Of the smaller groups, the protest activities of the Jews have received most attention, and rightly so. The Jews provide an interesting example of a people who are territorially dispersed and who are highly Russified both in language and culture yet have retained a strong sense of group identity and consciousness. They provide a salutary reminder to the Kremlin that even if general minority assimilation were achieved it might not mean the end of the nationality problem. Other smaller groups that are also at present highly active include the Crimean Tatars who are vociferously campaigning for the restoration of their national homeland; the Soviet Germans who, like the Jews, demand the right to emigrate; and the Meshetians, of whom some seek the restoration of territorial rights and others seek freedom to emigrate.

Georgian protest seems to have been triggered by Moscow-instigated purges against entrepreneurial elements in the Georgian community unleashed after the sacking of the local party secretary in 1972. This unrest has assumed literally explosive forms, with arsonist attacks on public buildings in Tbilisi and attempts to assassinate party officials. Moscow's intention, it would seem, is to bring Georgia more directly under central control, thus ending what at times has been virtually an autonomous existence.

One form of national expression, and one that could well have a critical bearing on the future evolution of the Soviet system, is unofficial Russian nationalism. It is distinguishable from the official variant in that, unlike the latter, it looks to the past, to orthodoxy and tradition, and sometimes to peasant society for its values and inspiration. It is still a rather inchoate movement embracing a number of different strands, from the extreme right-wing and anti-semitic variety to the liberal patriotism of an Osipov. A common meeting ground for its affiliates is the All-Russian Society for the Preservation of Historical and Cultural Monuments, which within seven years of its formation in 1965 attained a staggering membership of over seven million.[4] It is difficult to say how much support any of its tendencies may enjoy in party circles, or whether the moderation with which the KGB has dealt with it is an expression of official sympathy or simply prudence. Clearly the régime has an interest in enlisting patriotic forces to its side; Stalin did with obvious benefit during the war. At the same time, any excessive identification with this form of patriotism could have an alienating effect on other peoples; more important, it would place a severe strain on the unity of the multi-national party apparatus.

The recent upsurge of dissident nationalism within the Soviet Union has undoubtedly been a matter of major concern to the authorities and is reflected in the frequency with which the problem features in official pronouncements and in the dispatch with which the repressive agencies deal with it. Yet at the same time it is obvious that the régime has no clear idea of what it should do. According to the Party Programme now in force, the Soviet Union is in the phase of the 'drawing together' of nations, the prelude to their ultimate merger. The reality is that competing nationalisms within the state have never been so strong or so self-assertive and, as experience has shown, repression in itself is no answer. The underlying assumption was that the processes of modernisation would in time sap the roots of nationalist feelings. But this has patently not happened. If anything, modernisation has had quite the contrary effect, for it is precisely in those areas of the country that are most modernised (such as the Baltic) that nationalism is particularly acute. Similarly, in the Asiatic republics it is the very product of the modernising process, the new indigenous intelligentsia, that is in the forefront of the emerging nationalist movements. In this context it should be noted that it is in these eastern regions that the rate of population increase is fastest. Indeed, if present trends continue, within the foreseeable future Russians will have been reduced to a minority in the overall population, which will not only make their present dominance even more difficult to justify, but multiply the claimants for the positions they currently occupy.

Nationalism, we may conclude, is a deeply entrenched force in the USSR and carries a stronger emotional current than is sometimes appreciated by outsiders. It is one of the oldest and most enduring forms of dissent in the country, and unlike some of the more recent manifestations that have particularly engaged the attention of the West, it is not confined to intellectual circles. In the past it has been a major impediment to the totalist aspirations of the Stalinist state, helping to preserve 'islands of separateness' beyond its control. At present it can be said to constitute one of the key elements in the process of gradual 'pluralisation and re-politicisation' that is already perceptible in Soviet society. In the long run, unless the divergent aspirations of its various forms are somehow reconciled, it could have a devastating effect on the survival of the Soviet Union as a unified state.

YUGOSLAVIA

Yugoslavia is distinctive among communist states in that all its nationalities are in effect minorities. The Serbs are the most numerous, with about 40 per cent of the population; followed in descending order by the Croats (22 per cent); Moslems and Slovenes (8 per cent respectively); Macedonians (6 per cent) and Montenegrins (3 per cent). The remaining 13 per cent is spread over more than twenty other nationalities, the largest of which are the Albanians and the Hungarians.

Yugoslavia is distinctive also in being the only East European communist state since 1945 to follow Soviet practice in establishing a federation. Six ethnic groups are constitutionally recognised as 'nations' and form the constituent republics of the federation. The Hungarians and Albanians are regarded as 'nationalities' and are accorded the constitutionally somewhat inferior status of autonomous regions within the Serbian republic.[5]

In the first years of communist government the rights permitted to any ethnic group were limited. Modelling himself closely on Soviet example, Tito established an iron-fisted rule, characterised by the maximum centralisation of power and the subordination of state and governmental institutions

— both regional and federal — to the control of the party apparatus. The federal republics were in theory empowered to exercise self-determination right up to the point of outright secession, but as in the Soviet Union the party made sure that in practice the exercise of this right posed no threat to the continuing unity of the state.

However, the very degree of ethnic plurality in Yugoslavia, coupled after the 1948 departure from the Cominform with the need to mobilise the maximum possible popular support in the event of an invasion, pushed the régime into adopting more conciliatory policies. An additional incentive towards leniency on the question of national rights was the fact that several of the minorities were also the irredenta of now hostile Cominform powers. This bent towards a more tolerant stance accentuated as the Yugoslav leadership, stimulated by the deepening antagonism with Moscow, began to develop their own distinctive approach to the problems of 'socialist construction'. The new approach contained a number of different elements, which at first did not add up to a coherent programme, but emerged piecemeal as the régime gradually strengthened its resolve to abandon totalitarian methods in favour of a form of rule that was more genuinely responsive to the popular will. The net effect of the various changes was to bring the régime closer to the people, and to dissipate some of the tensions that had accumulated in the earlier years of harsh rule. Their ideological justification was a radical version of the doctrines of the state in socialist society, inspired by a growing conviction among party theoreticians that the root cause of Soviet bureaucratic deformations was Stalinist statism. Similar deformations could be avoided in Yugoslavia, it was argued, only by placing democratic checks on the growth of state power and by widening opportunities for popular participation in government. Educating and transfroming society in ways that would prepare it to absorb ever greater realms of state activity thus became a keynote of régime policy and a rationale of further decentralisation.

In line with the new thinking was the decision in November 1952 to change the name of the Communist Party to that of the League of Communists. This was symbolic of the intention of the leadership to change the relationship between the party and the state and to prevent the merger of party organisation and government into a single monolithic machine. Henceforth the party was to confine itself to defining the broad principles of policy, while leaving questions of administrative detail and application to other bodies. Equally, the details of personnel policy, save at the higher levels, were no longer to be considered the direct concern of the party managers. At the same time as the changes in the role of the party, reforms were carried out in the People's Front — a larger, more amorphous political organisation working under the direction of the Communists — to enlarge its membership and widen the scope of its activities. Overall, the effect of the changes was to loosen the structure of government, increase leeway for the functioning of bodies at the republic and grassroots level, and considerably improve opportunities for participation and initiative on the part of ordinary citizens.

Although it is true that the new anti-state, anti-central emphasis in régime policy worked to the advantage of the republics and other national agencies at the regional level, this was to some extent an incidental consequence rather than a direct intent. The aim of the reforms was to reach out to the people at large and draw them to the cause of a socialist Yugoslavia, not provide new opportunities for expressions of ethnic particularism.

The régime identified the cause of inter-ethnic difficulties as lying primarily in two sources: a peasant mentality and the economic disparities between different nationality regions. Industrialisation, they assumed, could provide a cure for both. It would help break down peasant parochialism and broaden horizons towards the larger community; and, just as important, it would generate the means of ironing out regional inequality. So, from the outset, industrialisation, in particular the industrialisation of the more backward regions, was given a high priority. Despite this, there was no consistent strategy underlying development policy. Investment choices were made on an ad hoc basis, as and when the money became available in the federal kitty. It was not until the 1961 creation of the Central Development Fund — formed by contributions from the social income of the richer republics — that anything like a sustained strategy came into operation.

As a solution to the nationalities problem, development policy has not been particularly successful. Like the gap between rich and poor in the world generally (of which, incidentally, Yugoslavia provides a reflection in microcosm) the gap between rich and poor republics has relentlessly widened. Thus, over the twenty-five year period from 1947 the gap — measured in per capita gross domestic product — between the most developed republics and the least developed widened from 3.1:1 to 5.7:1 in the most extreme case, and from 1.9:1 to 2.6:1 in the least extreme.[6] The reasons for this are manifold. On the economic side, probably the main cause is inadequate infrastructure and shortages of skilled manpower, which means that investment is used inefficiently and with poor returns. Politics also enter into it. Compared with the Soviet Union the rather loose political power structure that has developed in Yugoslavia over the years permits powerful local party bosses to press for concessionary investments in their particular areas. The acquisition of complex industrial plant is frequently seen as a matter of honour and a source of prestige to the locality, as well as a political feather in the cap of its party chief. This can lead to factories being sited in regions of such overwhelming disadvantage that they inevitably operate at a loss.

Misuse of funds is particularly resented in the donor republics, which are under statutory obligation to provide them at the expense of their own development. Croatia has been especially vociferous in condemning policies that expect her to put the general interest above her own, and a rampant nationalism is rarely far below the surface of the arguments advanced by her protagonists. During the early 1960s the most contentious issue was the decision to allocate extra investments to Serbia as compensation for the relative neglect that she, in common with other eastern regions of the country, suffered in the years of threatened Soviet incursion. The Croat leaders viewed this as an example of favouritism on the part of the 'Serb-dominated' federal government. They made a similar response to the 1965 economic reform, arguing that it unjustly favoured Serbia by rigging the new investment banking system to the advantage of Serbia and thus raising prices on Serbian raw materials to the detriment of the processing industries of Croatia.

Much more serious, however, was the crisis over foreign currency that erupted in 1970-71. The key issue was the distribution system of foreign currency earnings between the various republics by the federal authorities. According to figures quoted in the *Financial Times,* at the onset of the crisis Croatia accounted for 28 per cent of the country's export earnings, 39 per cent of its transport revenues, 72 per cent of its tourist revenue, and 35 per cent of the foreign exchange remittances from Yugoslav workers abroad. However, under the rules then in force, those who earned foreign currency were normally only allowed to retain between 7 and 10 per cent of it, the remainder being retained by central banks in Belgrade, which then resold the convertible currencies to enterprises on a commercial basis. The Croatian authorities deeply resented this and what started out as a purely financial grievance quickly assumed larger proportions as pent-up feelings of injustice began to boil over. A wave of protests and demonstrations broke out in the Croatian capital, and violence rapidly escalated to the point where Tito could speak of the imminence of civil war, a fear given added reality by a sudden upsurge of Ustashi terrorism. But for the unity of the League (apart from its Croatian section) and the continuing loyalty of the armed forces, Tito's forebodings might well have come true. After the disturbances had been quelled, the rules governing the distribution of hard currency were altered to accommodate Croatian objections.

Turning next to the cultural and linguistic aspects of nationality policy, it can be seen that Tito's approach has been both flexible and generous, relative to the Soviet Union's. A serious effort has been made to see that all minorities have an opportunity for education in their own language, with the exception of the more advanced subjects in the upper grades where lack of trained teachers makes it impossible. Provision of publications in minority tongues is good, within available resources. In 1969, for example, there were twelve newspapers and eleven journals being published in Hungarian.[7] And, apart from the Albanian and Macedonian irredenta who present special problems, there have generally been no complaints from neighbouring states in recent years about the treatment of their co-nationals in Yugoslavia.

The introduction of self-management principles, which have been steadily implemented in government and the economy, has provided minorities as well as other nationals with considerable opportunities for directing their own affairs. Likewise, the principle of pro rata representation and ethnic matching ensures reasonably equitable access for all nationals to public office. This principle is seen at the highest level in the recruitment to state and party offices, and in the creation of the ethnically balanced collective presidency. It should be said that the effect of this is not always desirable, for it sometimes means that utter incompetents are promoted simply because they are of the right ethnic group to complete a particular quota. Also, it tends to accentuate ethnic separateness and encourage officials to concentrate their attention exclusively on the interests of 'their own' people. Seemingly the principle does not operate fully in the armed forces, because the concentration of Serbian military talent and experience is not matched in other ethnic groups.

The overall thrust of Yugoslav constitutional change has been towards further decentralisation and strengthening the autonomy of lower bodies. The end result has been to make Yugoslavia more like a confederation than a federation. It is a policy that accords with the interests of the stronger republics, which are better able to take care of themselves. In the context of a market situation, however, it may work against the poorer republics who will find it increasingly difficult to survive in the battle for credit and investments against better placed rivals, unless protective cover is extended by the federal authority.

The goal of the Tito régime is 'socialist Yugoslavism'. This does not pre-suppose the eradication of nationality or full ethnic integration, but rather the creation of a multi-national community in which all nationalities have common interests. There is little evidence yet to suggest that this 'Yugoslavism' has achieved a lasting identity: given the centuries of bloodshed and fratricidal massacre, this is hardly surprising. The degree of devolution that Belgrade permits to her peoples is unparalleled in communist systems, and while this undoubtedly goes a considerable way to satisfy ethnic striving for autonomy, it is also to some extent counter-productive. For in passing so much of its power to the now virtually sovereign republics, the federal authority has not only dangerously weakened itself; it has also given institutional strength and protection to the very nationalisms that the régime wishes to weed out. One of the few really important national centralised organisations left is the party, but just how well its unity would stand up in the event of a really deep international crisis is debatable. In 1971 it was brought perilously close to a split. The charismatic presence of Tito has been a key factor in holding Yugoslavia together. The longer he remains in power, the more time those around him will have to prepare for an orderly succession, and the longer it will be before the fragile cohesion of the state is really put to the test. If it fails that test it may well be the army that will pick up the pieces, for, the party aside, the army is now one of Yugoslavia's strongest national institutions. Among European communist states there is no tradition of overt army intervention in politics, but Yugoslavia could be the first to break new ground here, just as she has done already in so many other ways.

CZECHOSLOVAKIA

From the outset, Czechoslovakia has been bedevilled by serious nationality problems, including those of significant German and Hungarian populations who resent their inclusion in the Czechoslovak state. By far the most serious, however, is that of the Slovaks and their relations with the Czechs. The friction between these two peoples goes back a long way and has its origin in divisive cultural, religious and other factors. Communist rule has not only failed to eradicate this friction but has in itself even aggravated it by adding new grievances. In fact, as is the case also in Yugoslavia, it is within the ranks of the party itself that signs of the continuing friction are most immediately displayed.

Leadership of the Czechoslovak Communist Party (CCP) in the interwar period was largely Czech based. Indeed, it was common practice to ignore Slovak sensibilities to the extent of appointing Czechs and even Germans to leading positions in the Slovak party organisation. Ironically, it was not until German occupation and the creation of the puppet clerico-fascist Slovak state that the Slovak party gained real independence from the Prague leadership. For much of the war the Slovak communists were left to their own devices; contact with Moscow and the émigré leadership was spasmodic, and real decision-making was left to men on the spot such as Husak and Novomesky. Through their activity in organising the Resistance, and in particular because of the role they played in the national Uprising in 1944, the Slovak communists had established themselves as a strong presence by the end of the war; and the Slovak National Council (SNC), in which they were the dominant element, had become the responsible government for the Slovak lands.

In acknowledgement of Slovak achievements and the strength of their unity in resistance to occupation, the SNC was recognised by the immediate postwar Czechoslovak government as the governing body of Slovakia, and the Kosice Programme — the blueprint for constitutional arrangements in the re-created state — made generous provision for it. It was promised that Slovaks would be 'masters of their own country'; that they would be permitted their own military formations; that the autonomy of Slovak culture would be respected and assured by an independent educational system. Slovaks were also to be accorded proportional representation in the central administration and in the allocation of important state offices.

As it transpired, however, the Kosice Programme was simply a vote-catching ruse, which the centrist party leadership in Prague had no intention of honouring. With their assumption of full power following the 1948 coup their true intentions became clear. The then existing quasi-federalist power structure was scrapped, and under the new state constitution Slovak autonomy was drastically abridged. Discretionary power was taken from the SNC and its competence was limited to secondary matters. Its executive organ, the Board of Commissioners, was made accountable to the Prague authorities, which in turn were now empowered to operate directly in Slovakia. The right of appointment to and removal from important Slovak executive positions was reserved to the central government and the process of constitutional amendment was fixed so as to prevent the Slovak deputies in the national parliament acting as a veto group. Administrative decrees issued from Prague quickly began to supersede SNC legislation, which as a result steadily diminished in quantity and in content.

Even more summary was the treatment of the Slovak Communist Party. By fiat it was re-absorbed into the Czechoslovak Party and its central committee subordinated to the central committee of the latter. Then, in order to pre-empt possible resistance on the part of the local leadership, a swingeing purge was unleashed against the Slovak party apparatus. In a bizarre and belated parody of the Soviet example, Husak, Clementis, Novomesky and other eminent Slovak communists were hauled before tribunals of 'justice' on a series of trumped-up charges and got rid of in various ways. Henceforth, attempts by Slovaks, or indeed any of the minority nationals, to protect themselves against centralist encroachment were treated as manifestations of 'bourgeois nationalism' and swiftly dealt with.

Strong centralist rule remained in force throughout the 1950s; even the events of 1956 — so cathartic for Czechoslovakia's neighbours — did little to shake it. In 1960, centralisation was taken a stage further, for in that year Novotny, the party leader, proclaimed Czechoslovakia a fully fledged socialist state, and in keeping with the greater social unity that this betokened set out plans for 'the further deepening of the central direction of [Czechoslovak] society'. The increased centralism that followed this pronouncement resulted in an emasculation of the remnants of power still enjoyed by the Slovak national institutions. The executive branch of the SNC was abolished and the legislative powers of the parent body further reduced; also, a number of local government organs were brought under the central authority. The fact that this adverse restructuring coincided with an economic recession that was having a disproportionately negative effect on the (in any case more backward) Slovak economy, added to the sense of injustice. Slovak outrage flared into open protest, which soon assumed strong nationalist overtones.

The prevalent view among Slovak protesters was that they were being subjected to a new form of Bohemian oppression. But this was not really the case. Slovakia was no more oppressed by Prague than was Moravia or even Bohemia itself. The problem was one of different perceptions. For what appeared to the Czechs to be simply the consequences of authoritarianism and bureaucracy, was invariably interpreted in Bratislava as a violation of national rights and a renewal of Czech hegemony. It should also be said that similar discrepancies in understanding the character of régime behaviour exist between Russians and other nationalities in the Soviet Union. Whereas, in fact, the problem in both countries is the existence of a centralised monistic system, which, even in a multi-national situation, cannot tolerate the presence of alternative centres of power or loyalty that may present a potential challenge to it.

In Czechoslovakia, this discrepancy of perception meant that Czechs and Slovaks tended to view the shortcomings of the system in rather different ways. For Czech reformers the problem lay in the workings of the system; the task as they saw it was to humanise and democratise the organs of power. The Slovaks, on the other hand, saw the problem in structural terms. Their object was to alter the system's institutional shape so as to provide possibilities for self-government. These underlying differences in attitude were to become important in 1968, when opportunities for thorough-going reform eventually presented themselves.

Aside from purely national grievances, Slovaks were also embittered by the existence of a number of unresolved economic problems. Although postwar economic advance in Slovakia was reasonably rapid, it had taken place from a very low base, and was as yet unable to generate enough employment.[8] The national government had attempted to meet this by offering Slovaks work in areas of the Czech lands where there were labour shortages. But this was rejected by the Slovaks, constituting in their eyes an attempt to denationalise their young people through induced 'emigration'.[9]

A further factor exacerbating Slovak feelings was the behaviour of Novotny. A true embodiment of the centralised bureaucracy, he seemingly refused to accept that Slovaks were entitled to rights of their own. Besides, in Slovak eyes he was deeply compromised by his involvement in the earlier persecution of Slovak nationals during the 'bourgeois-nationalist' witch-hunts. Not surprisingly, he was one of the most ardent opponents of attempts to investigate the validity of the trials and to rehabilitate victims subsequently admitted to have been wrongfully punished. It is said that he did not like Slovaks. At times he certainly could be gratuitously insulting towards them, as for instance when he prevented the Slovak National Council passing a bill that would have declared Bratislava the capital of Slovakia; thus, incidentally, confirming the utter impotence to which he had reduced this particular national body. It was fitting, therefore, that the Slovak party should have played such a central role in his eventual overthrow, and that the man who displaced him should be the first secretary of the Slovak central committee.

Though Czech reformists and Slovak party dissidents co-operated well in the early months of 1968 against the old leadership and in preparing the way for change, thereafter their ways parted. Economic reform, for example, though very important to the new Prague leaders, evoked little response in Bratislava. The reason for this was the disparity in the levels of economic development in the two parts of the country. The Czech economy was being stultified by the rigidities of Stalinist economic planning, and had little room for further growth under the existing system. The Slovak economy, on the other hand, being at a more primitive level of development, still had considerable slack; its problem was under-capitalisation rather than bad planning. Decentralisation and the introduction of market mechanisms, as being advocated by the Prague reformers, could in fact work against Slovakia, which would have to compete for capital and markets against better placed Czech enterprises. As was noted earlier, this is a danger too for the less developed regions in Yugoslavia and a factor that predisposes them to favour centralised economic regulation. One can envisage a similar response too from the more backward Soviet republics such as Kirgizia and Tadzhikistan, should the issue ever arise. The pointer from this is that local nationalism, while it attacks the centralist bureaucratic structure at one angle, can end up supporting it at another. A good example of this occurred in Czechoslovakia in 1968 when narrow nationalist elements in Slovakia conspired with reactionary centralists to oust the popular liberal, Smrkovsky — a man very sympathetic to Slovak grievances — simply because he occupied a post that it was felt should have gone to a Slovak. Likewise, the fact that the Slovak nationalists in 1968 were really only activated by the one cause — the introduction of a federal arrangement that would restore to them the constitutional rights denied them after 1948 — points not only to the short-sightedness of their outlook, but also to their failure to appreciate the flimsiness of constitutional guarantees in Stalinist-type systems.

The only enduring change to emerge out of the aborted reforms of 1968 has been the bipolar federalisation of the state between Bratislava and Prague. As far as the Soviet Union is concerned, this serves divide and rule purposes, and shows an understanding that Slovak national aspirations are less of a threat to bloc stability than Prague reformism.

Developments since 1945 indicate that a Czechoslovak nation — in the sense of a single community with a common national consciousness — does not exist yet. Neither have socialist development and ideological reorientation been sufficiently effective to permit the state to dispense with coercion as a key instrument of national unity. But although centrifugal forces still persist, the events of 1968 indicate that secession is not an immediate objective. In fact, the evidence suggests that meaningful devolution within the state — giving socialism an 'ethnic face' — together with some real substance in the constitutional declarations about ethnic equality, would go a long way towards alleviating the problem. However, devolution such as is implied here would be incompatible with the continuation of the present neo-Stalinist-type régime, and in fact would entail a return to something like the pluralist order that the 'Prague Spring' reformers were bringing about. In other words, 'solving the national problem' in Czechoslovakia is not simply a matter of institutional rejigging, as the Slovaks imagined, but demands fundamental political change.

ROMANIA

Of the four multi-ethnic countries being considered, Romania comes closest to being a one-nation state. The Romanian nationality makes up nearly 90 per cent of the population, and census returns show that in relative weight it is still growing. The other 10 per cent is spread among a number of minorities only two of which are numerically significant — the Hungarians located in the central and north-western regions, numbering around a million and three-quarters; and the Germans, a declining nationality, with now well under half a million. Of the remaining groups only the Gypsies, Jews and Ukrainians are present in any numbers.

Régime policy towards the minorities has altered considerably over the years, and has been differential in its application to the various peoples. With one exception, all groups were reasonably treated in the immediate postwar period. Their linguistic and cultural rights were respected and educational policy was framed to take account of their preferences. A factor at this time was probably the presence of several communists of minority stock in the party leadership. It has also been suggested that Soviet influence had a bearing. The claim is that the Kremlin leaders, recognising the strength of anti-Russian feelings among the Romanians, insisted on preferential treatment for the minorities in the hope of winning their support and perhaps using them as a check to Romanian nationalist ambitions. The Germans (Swabians and Saxons), not unexpectedly, were excepted from the general beneficence of this period. As a penalty for having backed the losing side in the war they were stripped of their prosperous farms and other property; some were expelled and a good many ended up as forced labour in Soviet prison camps. Rehabilitation came in the late 1940s, after which their condition appreciably improved.

Most capricious of all was the treatment of the Jews. With the Soviet occupation of Romania in 1944 active persecutions of the Guardist period ceased, anti-semitic laws were rescinded, civil rights and confiscated property were restored; and with the establishment of a communist government in which Jews were strongly represented at leadership level, prospects looked rosy. However, in 1948 Stalin unleashed his anti-Zionist campaign, and in Romania, in common with a number of bloc states, dormant antisemitism was given a new lease of life. Following a resolution of the Romanian party Politburo, a propaganda barrage was launched throughout the country against Jewish 'bourgeois-nationalism', with support, incidentally, from the pro-communist Democratic Jewish Committee. Jewish associations were broken up and applications to emigrate to Israel were treated as evidence of almost treasonable disloyalty. The purges of Ana Pauker and other leading Jewish communists in Romania were the high points of this sordid campaign. Since then treatment of Jews has improved and although their numbers are steadily falling because of emigration a fairly buoyant Jewish cultural and religious life survives. Emigration, however, is a contentious factor. The numbers seeking exit visas are much greater than the régime has been prepared to accept, and although a trickle has been let out — partly because their remittances to relatives form a useful source of foreign exchange, and partly to placate Israel, with whom Romania has good relations and strong trading links — the Romanian attitude to emigration has little to distinguish it from the Soviet.

Treatment of the Hungarian minority has shown similar, though less extreme, vicissitudes. The territory they occupy in the Transylvanian region has traditionally been disputed between Magyars and Romanians, and whichever dominated has generally pursued chauvinist policies at the expense of the weaker nationality. The fact that this region currently forms part of Romania and not Hungary is due to Stalin, who bestowed it as compensation for the annexation of other Romanian territories in Bessarabia and Bukovina to the USSR. Notwithstanding the animosity this action engendered among the Hungarian irredenta, the immediate policies of the new communist government in Bucharest seemed to make a break with the past pattern of hegemonic rule. Hungarian-language schools, theatre, press and cultural groups were encouraged to thrive; and the minority was even allowed to form its own political association (the MADOSZ), which was admitted as a member of the umbrella organisation, the National Front. Additional favour was conferred in 1952 with the establishment of the Magyar Autonomous Region, which incorporated a large part of the Szekler Hungarians into one area and gave it an 80 per cent Magyar population.[10] However, similar favour was not conferred upon the remaining Hungarians, who amounted to twice the number of those living in the Autonomous Region, ostensibly because they were less well concentrated, but more likely for the reason that they were located much closer to the Hungarian state frontier, and hence it was deemed prudent to keep them under direct central control. Not that possession of autonomous regional status would have given much opportunity for subversive behaviour in any case, for indeed, as the subsequent limitation on the activities of the Magyar Region made clear, the last thing the autonomous region had was autonomy. Nonetheless, the fact that even one region was set up meant that a significant number of Hungarians had a territory that was at least nominally their own, and a set of institutions with which they could more readily identify.

If the Magyar Autonomous Region was intended as a showpiece of Bucharest's tolerance and moderation towards her largest minority, the events of 1956 — the year of the Hungarian Uprising — put paid to this line of thinking. Fearing that the bitter struggle going on in Budapest would spill over the frontier and prompt a revolt among the minority, perhaps leading to attacks against Russian troop trains passing through Transylvania on their way to Budapest, the Romanian authorities decided to launch a preemptive strike against the local Hungarians. Martial law was declared in Transylvania, and the police were given orders to act ruthlessly against any signs of disturbance. Purges were launched against leading figures in the minority community thought to have become infected by Budapest liberalism, and numerous precautionary arrests were made.

The events of 1956 raised fears within the regime about the potential dangers of a fifth column within the country, and henceforth they decided to give top priority to integrating the minorities within the state. Appreciating that the greatest threat came from the intelligentsia, it was to these groups that the government gave first attention. Buttressed by appropriate quotations from Lenin about the undesirability of separate national schools, the authorities began phasing out Hungarian-language schools, and replacing them with special classes attached to Romanian-language schools. Other measures were also taken to restrict the education of children in Hungarian. Then, in 1959, a more damaging blow was struck with the closing down of the Hungarian university in Cluj, the Transylvanian Magyar centre, and the transfer of its faculty to the Romanian-language university in the same city. The move was initiated by party leader Gheorghiu-Dej himself, who specifically justified it as a necessary repudiation of ethnically based educational and cultural exclusiveness; and this justification subsequently extended to encompass the 'Romanisation' of a number of other specifically Hungarian institutes of higher education as well.[11]

These first actions were directed against the intelligentsia in particular, but in 1960 an important change was made that affected the whole minority community. The boundaries of the Magyar Autonomous Region were redrawn so that the new area contained more Romanians and fewer Hungarians. At the same time the name of the region was altered to the 'Mures-Autonomous Magyar Region': the addition of the Romanian word Mures signified its changed ethnic character. Also, as the proportion of Romanians in the revamped region was now greater, their numbers in the local administrative bodies had to be increased accordingly. Likewise, changes were made affecting cultural matters and media control, which were equally undesirable from the Hungarian point of view. Finally, in 1968, the Mures-Autonomous Magyar Region was abolished altogether, and a new territorial division of the country introduced that fragmented the minority population among numerous small districts, only a few of which emerged with Hungarian majorities.

The alteration of Romanian policy towards national minorities from the late 1950s onwards has to be seen in the context of development within the Communist bloc, the most important of which from the Romanian point of view was the emergence of differences between herself and the Soviet Union on key economic and political matters. In order to attract support against Moscow's hegemonic ambitions, including plans for an economic integration of the bloc along lines that would have consigned Romania to the status of a primary producer for her more developed partners, the Romanian party leadership found it expedient to make certain fundamental reorientations of policy. Hence her overtures towards China; the new policy of improving relations with the West; the development of close ties with the maverick communists of Yugoslavia; and more recently, attempts to strike an alliance with independent 'Eurocommunist' parties. But the most important force that the Bucharest regime sought to enlist was traditional Romanian patriotism. To this end they have promoted the concept of the identity of interests between party and people. Class criteria, and other ideological obstacles, standing in the way of this identification have been de-emphasised, and are no longer overt considerations in recruitment to the party or to public offices. National grievances have become party causes, such as the recovery of eastern territories annexed by the Soviet Union, and the safeguard of the nation's resources from Soviet exploitation. The position the regime seeks to establish in the popular mind is epitomised by the following remarks by Ceausescu: 'the Communist Party is the continuator [sic] of the secular struggle of the Romanian people for the attainment of national independence, for the formation of the Romanian nation, and the unitary national state, for the acceleration of social progress, and Romania's forward movement on the road to civilization'.[12]

The Romanian communist regime claims that it represents the interests of all the people regardless of race, religion and nationality. In practice, however, minority nationals have little say in the running of the state. And although the composition of the party fairly accurately reflects the ethnic break-down of the country, the all-powerful central organs are almost exclusively Romanian.[13] Jews have been particularly affected by the upsurge of nationalism that has affected the party and are entirely excluded from the major political posts where once they were numerous; they are now to be found only in positions of secondary significance. In its official voice the regime decries anti-semitism, but it is a factor in Romanian political life, and one that the past actions of the regime made more pronounced. Hungarians were never numerous at the upper levels of the state and party hierarchies, and consequently have been less affected by this aspect of Romanisation. But at the popular level, relations between them and their Romanian 'hosts' are sometimes difficult, and old grudges and resentments can easily flare up. There is a widespread feeling among the minority that the rich province of Transylvania is being milked by Bucharest to subsidise backward Romanian areas of the country. There is also a widespread feeling that the Bucharest regime aims in the end to become a state without any national minorities, and that cultural oppression and discriminatory educational policies are intended to obliterate ethnic consciousness and destroy their will to survive as separate national entities.

Conclusion

Broadly speaking, the communist states surveyed tend towards one of two strategies to maintain ethnic cohesion. At one extreme is the strategy typified by Yugoslavia, where the regime attempts to foster loyalty to the multi-national state by operating a loose-knit system that offers broad opportunities to the ethnic minorities to manage their own affairs. Here the state's role is more that of mediator and go-between. It uses its power sparingly, and so as to ensure that no one group acquires unfair advantages at the expense of others. Equally in the economy it acts as a 'visible hand' regulating affairs so as to promote regional economic equality and eradicate poverty. The image that the state presents is supranational and impartial. In cultural, linguistic and other matters bearing directly on national identity, official policy is tolerant and flexible. Overall the goal of the state is the *integration* of the communities, but not at the expense of social pluralism and ethnic diversity.

At the other extreme we have the strategy best typified by Romania. In this case the state is an active agency in promoting loyalty (obedience) to the system through the suppression of centrifugal forces and by the coercive enforcement of a common cultural pattern. The image that it presents is partisan and 'national'. The goal of the régime is not simply the integration of the communities, but their *assimilation* into the state nationality. The Soviet Union and Czechoslovakia would appear to lie somewhere between these two extremes, but, particularly in the case of the Soviet Union, closer to the Romanian than to the Yugoslav position.

With the decline in central authority within the communist bloc, nationalism has become a more pronounced force in all communist states. Contributory too has been the general inclination, post-1956, to substitute popular support for coercion as the mainstay of rule, which has encouraged régimes to adopt stances conciliatory to popular preferences. In the case of Yugoslavia and Romania an additional precipitating factor was the breakdown in relations with the USSR, and the consequent inability to rely on

Soviet backing for their survival; though, as we have seen, their nationalist reactions have taken markedly different forms. Communist nationalisms, however, are not simply updated versions of the nationalisms that pre-dated the communist take-overs. Ideology and residual internationalism have had a certain modifying effect and have at least softened the more xenophobic and racist aspects of the traditional forms.

As the fragmentation of the Soviet bloc proceeds, and as the synthetic unity provided by its declining ideology further dissolves, one can expect nationalism to become an even more dominant force in communist states. What form it takes, and with what consequences for the minor nationalities of these states, is as yet uncertain.

NOTES AND REFERENCES

1. See *Zarya vostoka,* 27 April 1973, for some examples.
2. Twelve out of the fourteen second secretaries in 1978 were Russians; one was a Belorussian (in Belorussia); and one a Ukrainian (serving in Latvia).
3. For some facets of this see *Voprosy ekonomiki,* no. 12, 1972; *Sovetskaya Litva,* 29 November, 1973; *Sovetskaya Kirgizia,* 20 Decemmber, 1973.
4. P. Reddaway, 'The Development of Dissent and Opposition' in A. Brown and M. Kaser, *The Soviet Union Since the Fall of Khrushchev,* London, Macmillan, 1975, p. 143.
5. Five of the six republics are based on a single nationality (Serbia, Croatia, Slovenia, Montenegro and Macedonia), the sixth (Bosnia-Herzegovina) is based on a mixed nationality region. If number and compactness had been the sole considerations in conferring republican status, then the Albanian and Hungarian minorities would have also been eligible, for both satisfied these criteria better than the Montenegrins when the latter were granted a republic.
6. *Yugoslav Survey,* February, 1974, p. 34. Another factor here is the high rate of population increase in the retarded areas, e.g. 22.8 per 1000 in Kosovo between 1950 and 1971, as against 6.5 in the developed Croatia.
7. R.R. King, *Minorities Under Communism,* Cambridge, Mass., Harvard University Press, 1973, p. 126.
8. Figures presented by Dubcek on one occasion showed economic advance to have been faster in Slovakia under the clerico-fascists than under the communists! See W. Shawcross, *Dubcek,* London, Weidenfeld and Nicolson, 1970, p. 120.
9. R. Selucky, *The Plan that Failed,* London, Nelson, 1970, p. 77.
10. There is some suggestion that the creation of this unit was sponsored by the USSR in order to place obstacles in the way of the full integration of the Transylvanian region into Romania, thus conciliating Budapest and also leaving the way open for a possible future transfer back to Hungary, if this became expedient.
11. This and recent more serious repressive measures against the Magyar minority have been the occasion of considerable friction between Romania and Hungary. For information on this and on recent repressions see H. Hartl, 'Das Minderheitenproblem zwischen Ungarn and Rumänien', *Wissenschaftlicher Dienst Südosteuropa,* 7, 1977, pp. 184-8; G. Schöpflin, *Sunday Times,* 10 April, 1977; *International Herald Tribune,* 2 March, 1978.
12. S. Fischer-Galati, *Twentieth Century Rumania,* New York, Columbia University Press, 1970, p. 190.
13. The ethnic break-down of the party in 1977 was: Romanians — 89%, Hungarians — 7.4%, Germans — 1.6%, other nationalities — 2%. Data from *RFE Report,* Romania, 18 April, 1977.

SELECT BIBLIOGRAPHY

Allworth, E. (ed.) *Soviet Nationality Problems,* New York, Columbia University Press, 1971.

Bertsch, G.K., *Values and Community in Multinational Yugoslavia,* New York, Columbia University Press, 1976.
Conquest, R. (ed.), *Soviet Nationalities Policy in Practice,* London, Bodley Head, 1967.
Fischer-Galati, S., *Twentieth Century Rumania,* New York, Columbia University Press, 1970.
King, R.R., *Minorities Under Communism,* Cambridge, Mass., Harvard University Press, 1973.
Simmonds, G. W., (ed.) *Nationalism in the USSR and Eastern Europe,* Detroit, University of Detroit Press, 1977.
Steiner, E., *The Slovak Dilemma,* London, Cambridge University Press, 1973.

CHAPTER 7

The State and the Economy in Eastern Europe

Hans-Hermann Höhmann

Every state and social order has its development and structure determined to a large extent by economic processes. This is true particularly of the countries of Eastern Europe. The very ideological foundation of Eastern European socialism, Marxist theory, attributes unequivocal priority to the economy over other determinant factors of political and social life (historical, intellectual factors) as being the material basis on which the structure of state and society is built. Furthermore, it has been postulated again and again since Lenin that the economic-ideological legitimation of socialist planned economy systems is closely linked to economic success; the superiority of socialism is best demonstrated in its successes in world competition with the capitalist West. This aspect is connected with the significance of the economy as a power factor. A strong position in foreign affairs, strong armaments, economic influence in the world (particularly in its underdeveloped parts), all depend on a powerful economy. Thus the targets of economic growth policies take pride of place amongst political objectives. Growth was also indispensable to attempts to surmount economic underdevelopment. So it was that the level of development of the economies of most of the Eastern European countries before and after the Second World War shifted the need to catch up on the industrialisation of the economy into the foreground of political activity. But there are also other factors governing the importance of the economy to politics and society in Eastern Europe. The rule of the Communist Party has been and still is supported to a great extent by economic institutions. The collectivist order of proprietary rights and the consequent political monopoly of the supply of jobs prevents society from retreating into an area beyond party influence where political resistance could develop, while the centralised administrative nature of the planning system creates a hierarchical structure that assures the political functionary of great influence. Finally, because of its wide range of action (planning and control of the entire economy) state economic policy is also a far-reaching instrument of social policy. Economic institutions — such as the system of proprietary rights or the planning system — and the priority given to economic policy and in particular to allocation policy, have a strong determining effect on the structure of Eastern European societies.

However, this widespread utilisation of the economy to further political aims has not been able to prevent the emergence of two phenomena: the increasing incompatibility between the various individual targets pursued by economic policy, e.g. between the targets of consolidating political rule and optimising the efficiency of economic expansion, and the increasing degree of de facto economic decentralisation, which has brought the political controllability of the economy into question.

These inconsistencies lie at the root of the economic reforms in Eastern Europe. The main causes of the reform movement that emerged in the 1960s were the deterioration in economic efficiency, which led to notable drops in the growth rates of the majority of Eastern European countries, and the decline in the ability to plan economic development. The latter development was itself due to ever more complex economic structures on the one hand and the limited effectiveness of planning techniques on the other.[1]

In some countries of Eastern Europe, the economic motives for overcoming these inconsistencies and difficulties were supplemented by political desires and hopes. In Czechoslovakia, particularly, economic decentralisation (the guiding idea of the reform) was seen not only as a way to improve economic performance but also as a means to attain 'socialist democratisation' (Ota Šik), i.e. towards relaxing the totalitarian methods and institutions associated with the traditional centralist economic system. Of course, it was not only the reformers who were aware of this interdependence between economic decentralisation and political democratisation. The conservative forces in Eastern Europe, particularly in the USSR, were induced, at least to some extent, by their knowledge of the connections between politics and economics to intervene in the process of reform in Czechoslovakia, admittedly at a time when the reform had long left the path of mere economic reform.

However, the fact that the desire to improve efficiency was by far the most important motive behind the Soviet reform does not imply that sociopolitical reform tendencies played no part at all in that country. Indeed, such motives were suggested by a number of advocates of reform, although in most cases they were brought forward in carefully veiled formulation. Neither does the subordinate role played by political and social motives in reforms in the USSR (as well as in the GDR) mean that economic reforms had no political and social effects whatsoever. As is the case with all institutional changes involving a shift in decision-making power, even conservative variants of reform affected the status and interests of many individuals and social groups. In this respect, processes of reform have been and still are going on in Eastern Europe in a field of social forces that has the effect of expediting or of retarding reform. In what follows, the extent, result and social relevance of the economic reforms in Eastern Europe will be analysed against the background of the traditional economic system, with its centralised administration and its dysfunctions. Particular attention is paid to the USSR and to Hungary as examples of two different approaches to reform.

In this differentiation between two models of reform, it must not be overlooked that in the course of the economic reforms major distinctions arose between economic institutions and policy instruments, even of countries using the same model. There were often great differences between both the formal structure of the administrative organisations of such countries as well as the form in which their enterprises were consolidated. For example, the production units of the USSR, the associations of people's enterprises (VVBs) of the GDR, the Polish 'pilot units' (*jednostki inicjujace*) and the Romanian industrial centres are not congruent in their organisational structure. This is true also of instruments of economic planning, such as the systems of plan indicators for steering and assessing the activities of the enterprises and combines. Assessed as to their economic functional mechanisms, however, they can be reduced to two models. Even the Polish reform developments of the 1970s, though revealing many interesting aspects as far as their institutions are concerned, 'have not distinguished themselves by a vision and originality which would put them into a separate category among East European countries.'[2] Despite their institutional peculiarities, they must be attributed to the conservative reform model.

THE TRADITIONAL SYSTEM OF SOCIALIST ECONOMIC PLANNING

The system of industrial economic planning (on which we shall concentrate) that was typical of the socialist countries of East Europe before the economic reforms were initiated, on the whole continues to prevail despite these reforms. So, the nature and extent of the economic reforms must be examined against the background of that system. Its basic features are, firstly, administrative state planning: co-ordination of the economic process by means of production and distribution plans prescribed by the government and monopolisation of foreign trade by the state. Secondly, it is characterised by imperative short-term planning — the compulsory character of administrative planning whereby the annual plans worked out by the authorities are binding upon the enterprises. Thirdly, there is comprehensive planning of production and distribution with official control of the macro- and micro-economic structure of all economic production processes; prices are fixed by the state, while consumers are free to choose what and how much they wish to consume and what professions, occupations and places of work are to their liking and advantage. Fourthly, there is a preponderance of quantity planning over price planning with passive (inactive) money circulation, performing the aggregating, co-ordinating, controlling functions that are typical of planning.

The system of socialist economic planning, in spite of all the economic progress achieved in the USSR and other East European countries, is marked by a number of typical functional inadequacies that are becoming increasingly obvious as the economic structure grows more complicated and, in many East European countries, are causing a slow-down of economic growth. These functional inadequacies have the effect of making the division of labour in the production sector less amenable to co-ordination and of gradually diminishing the effectiveness of production. Both these consequences impair the efficiency of the entire system. Two typical places where the functional weakness is concentrated are the administrative apparatus and the system of planning and distributing bonuses to the industrial enterprises (operational planning).

Models of Reform

In the mid-1960s the Communist parties and the governments of practically all the East European countries adopted reform programmes after previous preparatory experiments and discussions. Two models of reform are easily distinguished. Firstly, there is the model of a more flexible, rationalised, centrally administered and controlled economy (USSR, German Democratic Republic, Poland, Bulgaria and — with reservations — Romania). Secondly, there is the decentralised model tending towards a socialist market economy (Yugoslavia, Czechoslovakia until 1969, and Hungary). The first model — although differently institutionalised in the various countries concerned — is characterised by a reorganisation of the economic administration (changes in the degree of centralisation and in the principle of organisation); a modernisation of planning techniques (development of mathematical planning procedures); a modification and reduction of the number of binding plan indicators or targets (reduction of plan redundancies); a more exact orientation of operational profit and loss accounting (bonus system) by objective or synthetic standards of achievement (profitability); an improvement of the system of economic levers with a view to inducing the enterprises or operating units to increase the effectiveness of production and to bring production into more complete harmony with plans and contracts.

The model of a socialist market economy is marked by three sets of features. Firstly, there is a more or less complete liberation of the enterprises from the observance of direct plan indicators or targets (including those relating to foreign trade, albeit in a lesser degree); a relaxation of the foreign trade monopoly; a turning of the market into an instrument of short-term economic calculation; a decentralization of price-fixing. Secondly, there is skeleton planning by the socialist state with a view to securing the desired macro-economic structure (central responsibility for investment policy) and economic steering by indirect means (monetary, credit and financial policy). Thirdly, there is market organisation to support the overall organisational policy objective.

PROBLEMS OF IMPLEMENTATION

We shall now try to establish how far it was possible to carry into effect these various reforms. In other words, what changes have in fact taken place in the socialist economic system in East Europe?

Although, from the outset, the conservative type of reform could not be expected to produce a transformation of the socialist system, but merely (which means a great deal for East European economic policy) an increase in the system's effectiveness, the question of realisation is not an idle one. The tempo of even a limited or mild reform shows whether a system is open to reform and whether its leaders are willing to reform. On the other hand, it exposes the restrictions that hold back even the conservative variants of reform programmes. This makes it possible to evaluate the strength of the movement toward reform and the likely scope for future (modest or more ambitious) reforms.

The ceaseless discussions among economists, practical planners and socialist managers in the countries having embarked upon conservative reforms show that it is as yet impossible to speak of a completely organised, satisfactory steering system that leaves wider scope to managerial decision-making in the enterprises; works on a rationalised system of incentives (that is, one that is harmonized with plans and contracts); and effectively applies economic levers. Instead, a revival of centralised management and control is being observed, for example, in the USSR and the German Democratic Republic.

There are several reasons for the retardation of progress towards economic reorganisation, as a result of which the achievements fell short of even the limited aims of the conservative variants of reform.

Attitudes and behaviour are rooted in a tradition of orthodox socialist economic planning that makes it difficult to change the pattern of economic policy. The authorities responsible for economic administration (ministerial bureaucracy) are unwilling to relinquish their functions. The political leaders fear that a relaxation of the planning system may make it more difficult to enforce and uphold the supreme power of the party machine.

Additional centralised intervention is required even after the reform, on account of the vagueness and flexibility of the plan indicators. Finally, the lack of criteria by which decentralised management within the enterprises might be guided provokes administrative interference from above.

In spite of these inadequacies of economic policy, some of them deeply rooted in the system of centrally administered economies of the Soviet type, many economists think it is possible to make the planning and bonus system created by the reform workable by correcting procedural and organisational details. However, this seems very doubtful upon closer investigation. The combination of a partial extension of managerial discretion in the enterprises with a continuance of operational planning from above and with central price fixing shows the new system to be a half-way solution between centralised and decentralised planning, which would seem rather unstable. If the beginnings of decentralised economic processes are built into a centrally administered economy without at the same time creating criteria or standards for economically sound decision-making in the enterprises by introducing a comprehensive price reform, a 'functionally weak mixed system' is bound to emerge. This is made absolutely clear, despite partial improvements, by the experience gained from examining the Soviet economic reforms and the conservative reform model in other East European states. But it is equally plain that the Soviet leaders are not prepared to envisage a fundamental alteration of the planning system. Nor are we able to observe tendencies to replace the economic policy of 'step-by-step' reform by a comprehensive, farther-reaching reform model in the more immediate future.

THE 'NEW ECONOMIC MECHANISM' IN HUNGARY

As far as the realisation of the socialist market economy is concerned and the effects of this model of reform on the socialist economic order, it is necessary to remember first of all that the Czechoslovak leaders after 1969, partially under Soviet pressure and partially driven by their own conservative convictions, have given up the principle of skeleton-planned market socialism and have returned to administrative planning. A different kind of development is observed in Hungary,[3] but even there it is impossible to speak of a rapid transformation into a socialist market economy, despite the fact that the start of the reform on 1 January, 1968 was on more comprehensive lines than in other East European countries. Nor could a rapid transition have been envisaged or expected for several reasons. From the outset, Hungarian reformers had planned the implementation of the reform to be spread over a period of ten to fifteen years. During this long transitional period, while the elements of the 'new economic mechanism' were to be

The State and the Economy in Eastern Europe 147

gradually introduced, elements of the old administrative planning system were to be maintained. This decision would seem to have economic, ideological, social and general political causes. Firstly, it was impossible to expose an economic system that over two decades had been built up to the exclusion of an allocation system based on the market economy principle to the dangers of a 'sudden structural erosion' with its grave social consequences. Secondly, it was necessary gradually to change traditional attitudes and behaviour prevailing under an administrative planning system and, instead, to awaken and encourage 'entrepreneurial' behaviour (in Schumpeter's sense), of which preparedness to assume risk is an essential element. Finally, experience gained by what happened to economic reform in Czechoslovakia suggested an extremely cautious procedure and the avoidance of spectacular effects. For this reason it would be better for Western commentators on the Hungarian scene to be more careful in their utterances and to refrain from hailing the dawn of a market economy with undue and unjustified euphoria.

However, the beginnings of a transformation of the socialist planning system soon became visible in Hungary as a result of this careful and circumspect reform policy. The role of the market as an instrument for the current adjustment of production has been appreciably extended. The central system of plan indicators was considerably relaxed even in the first phase of the reform. This may be illustrated by information relating to production planning, investment policy, price policy and foreign trade policy.

As far as industrial production is concerned, only a small percentage of the total volume of production is controlled by binding instructions in the sense of the traditional planning system. Compulsory industrial production today is mainly concerned with exportable articles and with goods needed to satisfy the civil and military demands of the state. Thus, the majority of decisions on production are orientated by the market. In a few sectors of production (where shortages existed) the traditional allocation of production requisites (material and technological supplies) continued. Relatively strong state influence still prevailed in the field of investment policy. Nevertheless, decentralised decision-making became more important soon after the beginning of the reform. In the very important field of pricing policy a careful decentralisation of price determination proceeded, even if there have occurred some corrections in price formation, which were signs of a tendency towards recentralisation. In the foreign trade sector the traditional, very inflexible system has also been relaxed, although stringent restrictions continued in force (foreign exchange policy, quotas, compulsory licensing of foreign trade and payments transactions, import deposits and the like).

In summary, the result of the economic reform and the economic policy of the following years was certainly no market economy in the conventional textbook sense. The 'new economic mechanism' kept the only partially reformed socialist conception of property. The market mechanism stayed in some ways imperfect and a large area of economic interference by the state remained. Above all, the share of bonuses and wage supplements originally planned had to be modified so as to provide 80 per cent of monthly salary for managers, 50 per cent for other leading executives and only 15 per cent for workers. Also, the possibility of obtaining relatively high incomes in the growing private sector of the economy, led to resentment among some workers in the state sector. The extent of the participation in the decisions of the enterprise by workers' representatives has still not been settled. On the one hand, the Hungarian leadership is making efforts to maintain the technocratic character of the economic system, which is in favour of the enterprise management. On the other hand, it has had to make concessions regarding participation in the enterprises.

On the whole, a balance sheet after ten years shows that the concept and practical implementation of the reform in Hungary have had a stronger effect on the traditional socialist planning system than the reforms in other East European countries (with the exception of Yugoslavia). Also, the preparedness of Hungarian party and government leaders to go ahead with the reform process continues, though with changing priorities and with corrections to the course of economic policy. However, all will depend on keeping the friction caused by a gradual transformation of the system within as narrow bounds as possible, so as not to provide conservative quarters with arguments against the reform. It is necessary to make people understand that the difficulties arising during the transformation phase must not be looked upon as functional inadequacies of a decentralised socialist system. Further, care must be taken in the future that the social and political consequences of economic reform — which are inevitable owing to the interdependence of economic, social and political elements — are not regarded in Moscow and elsewhere as a breakaway from the principles of 'democratic centralism'. The future of the economic reform movement in East Europe does not depend, however, on the experiments with the Hungarian 'new economic mechanism'. Far more important is the extent of reform that the USSR is prepared to implement within its own country and to allow in the COMECON area. Therefore, the nature and limits of reform policy in the USSR have to be discussed.

REFORM POLICY AND THE ROLE OF SOCIAL GROUPS IN THE USSR

The remarkable slow-down of economic growth during the Ninth Five-Year Plan period led to persistent although limited efforts towards reform in three areas: administration, planning, plants. The importance of the traditional principle of administratively planned economies, which gives priority to vertical flows of information and directives over horizontal processes of consensus, is either to be reduced or at least this principle has to be complemented by the development of horizontal co-operative relations. However, the effectiveness of the measures that have been introduced is subject to some questioning because no substantial corrections have been made with respect to the basic principle of subordinating industrial plants and production associations to planning authorities. Better co-ordination of the various sub-sectors of the economy can only be expected if the importance of market controls in economic activity is more clearly recognised by the Soviet leaders and if effective mechanisms are created to this end. However, this can only be achieved within the context of a socialist market economy.

A thoroughgoing reform, based upon a combination of market mechanism, socialist property and overall state planning — such as has been implemented in Yugoslavia, is practised in Hungary with reservations, and was planned in Czechoslovakia in 1968 — still runs up against rigid barriers in the USSR. These barriers are of various kinds and they are found in the economic as well as in the political, social and ideological areas.

Economic policy risks

In terms of economic policy, the risk of a comprehensive reform in the sense of a transition to a socialist market economy in the USSR is much greater than in smaller, structurally more balanced socialist economies. The fact that the regional and sectoral production structure of the Soviet Union was created over a period of decades, with the complete exclusion of the system of controls of a market economy, contains the danger of 'structural erosion' in the case of a change to the functional mechanism of a market-oriented economy, and the social and economic ramifications of such a change cannot be foreseen. The necessity of considerable subsidies in unprofitable areas or of comprehensive regional and sectoral structural changes in order to ensure the requisite profitability at the level of the individual operations for a viable market economy would burden an extensive reform with such high transitional costs that the gains sought through such a reform — which might at any rate be attainable only in the long run — would appear less attractive by contrast. For the Soviet Union as a world power, which can live up to its international role only by harnessing all of its economic strength, the risk of economic setbacks is at least for the present too great and preclude gambling on the future success of reform, which is a matter of uncertainty.

In addition to risks associated with growth and structural policy, there are dangers in terms of stability. The controls of a market economy cannot function without flexible prices, and the inflationary pressure that already exists today in the consumer goods markets as well as in the area of raw materials would conceivably undergo a change from repressed or hidden inflation to open inflation.[4] The transition to a functional market economy would probably not be possible without a monetary reform. A comprehensive reduction of purchasing power (such as occurred when the German Federal Republic made the transition to a market economy) would, however, mean considerable risks in terms of political stability in the USSR.

Finally, the USSR is still pursuing developmental goals such as, for example, economically opening up the eastern part of the country. The completion of this developmental task is of considerable economic and strategic importance, both of which are subsumed under the terms 'raw materials supplies' and the 'Soviet-Chinese conflict'. Developmental goals would tend to make it seem expedient not to abandon central planning. On the whole, 'economic rationality' does not work exclusively in favour of extensive, market-oriented reforms. The reduction of the reform question to alternatives of economic or political rationality, often attempted by Western commentators, does not do justice to the complexity of the Soviet economy.

Political limits to reform

In the political area, there are several limits to reform.[5] In the foreign policy field, the administratively planned economy based upon a central administration is also an instrument of the policy of integration within the context of the Council for Mutual Economic Assistance and thus serves simultaneously as an instrument of the policy of hegemony pursued by the Soviets. Administrative economic planning provides three advantages in this respect. First of all, the bilateral coordination of plans between the USSR and other socialist countries links a considerable portion of the economic potential of the smaller COMECON countries to the USSR. In addition, the USSR can benefit from the technological progress of those COMECON countries that are more developed in this respect (German Democratic Republic, Czechoslovakia). Thirdly, the co-ordination of plans makes it possible to plan a great part of the USSR's international economic relations. A transition to socialist market economies in the countries of Eastern Europe with the concomitant possibility of a freer choice of trade partners in Western markets would endanger the USSR's predominant position in the COMECON area with respect to foreign policy, along with its dominant economic position (see below, chapter 11).

With respect to internal policy, the fact that the traditional administrative planning system has, from the very beginning, also been used as a means of securing power, militates against a more extensive reform. The subordination of extensive sections of society to rule by the party and state apparatus, as well as the socialisation of the means of production, has considerably limited the margins for democratic and participatory processes and has tended to stabilise the power structure. Both put society in a position of inferiority that in the final analysis provides the basis for the dominant position of the party. The Prague reformers had this relationship between bureaucratic planning and the suppression of democratic freedom in mind when they were designing their reform policy as both a way of increasing efficiency as well as a contribution to 'socialist democratisation' (Ota Šik). Abandoning the system of administrative compulsory planning would at the same time entail abandoning a substantial part of the power and controls exercised by the Communist Party. To accept this would mean that the thinking of Soviet leaders would have to undergo far-reaching changes in their understanding of leadership. It is of course true that totalitarian rule in the sense of Stalinism is no longer practicable today and the power exercised by the party has been transformed into an authoritarian system with a certain degree of legal security. However, the party is shying away from all-too-comprehensive reforms because it is aware of the existing interdependence between the system of power, the system of economic controls and the social structure. The political margin for thoroughgoing economic reforms in the sense of a socialistic market economy can only exist if the leaders of the Communist Party of the Soviet Union content themselves with shaping the political, social and economic framework.

Regional and nationality-related limits to reform

Factors having to do with the various nationalities also restrict the scope for extensive reform. It is highly probable that a transformation of the Soviet economy into a system incorporating market-oriented control principles would lead to greater differences in income between the various regions of the USSR and consequently also accentuate the problem of the various nationalities, which is already precarious today.[6] Centralised planning, on the other hand, is an effective instrument for compensating the differences in production or productivity between the various geographical areas of the USSR and therefore also serves to eliminate conflicts between nationalities. For the boundaries separating areas of greater economic capacity (such as in the north-west and in the central regions of European Russia) from areas of lesser economic capacity (such as Central Asia and the Transcaucasian republics) are in fact often also the boundaries separating various nationalities.[7] The differences in capacity that exist between the various parts of the country today would be exacerbated by a transition to market-oriented economies. The experience of Yugoslavia, for example, shows that market-oriented systems of control in socialist societies also exacerbate differences in income between developed and less developed regions and consequently sharpen the animosity that existed between various nationality groups in the first place. Such a development might be expected in the USSR too. The resulting centrifugal forces would then probably be difficult to neutralise and could, under certain circumstances, prove to be a threat to the USSR as a centralised superpower.

Another reason for retaining the instruments of a centralised administrative planning and controls system, as seen from the point of view of regional structural policy in connection with the nationalities problem, derives from long-term demographic trends and concomitant shifts in the regional structure of the labour supply. Demographic investigations have shown that growth in the labour market in the 1980s will shift more and more to the Asian and Transcaucasian union republics.[8] Since, however, it will probably only be partially possible to direct the labour supply to the existing industrial centres, a labour-oriented regional structural policy must be pursued to a greater extent. Optimum exploitation of the growth in the labour supply thus means creating employment in the areas in which the growth in the labour supply takes place. But since the areas showing high growth in terms of available manpower are also those areas with less productive capacity, such a policy would be impossible without the central control of investment resources.

Finally, one must not overlook the fact that the centrally administered planning and control system in its present institutional form, i.e. economic administration through separate ministries for various branches, also constitutes the most effective and at the same time the most inconspicuous means of Russian hegemony within the USSR. The institution of centralised ministries controlled by Moscow with industrial operations and production associations throughout the country make it possible to pursue a policy of Russification in the context of internal personnel policy within the administrative apparatus. A socialist market-oriented economy, on the other hand, would necessarily give increased importance to the local — and consequently also the national — element.

Vested interests of social groups

A comprehensive economic reform would also encounter resistance on the part of members of those groups in Soviet society whose social positions would be affected by the reform. This would apply especially to the administrative bureaucracy, the members of which would be concerned about their positions in the event of a transition to a market-oriented economy. However, the major social groups whose positions are affected by reform measures are not homogeneous. There are differences within these groups not only in how they are affected by reforms but also in the extent to which they are able to resist or promote them. This applies as much to the functionaries of the party and state apparatus as it does to enterprise managers and workers. Thus the lower-echelon functionaries bear the brunt of market-type reforms while the upper levels of the apparatuses would be able to retain a major part of their accustomed influence even in the event of a far-reaching reform. Nevertheless, it is true to say that a market-type reform 'is inconsistent with the exercise of power by officials of the party at all levels, at least in the arbitrary form in which they are accustomed to exercise it. The same is true of many state planning and finance officials.'[9] This stratum no doubt brings its influence to bear within the party against any comprehensive reform. However, even more modest reform measures, e.g. a reorganisational change within the economic administration, are scarcely applauded by the officials they affect. Thus, by way of example, the formation of industrial associations encounters resistance from the ministerial bureaucracy because it would be carried out at the expense of the traditional administration of industrial branches within the ministries.

The reservations voiced by leading planning officials, for example, regarding the intensified employment of mathematical models and electronic data processing in economic planning, cannot be accounted for merely by the limited uses of mathematical instruments and by the continued inadequacy of computer technology. This situation is aggravated by the old-guard planners' fears of being replaced, in the wake of the ever-progressing modernisation of the planning instrumentarium, by freshly trained 'planning engineers' with a high standard of theoretical knowledge. Competition and computation are hardly compatible with the interests of the traditional party and state bureaucracy. The Czechoslovak experience shows how strong and how much of a barrier resistance on the part of the administrative bureaucracies can be in the face of reforms that have already been approved by the party leaders.

The attitude of management towards reform is ambivalent. Frequent complaints in the Soviet press make it clear that numerous managers are dissatisfied with the existing system of operational planning. The source of this dissatisfaction is, however, hardly to be found in a general rejection of the traditional system and a desire to replace administrative planning by a market-oriented economy. The source of management's complaints is more the existence of contradictions in the present system than the system itself. The difficulty of meeting all of the authorities' plan quotas simultaneously, the incessantly recurring problem of finding the right combination of fulfilling and not fulfilling official plans, the lack of stability of official plans, the chronic lack of regularity of material and equipment deliveries and similar difficulties are indeed responsible for the fact that management is in favour of reforms in order to create less ambiguous channels of information, more reliable allocations and uninterrupted supplies. However, reforms in the direction of a market-oriented economy would entail new risks for traditional management. For one thing there are economic risks. The market demands profitability, but this can often be achieved only with difficulty, not least because of structural phenomena over which the individual operation has no influence. Thus the attitude of the managers towards reform could well depend heavily on the economic situation of their enterprises, the probable effects of the reform on the profit and loss performance of their enterprises and their own personal ability to take the initiative and make correct decisions on the basis of their own aptitude and training. On account of their traditional behavioural role as executors of ready-made planning decisions, many managers of minor industrial enterprises would be unable to cope with the economic conditions imposed by a market-type reform. In addition, it is questionable whether a technocratic market economy, i.e. forms of a market-oriented economy that are shielded against any sort of democratic participation, could prove to be lasting in a socialist environment. For once individual decision-making responsibility for an operation is based upon the market, the question is soon asked as to who is to be responsible for this decision-making autonomy. Discussions in Eastern Europe as well as the Yugoslav and Czechoslovak experience show a more or less marked tendency toward participatory management models as decision-making processes in socialist market-oriented economies.

To the same extent that centrally administered planning exerts pressure upon management from above on the one hand, it also protects management's position from too much pressure from below, on the other. Centrally administered planning protects not only the party and the officials within the economic administration from genuine democratisation, but management as well.

For the workforce, too, a reform would bring not only advantages. On the one hand, the Soviet worker as a consumer is interested in an increase in economic efficiency, in a greater supply of consumer goods and in improved quality and a wider selection of goods. On the other hand, market-type reforms, if they are to be successful, depend upon a high degree of mobility on the part of the labour force and on a productivity and performance-based system of pay differentials. Both of these could only be in the interests of capable and motivated sections of the workforce.

Finally, advocacy of a market-economy solution is not common even among the economists themselves. Admittedly, there is some criticism of the present system. But the alternative suggested in most cases takes the form of a reduced, modernised centralism and not of a market-type model. This is due in part to the lack of market-economy traditions within Soviet economics and in part to the fact that economists clearly see the difficulties that a market-economy solution would entail, even if they do not support, or are not forced to support, the official rejection of a market-type reform, by virtue of their political views and/or professional position.

Ideological barriers?

Ideological barriers would in the final analysis probably prove to be less important. Marxism as a basic ideological system is amenable to quite varied interpretations, as evidenced by the international socialist movement, and can, as is for instance the case in Yugoslavia, also be combined with a market-oriented system of controls. Contemporary Soviet Marxism-Leninism has, however, not yet attained this interpretive elasticity, which means that it has the effect of inhibiting reform. However, two basic postulates of Soviet ideology that have not been abandoned continue to inhibit reform and both of them are of substantial importance in terms of legitimising the dominant position of the party. These two postulates can be described as the postulates of planability and harmony.

The postulate of planability states that the course of economic and social processes can be planned under socialism, in contrast to the anarchy of capitalist market systems. This postulate of planability is the source both of the justification of the leadership role claimed by the party and state apparatus, as the conceptual and organisational agent of planning processes, and of aversion to spontaneous market-instigated processes, which would result in unplanned economic trends and, more importantly, would at the same time also constitute an admission of the existence of limits to planability.

The postulate of harmony is based upon the fiction of a society free of conflicts that reflects a complete harmony of interests. This postulate was questioned during the Soviet reform discussions, although to a lesser extent than in other Eastern European countries. Official ideology has, however, still not abandoned this concept. The fiction of harmony continues to be maintained. As far as practical reforms are concerned, this means that a society that is characterised by uniform interests needs no institutions to resolve conflicts and develop compromises, such as those that constitute part of the nature of market-oriented systems.

The planability and harmony postulates serve in the final analysis to stabilise the power of the party, but quite independently of the party they also block new developments in economic thinking. They are a concrete case of the phenomenon described in Keynes' famous statement to the effect that ideas that have become obsolete retain the ability to exert influence on politicians.

Conclusion

The limits to reform described above clearly demonstrate that no alternative exists to the present course of Soviet economic policy. The policy of relaxed rationalised centralism, which has been pursued since the end of the 1960s, may be expected to continue in the future. It means, also, that the scope for reforms in the other East European countries remains limited. Though the Hungarian system represents an alternative to the modernised centralism of the Soviet type, it is hard to believe that the USSR will allow a 'Hungarianisation' of economic systems in its sphere of influence. In that event, the resultant revisionism would reach dimensions that would not only endanger the foreign trade interests of the Soviet Union in the COMECON area but would also call into question the existence of the communist governmental system and its ideological legitimation. The USSR can hardly afford to permit broad economic reforms in other countries as an expression of advanced adjustments to changed economic conditions, so long as the Soviet Union itself as the hegemonic socialist power keeps to economic conservatism for the reasons already mentioned. These limits to changes in the economic system in Eastern Europe, however, do not exclude partial reforms. The economic situation makes it necessary to look for new ways in economic policy. This will lead the East European economies to explore areas of different, permanent, but at the same time limited reforms.

NOTES AND REFERENCES
1. See H.-H. Höhmann, M.C. Kaser and K.C. Thalheim (eds), *The New Economic Systems of Eastern Europe,* London, C. Hurst, 1975.
2. W. Brus, 'Economic Policy in Poland, 1970-1976', to be published in *Berichte des Bundesinstituts für ostwissenschaftliche und internationale Studien,* Cologne, 1978.
3. See O. Gado, *The Economic Mechanism in Hungary — How it works in 1976,* Budapest, Akadémiai Kiadó, 1976; A. Nove, *The Soviet Economic System,* London, Allen and Unwin, 1977, pp. 290-8 ('The Hungarian Reform Model').
4. See Jakov N. Khanelis, 'Ursachen und Erscheinungsformen der Inflation in der Sowjetunion', *Arbeiten aus dem Osteuropa-Institut Munchen,* no. 6, January 1976.
5. See R. V. Burks, 'The Political Implications of Economic Reform' in M. Bornstein (ed.), *Plan and Market,* New Haven, Conn., and London, Yale University Press, 1973, pp. 391 ff.
6. *ibid.,* pp. 391 ff. See also chapter 6 in this volume.
7. See Hans-Jürgen Wagener, 'Regionalentwicklung und Regionalpolitik in der Sowjetunion', *Forschungsberichte des Wiener Instituts für Internationale Wirtschaftsvergleiche* of the *Österreichisches Institut für Wirtschaftsforschung,* no. 25, April 1975, on the differences in the economic development of the various union republics of the USSR.
8. See Murray Feshbach and Stephan Rapaway, 'Soviet Population and Manpower Trends and Policies', *Soviet Economy in a New Perspective,* Washington, US Government Printing Office, 1976, pp. 113 ff.
9. Alec Nove, *The Soviet Economic System,* London, Allen and Unwin, 1977, p. 312.

SELECT BIBLIOGRAPHY
Bornstein, M. (ed.), *Plan and Market, Economic Reform in Eastern Europe,* New Haven, Conn. and London, Yale University Press, 1973.
Fallenbuchl, Z. M. (ed.), *Economic Development in the Soviet Union and Eastern Europe — Reforms, Technology and Income Distribution,* New York, Praeger, 1975.
Höhmann, H.-H., Kaser, M. C. and Thalheim, K. C. (eds), *The New Economic Systems of Eastern Europe,* London, C. Hurst, 1975.
Nove, A., *The Soviet Economic System,* London, Allen and Unwin, 1977.

Selucky, R., *Economic Reforms in Eastern Europe — Political Background and Economic Significance,* New York, Praeger, 1972.
Thornton, J., *Economic Analysis of the Soviet-Type System,* London, Cambridge University Press, 1976.

CHAPTER 8

Yugoslavia: A Special Case

Robert K. Furtak

The Origins of Yugoslav Socialism

In spite of several similarities, Yugoslavia's political and socio-economic system constitutes a deviant case among the East European states dominated by a Communist party. The essential divergencies are:
1. Administration of the means of production and regulation of individual and common affairs by the citizens at their workplace (workers' self-management) and at their place of residence (territorial self-government) on their own responsibility;
2. Direct democratic institutions at all levels of decision-making, with limited competition in elections;
3. A relatively strong legislature vis à vis the administrative organs;
4. A stronger emphasis upon the democratic component in the Leninist principle of democratic centralism;
5. Recognition of pluralist interests and possibility of conflict even in a socialist society;
6. An organisation of production, distribution and consumption according to the principles of a market economy; indicative planning of the economic process;
7. The existence of a constitutional judicature.

Let us first examine the origins and historical conditions that have led to the emergence of these peculiarities before characterising them in detail, examining their problems and evaluating their consequences for the singular and somewhat precarious relationship between state, party and society in Yugoslavia. Three variables can be distinguished that determine the specific features of the Yugoslav political system: the ethnic, cultural and socio-economic setting; the way communism attained power; and the Yugoslav interpretation of Marxism. We should at the start note the ethnic, cultural and religious heterogeneity of the peoples who established themselves over centuries in the part of Europe that became Yugoslavia in 1918. At the 1948 census, six 'nations' and eighteen 'nationalities' were recognised.

For centuries, the diversities as well as dynastic power struggles had created animosities that ultimately led to bloodshed and expulsions. These conflicts impeded the appearance of something like a commonly shared historical consciousness and a common system of values as prerequisites for a stable state. Only a part of contemporary Yugoslavia has been industrialised and modernised. The economic gap between north-west and south-east Yugoslavia even increased as the interwar governments totally failed to pursue a development policy.

Secondly, the partisan forces organised during the Second World War by the Tito-led Communist Party of Yugoslavia (CPY; in 1952 the CPY changed its name to the League of Yugoslav Communists — LCY) were based on a broad anti-fascist front, comprising all Yugoslav nations and nationalities. In spite of feelings of hatred, especially between Serbs and Croats, the 'Yugoslavism' of the partisans was welcomed by the population. Having striven before the war for a federal structure of Yugoslavia, the CPY created an image that it could successfully use for the legitimation of its leadership in the Liberation War. Yet it would be misleading to believe that the CPY would have restricted itself to the expulsion of the German and Italian invaders. It also had revolutionary purposes. As in China, the Yugoslav communists in the liberated areas created the institutional conditions for a take-over later on and initiated a series of social changes. After having seized power, the Yugoslav communists at first strictly followed the Soviet model of socialism. Yet the victory over the fascists, without any substantial support by the Soviet Union, and the independent take-over of power — both unique among East European countries that became communist after the war — created within the CPY a demand for equal relations with the Soviet Union and its Communist Party. The increasingly hostile attitude of the Soviet Union and other socialist countries — which culminated in the exclusion of Yugoslavia from the Cominform in June 1948 — gave the impetus for second thoughts resulting in the rejection of the Soviet model.

Thirdly, the new policy of the CPY leaders began by seeking an explanation of why the Soviet Union applied to a socialist country diplomatic and economic pressures that are characteristic of relations between capitalist countries. The leaders of the CPY came to the conclusion that a system not differing in this respect from a capitalist one would show similar political and socio-economic structural characteristics. The characteristic found common to both was the monopolisation of economic decision-making. Rejecting this, the Yugoslavs sought to rediscover for themselves the 'true' path to socialism, which they gradually came to believe must be based on the principles of community self-management.

The theoretical foundation of the system of workers' self-management, introduced on 26 June 1950, resulted from an independent exegesis of the Marxist classics, especially the early writings of Marx. Apart from Marx, Engels and Lenin's work *State and Revolution,* the Yugoslav communists could also draw upon the thinking of the so-called utopian socialists such as Robert Owen, Charles Fourier and Louis Blanc and likewise upon some of Proudhon's views about the co-operative character of production and the decentralised structure of the state. They rejected, however, co-operative ownership of the means of production. Further, the conceptions of the German and Dutch theorists of direct democracy such as Karl Korsch, Herman Gorter and Anton Pannekoek, as well as some ideas of Antonio Gramsci, paved the way for the new political design.

The founders of the Yugoslav system of self-management could, however, also rely on traditional institutions and ideas of their compatriots. The opposition to foreign rule had been organised for centuries in a decentralised form. In nineteenth-century Serbia the commune was administered autonomously by the citizens. Influenced by Western socialist concepts and the Paris Commune, the Serbs Svetozar Marković (1846-1875) and Dimitrije Cenić (1851-1888) had already considered the participation of workers in the administration of factories and social self-government in general. Marković thought the latter to be the best way to lead man to individual self-determination. His conception was not that of a dualistic relationship of local self-government and state, but that of a comprehensive system in which all territorial administrative organs, communities and organisations should be organised according to the same principles.

The Yugoslav communists had, when exercising the 'dictatorship of the proletariat', essentially eliminated private property of the means of production (temporarily also in agriculture), but they had not converted power 'on behalf of the workers' into a 'power of the workers'. The consequence was the formation of a layer of professional administrators of the means of production, formally in the hands of the working class, who decided on the use of surplus value, thus obtaining a privileged social position independent of the workers.

Although the Yugoslavs did not employ a complete Marxist model of a classless, self-managing industrial society, they could find an essential criterion for their conceptions in the *Communist Manifesto* of 1848, in which Marx and Engels defined the concentration of production in the hands of associated individuals as a precondition for the free development of man. Although they envisaged a transfer of all means of production to the state, this was only for a transitional phase, when the state was the instrument of the proletariat's power.[1] But at the same time, in common with other socialist regimes, the Yugoslav leaders took the view that it would be ideologically inappropriate at any time to transfer ownership of the means of production to associations of producers, i.e. to create group property. This is why they insist that the worker collectives are only given the administration of a common social ownership of the means of production.[2]

Self-management contains, however, a source of conflict, owing to the strained relations between the interest of the workers' collectives aimed at a particular advantage and the necessity of satisfying social needs. Marx found the synthesis between self-management and centralised planning in a central authority, which should be legitimised by delegated power. Therefore this central power should derive from the basic units of society; the deputies, judges and the holders of central posts should be bound by the instructions of their constituents, be held responsible to them and subject to recall at any time.[3]

However, while the introduction of democratic checks at various decision-making levels may help prevent the growth of excessive power within the central organs, this will not necessarily ensure an identity of interest between the individual and the group, or between either and society as a whole. This the Yugoslavs clearly recognise, and instead of trying to hide conflicts that arise behind a fiction of social harmony, they institutionalise them in the form of self-management and self-government.

THE SYSTEM OF SELF-MANAGEMENT AND SELF-GOVERNMENT[4]

The Yugoslav people have the right to associate for the purpose of engaging in work, to utilise the means of production belonging to society, to share the income from associated work among themselves and to settle their affairs at their workplace and at their place of residence, as well as to regulate them in so-called self-managing interest communities.

Workers' self-management is achieved through the *Organisation of Associated Work* (OAW) and the work community. They are founded by people working in industrial, handicraft, commercial, service and agricultural enterprises as far as they use means of production regarded as social property; by people working in schools, clinics, research institutes, publishing houses; in the field of banking and insurance; by persons belonging to the administrative staff of state and socio-political organisations; artists, journalists, lawyers, etc. The forms of organisation of territorial self-management are the local communities and the socio-political communities: communes, republics (in Serbia also provinces) and finally the federation.

The rights of self-management of the workers are determined by the combination of the three structural elements of the Yugoslav socio-economic order: the mainly social property of the means of production, the market mechanism and indicative economic planning. They include among others: the administration of the OAW; the utilisation of social means on behalf of the organisation and the whole society; the regulation of the kind and scope of production, the distribution of income, fixing working conditions, the arrangement of vacations, advanced training and safety provisions; decisions on the possible exclusion of parts of an OAW or their fusion with others and the guarantee of the rights of self-management by control over their observation. Details are regulated autonomously in accordance with the constitutions, laws (in particular the Law on Associated Work, promulgated on 25 November 1976), self-managing arrangements and social agreements. The association of work principally takes place by the organisation of a Basic OAW, where the working process and its implications can be observed by the worker, so that he does not only have to execute orders but is supposed to be in a position to participate in the decision-making. The criterion for setting up such a basic organisation is the capacity to measure the economic result of its work.

The workers' collective makes use of its rights either directly at meetings or by referendum or indirectly by elected or appointed executive and administrative organs. Meetings may consider reports of the administrative organs, the distribution of income, the economic plan, working conditions or the foundation of Basic OAWs. The worker collective decides by referendum matters such as the separation from or fusion with other organisations into trusts.

The OAWs generally have two organs of self-management: one administrative — the workers' council; one executive. The numerical composition of a workers' council, the procedure for the election and the recall of its members, the detailed determination of its functions, are the concern of the organisation. The Constitution fixes the term of office. At present, it is limited to two years. Further, by the principle of rotation, nobody can be elected more than twice successively to the same workers' council. Implementation of the resolutions passed by the worker collective or by the workers' council generally is the duty of the director appointed by the workers' council after public competition and on the recommendation of a committee of the OAW, the trade unions and a socio-political community. The term of office lasts four years, but it can be renewed as often as convenient.

Another form of self-management, the *interest communities,* are based on the conception of a comprehensive self-managing satisfaction of social needs. They are established where social services cannot be evaluated by the market mechanism alone. This is the case in education, research, health, construction, transport, power and water supply. The interest communities are established by arrangement between working people who offer material and cultural goods and their beneficiaries: citizens, OAWs, local communities, communes, provinces and republics. They are financed by income obtained for their services, by contributions made from the personal income of the citizens, as well as from funds and budgets of the local and socio-political communities.

Then there are the *local communities,* which are the basic territorial units of self-management. When the broader interest is not concerned, citizens can regulate their affairs within them autonomously and directly at their place of residence. The local communities work out programmes that —

taking into account the requirements of the citizens, households and communities — stipulate instructions concerning the housing sector, education, health service, sports, social welfare services and defence. The local communities are in charge of the administration and the maintenance of the tenement houses, roads, public lighting and other services of local concern.

The direct participation of the citizens in local decision-making is achieved by the electors' meeting. It elects the Council of the local community, which carries out the citizens' resolutions. The administrative staff is not professionalised. Via their delegations in the Communal Assemblies, the citizens living in the local communities are able to ensure consideration of their interests in the communal process of decision-making.

On a somewhat higher plane is the *commune,* defined in the Constitution as a self-managing and basic socio-political community, which is mainly responsible for the regulation of social matters. Within the system of self-management the commune is the framework integrating the OAWs, the local communities and the interest communities within their territories. It is an institution comprising numerous OAWs and work communities for the satisfaction of the population's requirements. It is also an institution exercising state power.[5]

The communes are charged with the task of creating the conditions for the satisfaction of the material, cultural and social needs of the citizens. They co-ordinate the activities of the self-managing organisations and local communities in the economic, educational, cultural, sporting, health, social welfare, construction and public utilities fields. They protect the human rights of the citizens and regulate their social and legal affairs. They look after public order and security, guarantee the cultural development of minorities, regulate the utilisation of land and protect the environment. The communes also set up units for territorial defence and raise funds for their equipment, training and maintenance, because 'general people's defence' is an integral part of the right of the citizens to self-management. Commune expenditures are financed by the OAWs, from the personal income of the citizens working in the social and private sector, by taxes (especially purchase tax) and by fees.

Local policy is decided by the Commune Assembly. It is carried out by the Executive Council, whose members are elected or appointed by the Commune Assembly and are responsible to it, as well as by administrative organs, concerned with the detailed implementation of laws and decrees.

Federalism and self-management are interrelated; both render possible the preservation of ethnic and cultural specificities. The system of self-management also shapes the Yugoslav conception of state, sovereignty and the relationship between republics and the federation. According to this conception sovereignty is self-determination by self-management at the workplace and at the place of residence. The nations and nationalities are supposed to exercise their sovereign rights according to the principles of equality, solidarity, reciprocity and responsibility for the maintenance and the development of the republics and provinces as well as the federation in its entirety. The republics are the main repositories of sovereignty, recourse to the federation only being made when common interests make it necessary.

The six republics (Bosnia—Herzegovina, Croatia, Macedonia, Montenegro, Serbia, Slovenia) have an ambivalent place in the political structure of Yugoslavia. According to Yugoslav constitutional law they are called states and self-managing communities of the nations and nationalities living on their territories. They are exclusively responsible for education, research, health, social care, the means of mass-communication and sport. They are also responsible for the organisation of the judiciary and of the communes. Furthermore, they are responsible for planning the socio-economic development on their territory, for aid to economically backward regions and for the determination of the allocation of the national product. In the field of social and economic policy they are autonomous except when the need for uniform regulations justifies the intervention of the federation. Special stress has to be laid upon the rights of the republics within the system of national defence, which derive less from their statehood as from the fact that they are also conceived as self-managing communities and national defence is a matter of self-management.

The federation, likewise defined as a state and self-managing community, is an instrument for the pursuit of joint interest. It should guarantee the equal rights of the nations and nationalities, the further development of self-management, the maintenance of a homogeneous market as well as the independence and territorial integrity of Yugoslavia through a common foreign and defence policy. The key federal organ is the Assembly of the Socialist Federal Republic of Yugoslavia (SFRY) in whose chambers republics and provinces are represented in equal numbers.

As in other socialist countries, there are numerous *organisations and associations* in Yugoslavia. Three types can be distinguished. There are 'socio-political organisations' (besides the LCY) such as the Socialist Alliance of the Working People of Yugoslavia, the Trade Union Federation, the Socialist Youth Federation and the Federation of Participants in the People's Liberation War. There are also two kinds of promotional groups, the 'social organisations' and the 'citizens' associations'. Whereas the LCY and the Socialist Alliance are supposed to articulate and defend common interests, the remaining socio-political organisations also articulate special interests of particular segments of the population and exercise a protective function. The trade unions, moreover, exercise an arbitration function in the case of strikes, which in Yugoslavia are tolerated though not legally allowed. Although the social organisations and associations articulate special interests, they do not exert pressure on the decision-making process, so that it would not be correct to call them pressure groups. Nevertheless, they are in a position to introduce the interests of their members into this process through the Socialist Alliance, of which they together form a part. This kind of 'united front', which in 1975 numbered some 12.6 million members (roughly 90 per cent of the population aged 18 and above)[6] coordinates and aggregates the interests of these organisations, bearing in mind the 'objective interest of the working class',[7] whose leading organisation, the LCY, is also the dominant organisation within the Socialist Alliance.

The feature essentially distinguishing Yugoslavia from the other socialist societies is, however, that the real and to a high degree autonomous structures for the articulation of particular interests are the self-managing organisations and communities and their delegations, this arrangement being described as a 'pluralism of self-managed interests'.[8] By the system of self-management, as well as by the decentralisation of decision-making through federalism, the pursuit of particular socio-economic and national group interests has been openly institutionalised. This, however, facilitates their integration and harmonisation, and also their control. Self-management promotes the pursuit of personal material interests, which is considered a rational means for the further development of the whole society. As the LCY Programme of 1958 puts it 'the highest goal of socialism is the personal happiness of man'. However, the workers' right to decide the distribution of the enterprise's income encourages the tendency to strive for a maximum personal income. Workers' self-management in the context of a market economy makes for competition, producing different incomes for equal work and generating privileges. Furthermore, federalism acknowledges rivalries between the nations and the nationalities and widens the gap between the more and the less developed territories.

The amount of personal income depends, on the one hand, on the quantity, quality and price of the products and services sold by the OAWs. These are influenced by several internal and external conditions such as productivity, the qualifications of workers and management, capital, technological standards, the location of the enterprise in a greater or less developed region or by market opportunities. Thus the OAWs have unequal opportunities to earn income. Let us consider some examples of such disparities. In 1971 the average monthly income of a worker with high school education in Slovenia amounted to 3285 dinars, but in Macedonia it was only 2359 dinars; that of a skilled worker in Slovenia was 1735 dinars, yet in Macedonia it was only 1142 dinars. Unskilled workers earned an average of 1260 dinars in Slovenia but in Kosovo only 865 dinars.[9] In March 1976, under 1800 dinars were earned by 0.6 per cent of the employed in Slovenia, yet in Montenegro the percentage went up to 17.7. An income over 4500 dinars was earned by 23.5 per cent of the employed in Slovenia and by only 8.9 per cent in Montenegro.[10]

The amount of personal income depends on the allocation of remuneration between work and capital. The workers are free to choose between consumption and investments but favour the former and neglect the latter, though this is clearly a precondition of economic growth and the welfare of the whole society. The attitude of individualism and 'groupism', resulting in the absence of social responsibility, is the consequence of the individual worker's inclination to identify himself with the communities closest to him: the family, group or at most the nation or nationality to which he belongs. He has a stronger commitment to the republic or province he lives in than to the federation.

This especially applies to the wealthiest republics, Slovenia and Croatia, whose relatively high degree of industrialisation offers favourable conditions for high incomes. In 1974 the national income per capita amounted in Slovenia to 32,320 and in Croatia to 21,000 dinars, whereas in Bosnia–Herzegovina it was only 11,513 and in the province of Kosovo only 5719 dinars. (The Yugoslav average was 17,174 dinars.)[11] Workers' and national egoisms are supplementary factors. Each republic is inclined to preserve and even enlarge the conditions for high incomes by distributing capital for investment and foreign currency among the enterprises situated in its territory. Separate national interests promote co-operation between enterprises within each republic, rather than the conclusion of agreements between the republics in order to diminish disparities in their economic development. In 1974 investment in economic installations amounted in Slovenia to 7070 dinars but in Macedonia to only 2420 and in Kosovo to only 2112 dinars per capita.[12] However, the rich republics find themselves confronted with the demands of the less developed republics and provinces for subsidies from their budgets and for a greater share in the federation's development fund.

It is noteworthy that interest groups also try to achieve their particular goals with the assistance of the Leagues of Communists (LC) in the republics and provinces and national egoisms are sometimes sponsored by the latter. (This was particularly true of the leaders of the LC of Croatia in 1971.) It could be observed furthermore that within the LCY temporary interest coalitions were formed between the Leagues of the most developed and of the least developed republics. In their attitude towards the freedom of opinion republic Leagues reflected the political culture of the different nations and nationalities, based on a more 'western' or 'eastern' tradition. Thus the conduct of the LCs is rather similar to that of political parties in a multi-party system.

The concept of self-management provides for the citizens to settle their affairs principally themselves in their place of work, place of residence and socio-political organisation. However, the planning and control of social development requires the *co-ordination of particular interests* and the perception of general interests at the regional and central level. This is achieved more and more by the so-called self-managing arrangements and social agreements, as well as by what Easton called the authoritative allocation of goods and values in the form of laws and decrees. These legal acts should, however, be legitimated by the social base in a way that citizens can identify with, thereby avoiding political alienation. This is meant to be guaranteed by the delegation system introduced in 1974, which in itself is regarded as an institutional element of self-management and as the expression of the 'pluralism of self-managed interests'.[13]

In simplified form this complex system has the following constituent elements. Members of the organisations of workers' self-management, local communities and socio-political organisations elect delegations, which themselves elect delegates to the Council of Associated Work and the Council of the Local Communities of the Commune Assembly. The delegates of the Socio-Political Council of the Commune Assembly are elected by all citizens directly. The Councils of the Commune Assembly elect from among the delegations (not from their own members) delegates to the Council of Associated Work, the Council of the Communes and the Socio-Political Council of the Republic Assembly and the Province Assembly. The Commune Assemblies elect the Federal Council of the Assembly of the SFRY from among the members of the delegations, while the Council of the Republics and Provinces of the Assembly of the SFRY is formed by delegates of the assemblies of the republics and provinces (see Figure 8.1).
In all elections, more candidates can be nominated than the seats available, allowing contests.

The self-management character of the delegation system is meant to be preserved by the delegates acting as a link between the social base and the assemblies. The delegates should, on the one hand, express the particular interests of the members of the organisations and communities of self-management on the various territorial levels of organisation; on the other hand, they should co-ordinate these interests in the assemblies in such a way that a decision can be reached. With the right of the self-managing, local and socio-political organisations and their delegations to give directives, with the duty to provide information and assume responsibility of the delegates, the influence of the workers and citizens on the decision-making in the assemblies should be secured. Through the institutions of recall and rotation, a professionalisation of the elected and their separation from the electors should be prevented. The duration of elected office is four years, election to the same assembly being restricted to two successive periods. The delegate does not give up his job but is merely given time off for his work in the assembly.

If a delegate has an explicit instruction, he can bring forward in the assembly a motion for the adjournment of the debate in order to consult his organisation and/or the delegation. He is, however, not bound by an imperative mandate, and is free to vote as he pleases. (An exception exists,

FIGURE 8.1   *The Yugoslav delegation and assembly system*

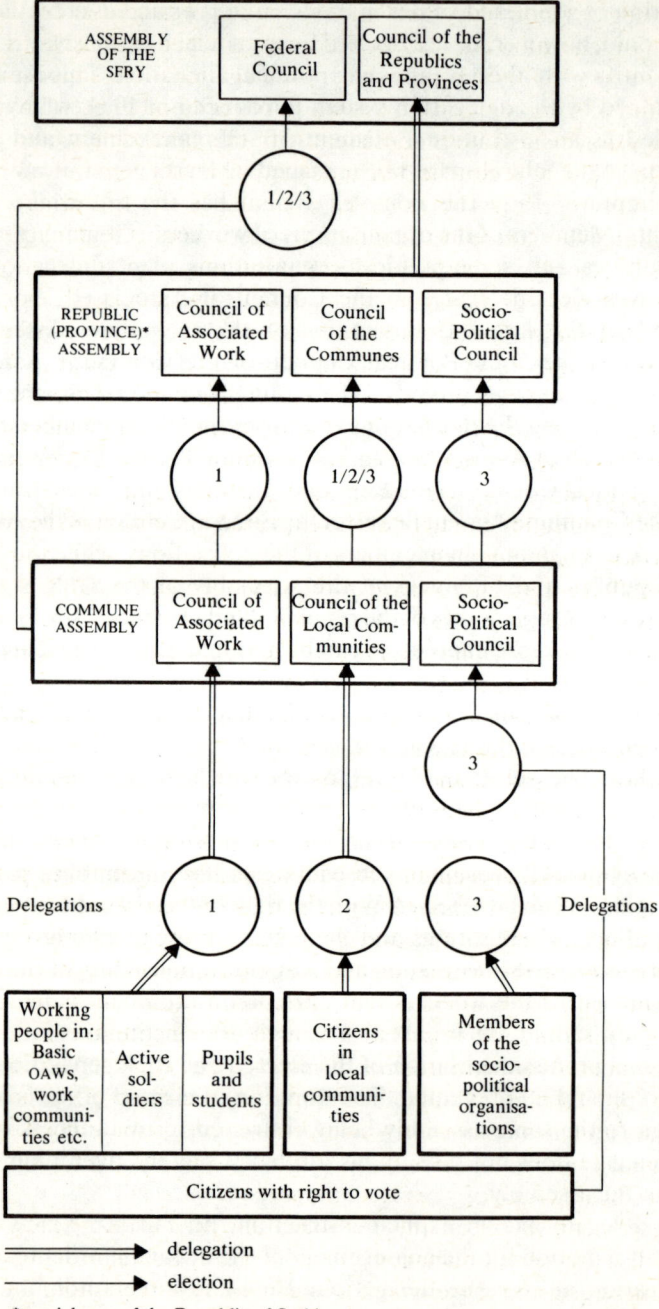

however, for the Council of the Republics and Provinces of the Assembly of the SFRY.) The Constitution in addition provides that the instructions given to the delegates not only take into account the interests of their self-managing organisation but also the interests of other organisations and the 'general interest'. For this purpose the delegations are supposed to co-operate and to seek solutions to questions of common interest. Avoidance of the imperative mandate is consistent with this because it would not give enough flexibility to reconcile demands and achieve a generally acceptable decision. Discrepancies between a particular interest and the general interest should be reduced to a minimum right from the beginning, to avoid delegates becoming victims of conflicts of interest.

By the so-called self-managing arrangements and social agreements, it is intended that the atomisation of decision-making in the economic field, which might arise from workers' self-management dominated by the narrow interests of the OAWs, would be counteracted without the organs of the socio-political communities having to intervene. These arrangements and agreements operate particularly in the planning of the middle- and long-term development of an economic branch and/or region. They provide the investment required in the light of the expected demands and the timing of socio-economic development.

Workers have the right to share in self-management, notably by entering into contracts with other self-managing bodies. Thus the fusion of Basic OAWs into a Work Organisation takes place on the basis of a self-managing arrangement as well as the fusion of enterprises into Combined OAWs. The OAWs of one branch come to an understanding by self-managing arrangements to ensure that the same remuneration is paid for the same work. It is furthermore guaranteed that Basic OAWs with a budget deficit are subsidised from the joint income of an OAW.

Besides the OAWs, corporations, institutions and organisations also participate in social agreements as well as bodies not forming part of the system of workers' self-management, such as the socio-political communities, economic chambers and trades unions. It is especially the duty of the latter to convince the worker collectives of the necessity of these social agreements and to guarantee that their realisation does not result in advantages for some with regard to income, working conditions and security of employment. By social agreements (instead of by control over incomes by the state) the distribution of income is agreed upon in an economic branch or several branches within one or several regions, stipulating a minimum income and a maximum income as a multiple of the average income in determined categories of workers and employees.

By agreements between the republics and provinces, which are also described as acts of self-management, a decrease should be achieved in the development gap and thereby also of the income gap between them. Such agreements, in which they commit themselves to take over special tasks with respect to the development of the whole federation, are a precondition for the realisation of the Federal Social Plan for 1976-1980.

By all these co-ordination procedures, essential rights of the OAWs are limited. However, as all participants are considered part of the system of self-management, the Yugoslavs believe they have found a way within the system to overcome or at least to diminish social inequality resulting from different incomes in spite of equal work and regional discrepancies resulting from different levels of socio-economic development.

LIMITS AND OBSTACLES TO SELF-MANAGEMENT

The Communist Party

It is obvious that self-management and the monopolistic position of the LCY, which is organised according to the principles of 'democratic centralism', are incompatible. The conviction that a political organisation advocating a particular socio-political system should itself act in conformity with this system, led the Yugoslav communists to redefine the party's functions at their Sixth Congress of 1952. Invoking the *Communist Manifesto,* according to which communists are theoretically superior to the proletarian masses but have no interests differing from those of the whole proletariat,[14] they argued that the party should not handle social affairs in the name of the working class but should only exert influence on it. The instrument of this influence would be the strength of ideas and arguments founded on high moral standards and on the consciousness of the direction in which a socialist society would evolve. After a phase in which the party had placed itself above society, it was supposed to be brought back into society. The organisational structure, the mode of working of their organs and the process of decision-making would be based upon the same principles as those used to establish the institutions of self-management. The party was supposed to continue 'leading' but no longer 'interfering'.[15] The renunciation of the 'leading role' of the party was linked in its Programme of 1958 to the 'withering away' of social antagonisms. Yet how the functions of the party can be adapted to the new system of socio-political relations, the question of the compatibility of a one-party system (and the existence of parties at all) with a society founded on the principles of self-management, are still a topic of inner-party discussions.

Particularly because of individual and group egoism, and social and regional inequality, the LCY believes it has to interfere in the political and economic decision-making in order to avoid even sharper disparities. Party directives not only bind the organs of state and self-management as well as those of the other socio-political organisations directly; it is further guaranteed that the ideas, conceptions and the will of the party are given due attention by the occupation of leading positions in all fields by reliable members of the LCY who are subject to party discipline.

At least three channels can be distinguished through which the party can exert influence upon the organs of self-management. First, directly, from within the organs by its members elected to the workers' councils and the Councils of the Assemblies of the socio-political communities, especially their Socio-Political Councils, whose task consists in safe-guarding the general interest. Second, by party members in the trade unions, which have their basic organisations in the OAWs and influence the composition of the workers' councils. The trade unions, though generally considering themselves as intermediaries between the workers and the management, according to their Statute of 1974 'are guided by the programme and the ideal-political orientation of the LCY'. The unions are thus bound to help enforce the party's (and the management's) interest, e.g. to increase investments instead of personal income. (It can also be observed, however, that they support the workers' desire for an increase in income.) Management provides the third channel of influence. Appointment as a director necessitates not only expert qualifications but also adhesion of the candidate to the party's principles and goals. In 1972, 70.5 per cent of the directors of enterprises with a workers' council were members of the LCY.[16] There is some evidence that directors conceive their role primarily in the light of professional criteria and let themselves be guided by group interests and the specific interests of the enterprise.[17] However, insofar as they show obedience to party discipline, their decisive part in the enterprises' decision-making may guarantee at least a certain influence of the party upon workers' self-management.

Although in the LCY Statute of 1969 the separation between party and state offices was strictly established, the party is far from having retreated from active political power. This is demonstrated especially by the fusion of top organs of party and state in one and the same person. The Chairmen of the Republics' and Provinces' LCs are officially members of the State Presidencies of the Republics and Provinces. The members of the Presidency of the LCY constitute the Presidency of the SFRY. Moreover, Tito united in his person the functions of the President of the Republic and that of President for life of the LCY.

The central organs consider themselves, although not rigidly dogmatic, as the sole binding interpreters of the tenets of Marxism-Leninism and as guardians of the specific Yugoslav socialist order. They sponsor the delegation of decision-making power, however, only to the extent that their control remains unimpaired. As against the Programme of 1958, where self-management was raised to a principle of organisation of any socialist society, the LCY in its 1974 Statute considers self-management not as an aim but merely as a form of the dictatorship of the proletariat 'in the present stage of development of Yugoslav society', by which the party again in fact claims to replace the proletariat. The LCY does not confine itself to educating the people in the way in which particular and common interests can be reconciled but becomes a superstructure over and above the system of self-management. The anti-hierarchical structure of the latter and the hierarchically structured party are in irreconcilable conflict.

The tendency towards centralised, authoritarian decision-making observable since 1974 has, however, been criticised by top party leaders because it would undermine self-management. The party should guarantee the achievement and functioning of self-management but the party should not be allowed to replace it. Being considered as an integral part of the socialist self-management system, the party should act only within its framework.[18] If the party is not supposed to be a foreign body within self-management, this implies inner-party decision-making from bottom to top, responsibility of the higher organs to the lower ones, rotation and recall of the office holders. The conception of the LCY as a 'specific form of an interest community of the working people'[19] would necessitate a redefinition of its claim to the leading role.

State intervention

Although self-management implies the regulation of social goals by basic organisational units of the citizens and thus fundamentally differs from a mere delegation of responsibility by administrative decentralisation, it is a fact that the right to self-management was transferred by the state. Workers' self-management was introduced by law at the instance of the Communist Party. The fusion of Basic OAWs or of Work Organisations into Combined OAWs is mainly voluntary and with the agreement of the workers. It can, however, be induced by the commune or the republic or even be decreed by federal law, if such a measure is considered to be in the interest of the whole country. Local communities are constituted by a corresponding resolution of the residents. They have the right to do this but also the duty. Along with the responsibility of the commune to regulate the procedure concerning the foundation of a local community and to ensure compliance with its statute, it is clear that local communities are not simply the result of the freedom of organisation presupposed by the conception of self-management. Furthermore the constitution, dissolution and fusion of communes, the separation of individual settlements and their incorporation into another commune, falls within the legal responsibility of the republics. The citizens and assemblies of the affected commune are only consulted on these matters.

Furthermore, state bodies have several rights of intervention in the affairs of the self-managing organisations and communities, rights that are stipulated particularly by the federal and the republics' constitutions and the Law on Associated Work. The socio-political communities, as well as the republics and communes, are entitled to intervene, e.g. when an OAW does not fulfil its legal obligations or harms interests described as general ones. The intervention may consist in the dissolution of the workers' council, in the recall of the director, as well as in the suspension of acts of self-management. It may involve the liquidation of an OAW, if its income is not sufficient to guarantee the material and social security of the workers. Interventions of state organs are particularly problematic when they try to impose on the organs of self-management a certain behaviour, as happened with respect to the modification of the Serbian law on high schools, in November 1974, to overcome resistance of the self-management organs to the dismissal of teachers who criticised 'bureaucratic' symptoms in party and state.

Finally, the scope of self-managing decision-making is subject to legal limitations. OAWs cannot freely dispose of their income. They are obliged by law or by contract to levy and pass on purchase tax on goods and services, which goes into the budgets of the socio-political communities. Further, they have to pay duties for the financing of social needs provided by the socio-political communities on administration, courts, social services, defence. It can be stipulated by law that incomes that result from particularly favourable natural or market conditions have to contribute towards financing economic projects in the communes, provinces and republics. The plans for the development of the federation are not obligatory. Nevertheless, they limit the right of the enterprises to distribute their income insofar as they require the transfer of a certain percentage of the social product to the Federal Development Fund (1.97 per cent in the 1976-1980 plan) to help the less developed republics and provinces. For defence and the elimination of market fluctuations, the republics are entitled to prescribe to the communes the amount they can draw upon the incomes of the OAWs and from the purchase tax, the formation of reserves, the temporary stoppage of expenditures and the way in which expenditures in excess of the budget should be treated.

The right of self-management is, however, also protected by the constitutions, laws and courts of the federation, the republics, the provinces and the communes, as well as by special organs of self-management and of the state. So-called workers' control watches over how the director respects the right to self-management; courts of associated work regulate controversies emanating from self-managing arrangements; attorneys for self-management affairs in communes, provinces, republics and at the federation level are supposed to supervise the strict observance of the rights deriving from self-management.

Lack of participation

The framework of self-management offers citizens vast possibilities for participation in decision-making. In 1972, 6130 workers' councils were in operation with 135,171 members.[20] In 1974 there were 72,521 delegations in existence (58,400 from workers' self-managing organisations and communities, 11,583 from local communities and 2538 from socio-political organisations), comprising about 840,000 members; 53,371 citizens were elected members to the 510 Communal Assemblies.[21] However, the real exercise of grassroots participation in the economic and socio-political decision-making proves to be rather weak. The referendum and the workers' meeting, forms of direct participation in OAWs and significant because their results are binding for the workers' council and the management, are very rarely used. In 1971 only in 7 per cent of the enterprises were referenda held; in nine out of ten enterprises there was only one referendum. In the same year, 16 per cent of the enterprises with a workers' council and 11 per cent of the enterprises without a workers' council did not have a single workers' meeting.[22]

According to the results of a participant observation survey of the sessions of workers' councils in twenty enterprises during the years 1966 to 1969, the members of the management clearly dominated the discussions and decisions. With respect to the market relations of enterprises, the frequency of the management's participation in the discussion amounted to 75 per cent and it occupied 85 per cent of the discussion time. About 75 per cent of the suggestions submitted to the workers' councils and the same percentage of the suggestions approved by the workers' councils came from within the management. These results may well be in accordance with expectations because of the highly technical character of the matter. However, it is surprising that similar results were obtained regarding questions connected with the enterprises' income distribution.[23] This attitude of the workers is obviously not just the consequence of an inability to understand and evaluate information due to their generally low educational standard. It is also a consequence of the absence of any motivation based on the conviction that they are able to exert effective influence in the decision-making process and of uncontrolled, secretive, oligarchic and technocratic tendencies within the enterprises. Similar observations regarding the influence structure have been made with respect to the decision-making process in the communes. The greatest influence is exerted by the president of the Commune Assembly and leading officials of the administrative apparatus.[24]

Widespread resignation and apathy are also characteristic of citizen participation in the voters' meetings in the local communities. Though local communities deal with problems that are very close to the citizens' interests, it has been observed that out of 4000 persons of voting age only about 40 — usually the same people — attended each meeting.[25] This was also due to a sense of impotence in influencing decision-making, the reasons for which cannot be examined here.

Yugoslav citizens also showed little interest in the approval of candidates for the assemblies' councils in the federation, republics and communes. In 1969, in the meetings for the confirmation of the candidates for the then existing Economic Council of the Federal Assembly, 30.6 per cent participated; 36.3 per cent for its Cultural Council; 36.1 per cent for its Social and Health Council; and only 12.1 per cent for the directly elected Socio-Political Council. Citizens had been even less interested in the candidates for the Republic councils. Participation oscillated between 6.5 per cent in Slovenia and 20.4 per cent in Montenegro. As far as the directly elected Commune councils were concerned, citizen turnout amounted only to 11.7 per cent.[26] These observations can be supported by numerous other findings. Obviously, structural and institutional modifications have not yet created a political culture corresponding to the formally vast possibilities of participation in decision-making offered by the institutional framework of self-management.

Conclusions

In the Yugoslav Constitution the federation and the republics are defined as states and as self-managing communities. The communes, the provinces, the republics and the federation exercise power as well as settle social matters according to self-management principles. Thus they are organs both of power and of self-management as well. It is therefore impossible to separate institutionally the state and self-management from each other.

From the standpoint of the Yugoslavs' conception of their political system, it would be inappropriate to separate state and self-management by the criterion of centralised and decentralised decision-making. The step-by-step replacement of the state by self-management should not imply either the renunciation of central decision-making or the elimination of generally binding decisions. Mere decentralisation would only accentuate the disintegration of an already extremely fragmented society. The conception of self-management should not only provide for the pursuit of particular group interests but include their co-ordination and the realisation of general social goals by means of a horizontal and vertical integration of the individual self-managing organisations and communities. Thus self-management is not supposed to be an alternative to the existence of central institutions as such but to the existence of a type of state that is superimposed upon society, is organised on bureaucratic lines, acts in an authoritarian way and is not responsible to the citizens.

The criteria that demarcate the state from self-management are rather structural and procedural. The participants in the self-managing process of decision-making should have equal rights and not dominate one over the other. They should arrive at decisions by conviction and compromises, by what Lindblom has called mutual adjustment. They should identify themselves with the decisions by determining them directly. It is a fact that in the course of decision-making majorities form themselves, but they are not organised and are subject to constant change, which should counteract the petrification of power. It is not a matter of eliminating all power but legitimating it by a new institutional and procedural network and limiting it.

The idea of self-management is to transfer the function of mediating and reconciling conflicting interests to society. Interests transcending the individual and group interests should be expressed by membership not of the state but of an organised self-managing community. Although the institutional and procedural prerequisites for attaining social goals by the organised society itself have been created, the state as an authority structure still retains not only residual functions, such as the safeguarding of the country's internal and external security; it also exercises power when the institutions of self-management are not able to settle their affairs and those common to the whole society. This may be either because they lack the will to do so or because of difficulties of an organisational and technical kind. Thus, for the time being, the state and the institutions of social self-management constitute a dual system of decision-making, a situation that is further complicated by the existence of a Marxist-Leninist party that claims a leading role in state and in society as well, though this is disputed.

The LCY considers that it unifies within its ranks the most conscious and progressive members of society, thus having legitimacy as the leading moral force and the most important socialising agency. In its hierarchical organisation and decision-making structure and bureaucratic behaviour it has much in common with the state, in whose institutions it occupies leading positions, the same also being true in the institutions of self-management. It is therefore a state within the state and within the system of self-management. Because the state functions are gradually diminishing but the producers and citizens are not yet fully able to co-ordinate their interests and to recognise and implement common goals, the party considers itself to be, and really is, an indispensable structure for aggregating the particular interests of the self-managing organisations and communities as well as of the nations and nationalities, thus safeguarding the unity of Yugoslav state and society.

Yugoslavia represents, despite its imperfections, a relationship between state and society that differs in a singular way from that prevailing in both Western European and Eastern European countries. It therefore deserves attention, not only as a deviant case among socialist countries, but also and above all because of its innovative design for an original type of political and social change in both socialist and capitalist industrialised societies and in developing societies as well.

NOTES AND REFERENCES
1. K. Marx and F. Engels, *Werke,* East Berlin, Dietz Verlag, 1956 ff; vol. 4, pp. 481 ff., and vol. 20, pp. 261 ff.
2. E. Pusić, *Samoupravljanje: Prilozi teoriji i praktični problemi,* Zagreb, Narodne Novine, 1968, pp. 52ff.
3. Marx and Engels, *op. cit,* vol. 17, pp. 339 ff.
4. The term self-management — according to the Serbo-Croat *samoupravljanje* — will cover both workers' self-management and territorial self-government.
5. E. Pusić, *op. cit.,* p. 242.
6. *Statistički kalendar Jugoslavije 1977* (German ed.), Belgrade, Savezni zavod za statistiku, 1977, p. 22.
7. M. Kešetović, *Gesellschaftspolitische Organisationen in Jugoslawien,* Belgrade, Mejdunarodna politika, 1968, p. 30.
8. E. Kardelj in *Politika,* 14 June 1977.
9. *Materijalni i društveni razvoj SFR Jugoslavije 1947-1972,* Belgrade, Savezni zavod za statistiku, 1973, p. 263.
10. *Statistički kalendar, op. cit.,* pp. 43 ff.
11. *ibid,* pp. 24 and 48, computed from national income figures and from population estimates for 1974.
12. *ibid,* pp. 24 and 49, computed from investment figures and from population estimates.
13. E. Kardelj, *op. cit.*
14. Marx and Engels, *op. cit.,* vol. 4, p. 474.
15. Resolution of the Sixth Congress of the CPY/LCY according to I. Perić, 'Teorija partije radničke klase i SKJ' in *Naše teme,* vol. 10, no. 12, 1966, p. 2047.
16. *Materijalni i društveni razvoj, op. cit.,* p. 29.
17. J. Županov, *Samoupravljanje i društvena moć: Prilozi za sociologiju samoupravne organizacije,* Zagreb, Naše Teme, 1969, pp. 242 ff. and p. 263; J. Obradović, 'Distribution of Participation in the Process of Decision Making on Problems Related to the Economic Activity of the Company' in *First International Conference on Participation and Self-Management* (Dubrovnik, 13-17 December 1972), vol. 2, Zagreb, 1972, pp. 159 and 161.
18. S. Dolnac in *Delo,* 30 December 1976.
19. E. Kardelj, *op. cit.*
20. *Statistički godišnjak Jugoslavije 1974,* Belgrade, Savezni zavod za statistiku, 1974, p. 70.
21. *Statistički kalendar, op. cit.,* pp. 14 and 16.
22. *Materijalni i društveni razvoj, op. cit.,* p. 30.
23. J. Obradović, *op. cit.,* pp. 145 ff. and 157 ff.
24. R. Marinković, *Ko odlučuje u komuni,* Belgrade, Institut društvenihnavka, 1971, pp. 250 ff; P. Jambrek, *Development and Social Change in Yugoslavia: Crises and Perspectives of Building a Nation,* Westmead, Saxon House, 1975, pp. 162 ff.
25. S. Zukin, *Beyond Marx and Tito: Theory and Practice in Yugoslav Socialism,* London, Cambridge University Press, 1975, p. 158.
26. M. Matić *et al., Skupštinski izbori 1969,* Belgrade, Centar za istraživanje jarnog mnenja, 1970, pp. 84 ff.

SELECT BIBLIOGRAPHY
Clissold, Stephen (ed), *A Short History of Yugoslavia from Early Times to 1966,* New York, Cambridge University Press, 1966.
Denitch, Bogdan D., *The Legitimation of a Revolution: The Yugoslav Case,* New Haven and London, Yale University Press, 1976.
Furtak, Robert K., *Jugoslawien: Politik. Gesellschaft. Wirtschaft* (Yugoslavia: Politics, Society, Economy), Hamburg, Hoffman und Campe, 1975.

Horvat, Branko, *An Essay on Yugoslav Society,* New York, International Arts and Sciences Press, 1970.
Jambrek, Peter, *Development and Social Change in Yugoslavia: Crises and Perspectives of Building a Nation,* Westmead, Saxon House, 1975.
Vucinich, Wayne S. (ed), *Contemporary Yugoslavia: Twenty Years of Socialist Experiment,* Berkeley, University of California Press, 1969.
Zaninovich, M. George, *The Development of Socialist Yugoslavia,* Baltimore, The Johns Hopkins Press, 1968.
Zukin, Sharon, *Beyond Marx and Tito: Theory and Practice in Yugoslav Socialism,* London, Cambridge University Press, 1975.

PART III

The International Context

CHAPTER 9

Great-Power Involvement in European Systems

Stephen Kirby

In 1914 a recently issued and widely used British school-textbook described Europe as 'the smallest of all the six continents except Australia, but it is the most populous of all except Asia. It is also the most civilised, the most wealthy, and the most powerful.'[1] In 1945 Europe remained small and populous, but the quality of its civilisation was debased, its wealth squandered, and its power overshadowed by two quasi-European powers; powers upon which the states of Europe were to become dependent for new standards of civilisation, for economic recovery and, most of all, for their security. Within a decade of the end of the Second World War, the United States of America helped revive liberal democracy in the West and the Soviet Union created or reinforced Marxist-Leninist socialism in the East; the United States helped rebuild the Western economies through the Marshall Aid programme and by the encouragement of European economic unity, and the Soviet Union transformed and tied the economies of Eastern Europe to her own through extensive bilateral links, which were later overlaid by the Council for Mutual Economic Assistance (CMEA or COMECON). Through the North Atlantic Treaty Organisation (NATO) and the Warsaw Pact (WTO) the security and inviolability of the two halves of Europe were guaranteed.

The process by which the two great powers became involved in the European system is complex but rests essentially upon the new configuration of power in the twentieth century, in which the pre-1939 multi-polar world was transformed into the essentially bi-polar world of 1945. As great powers, America and the Soviet Union quite naturally and inevitably developed interests in Europe, and the Second World War did no more than accelerate that development. What was crucial about the outcome of the war was that European states emerged from the conflict defeated or exhausted, but America and Russia emerged stronger than before. Although their military capabilities were asymmetrical, only they were capable after 1945 of making a military effort that could decisively affect the European or global order. The war confirmed rather than caused the change of power.

It is true that Great Britain and France retained the title and some of the substance of great powers in the immediate postwar period, indeed Britain was even once called a 'superpower',[2] but the abortive Four Power Summit meeting at Paris in 1960 was the last time that the United States and the Soviet Union were prepared to involve the United Kingdom and France as equals in issues that were global in their importance. Even before this, it had become clear that the United Kingdom and France were unable to fulfil the roles and meet the requirements traditionally expected of great powers within the international system. Great powers are states that can authoritatively resolve the great international political issues of the day.[3] Their authority stems from a mutual recognition of their dominance in, and responsibility for, the international order, from their position in the front rank of military power, and most of all from the recognition of other states that they have certain rights and duties in the international system. Among the most important rights is that to be consulted, and the Munich Agreement of 1938 remains the last occasion on which European states changed the European order, and the Suez operation of 1956 the last *attempt* to change the extra-European order without involving or consulting America or Russia. Hedley Bull notes that after 1945 there was 'the appearance of a new class of power, superior to the traditional European great powers, and alone capable of undertaking the central managerial role in international politics they had played in the past'.[4] In General de Gaulle's contemporary and more forthright view, Europe had fallen 'under the two hegemonies'.

The way in which each of the great powers has exercised its managerial role is very different but the difference in reality is not nearly so marked as that in rhetoric. The United States has projected an image of an international system of sovereign states in which common goals and a recognition of moral and legal rules provide the ordering element in world affairs. Leadership over allies is explained as a consequence of their own requests for American protection, so that leadership in Europe has been described as 'situational not deliberate'. Great-power management of inter-bloc relations has been described most often as America successfully countering Soviet challenges. On the other hand the Soviet Union projects an image of itself as the vanguard in an international revolutionary movement that will transform the international system, in time, into a global Soviet order. The managerial role when applied to allies is explained as the purging of revisionism, as in the Brezhnev Doctrine, and when carried out in conjunction with the United States as no more than tactical co-operation that leaves the fundamental ideological conflict undiminished, as in the doctrine of peaceful coexistence. Yet, throughout the postwar period, unbroken diplomatic contact between the great powers has been maintained, spheres of influence have been recognised and rarely breached, direct confrontation has been avoided, and great-power deliberations have produced a regular series of agreements and treaties that have reinforced and maintained an ordered international system. The differences expressed in the rhetoric serve, however, to highlight the fact that for most of the postwar period the central managerial role of the United States and the Soviet Union has been an essentially competitive rather than a cooperative one. The stability of the postwar international system arose not from great-power condominium but was achieved by the organisation of regional balances, the most pronounced and the most important of which was in Europe.

THE WEST

The links that bind the Western European nations to the United States, and that provide the foundation of her leadership are multi-faceted and have changed constantly during the postwar period, as has the unity and the solidarity that these links produce. Hoffmann has described Atlantic relations as 'a mass of ambiguities in motion',[5] and in April 1973 Henry Kissinger explained that problems '. . . have arisen in part because during the fifties and sixties the Atlantic community organised itself in many different ways in the many different dimensions of its common enterprise'.[6] The constantly changing pattern of transatlantic ties and the waxing and waning of Western solidarity have made a precise definition of 'the West' impossible, but the concept of the 'Atlantic Community' was and is intended, by America at least, to express those fundamental values that serve to identify a state's attachment to the West. The concept was developed from the Truman Doctrine and the Marshall Plan, and these two speeches made explicit the notion of an American-West European partnership in world affairs, and looked towards an eventually United States of Europe, acting together with the United States of America to carry out a world role in the economic, security and diplomatic spheres. The assumption of partnership was reformulated in John Kennedy's 'Grand Design' and was expressed more recently and more powerfully in Henry Kissinger's 'Year of Europe' policy, which he hoped would produce a new Atlantic Charter. In April 1973, Kissinger noted America's support for European unity and that

> . . . we assumed, perhaps too uncritically, that our common interests would be assured by our long history of cooperation. We expected that political unity would follow economic integration; and that a unified Europe working cooperatively with us in an Atlantic partnership would ease many of our international burdens.[7]

The significance of the concept of partnership within the Atlantic Community has been that many of the core institutions of 'the West' have a purely European membership. The United States strongly encouraged and supported the creation of Western Union in Brussels in March 1948, the Council of Europe in Strasbourg in August 1949 and the European Economic Community in Rome in March 1957, all of which were regarded as building blocks of Western unity. NATO on the other hand was first devised as a short-term solution to the defence of Western Europe, and when the North Atlantic Treaty was signed in April 1949 no permanent political or military institutions were established; the treaty was essentially a guarantee of United States' assistance to the Western European states, should their security be threatened. Even in the aftermath of the Korean War, when permanent political and military institutions were set up, the acceptance of the principle of national sovereignty, the creation of an international secretariat restricted to administrative functions and the acceptance of national responsibility for the equipping and training of forces, ensured that NATO could not assist the process of European unification. America had supported French proposals in 1950 for the creation of a European Defence Community (EDC), and this would have complemented the idea of an Atlantic partnership in defence, but this aim was undermined by European resistance to military integration and by America's desire to find some quick relief from carrying the main burden of defending Europe. That relief was provided by the creation in 1954 of Western European Union (WEU), which had the virtue of making West German manpower available to NATO but the vice of creating yet more purely national armed forces. From the mid-1950s the dominance of the United States in the affairs of the NATO Council, and the reliance of Europe on America for a nuclear guarantee and a substantial proportion of allied ground troops and arms supplies, have all inhibited rather than enhanced European independence within the allied framework. The inclusion in the alliance of the small states of Europe like Iceland, Portugal, Greece and Turkey made, and still makes, the European grouping in NATO too diverse in economic, political, and military terms to create a viable European world-partner for the United States.

American hopes for an Atlantic partnership have therefore been invested in the products of the process of European integration. The achievements and the failures of that process are well known, but what is noteworthy is that the European Communities, even after enlargement in 1972, show no signs of creating a supranational Europe that is able to co-operate with America in a world role. The ability to articulate a European foreign policy remains a fundamental requirement of either a joint world role with America or an independent world role for Europe, but the European Communities have been reluctant to deal effectively with 'high politics' and this is reflected by the limitation of the Davignon Committee and its successors to a purely co-ordinating role in the external policies of the Nine. The best achievement so far has been the engineering of joint foreign policy positions on single issues, like the decision to have a single representative at the Helsinki Conference on Security and Cooperation in Europe in early 1972 and the initial reaction to the 1973 oil crisis. Even these co-ordinated foreign policy positions have proved fragile and have been directed most often against the United States. The failure to devise a *European* foreign policy leaves the United States without a viable partner, and taken in conjunction with Europe's acknowledged dependence on United States' arms means that there is little alternative to American protection when the interests of Western Europe are seriously threatened from outside.

Membership of institutions, both transatlantic and exclusively European, has served to identify states with the West, but for many states the strength of their bilateral links with America has been an equally important indication of their 'Western-ness'. This was certainly true of Britain's 'special relationship' with America before she committed herself fully to European defence after January 1968, and to the European Communities after January 1972. Even when asserting an independent world role, the 'special relationship' made Britain one of the pillars of the West. The particular vulnerability of the Federal Republic of Germany (FRG) to Soviet power and America's involvement in the constitutional development of Germany, has made the bilateral link with the United States fundamental to German foreign policy and central to the unity of the West. Indeed, the strength of the American-German link facilitates American leadership in the alliance and Germany's powerful military position and her influence in the ranks of the European allies is much valued by America. This was clearly implied in a statement made by the American Secretary of Defense James Schlesinger at a time when American-European relations had been shaken by the consequences of the 1973 oil crisis: 'Germany . . . plays a critical role in the Alliance at the present time. Its role is critical, partly because it is a forward defense area, but for a variety of reasons, *given the overall state of European politics,* Germany turns out to be the bastion of NATO.'[8] For smaller European states like Spain, the bilateral link with the United States has served to identify her unambiguously with the West, even though the other European states have so far successfully kept Spain out of the European Communities and out of NATO.

From this complex of relationships it is possible to identify a hierarchy below the leading role of the United States. Britain, France and Federal Germany are the leading states of Europe and their combined resources are of superpower proportions. Their position is demonstrated by a preferential status in the institutions of the European Communities and also by the fact that the United States devolves some of its responsibility for the management of the European system upon them. These states are also important for their trade and security links with the Soviet Union. Russia has looked to them in particular, to satisfy some of its needs for modern technology and for expanded international trade and credits. Also, until the successes of *Ostpolitik,* Russia looked to France and Britain to place a restraining hand upon a militarily powerful FRG.

Beyond this, the European Communities collectively are regarded as the next most significant core group of the West, even though Ireland is not a member of NATO and several members of NATO do not participate in the European Communities. The significance attached to these states stems in part from the American assessment that with them lies, or lay, the best hope for an independent world-partner, but also from the massive and growing economic importance of the Communities, which some Europeans hope will lay the foundation for the creation of a European superstate in its own right.[9] The European Communities have sometimes acted as an alternative centre of loyalty and interest for the European members of the West and this has often weakened the bonds of the Atlantic Community, but the Communities are an expression of Western vitality that America can neither disregard nor afford to undermine. In some ways the United States is an ideological hostage to the success and independence of the European Communities, since their dynamism vindicates and expresses many of the West's core values. NATO, despite the institutional limitations outlined above, is an important link with the West for some of the smaller European states. This was particularly true for Portugal and Iceland when membership of the alliance became the focus of conflicts between communist and pro-Western ministers of their coalition governments. At the very fringes of the Western system in Europe lie states like Switzerland, Sweden, Austria and Spain. Their commitment to non-communist governments and capitalist economies identifies them with the values of the Atlantic Community, but they lack sufficient institutional links to place them near the centre of the Western system.

The complex nature of the web that enmeshes the members of the West, especially the concept of partnership, produces both strength and weakness. One of the strengths is that states may vary the emphasis they place upon the different strands of Western unity and may thereby achieve a degree of foreign policy flexibility without necessarily detaching themselves from the bloc. Many states have relaxed or even severed the institutional and bilateral links with America without questioning their commitment to the Western camp that America leads.

The France of General de Gaulle is the best example of this phenomenon. One of the most celebrated challenges to American leadership was de Gaulle's decision to withdraw from the integrated military structure of NATO in March 1966. This decision reflected his belief that national autonomy rested upon an independent foreign policy, which in turn required a credible independent nuclear deterrent. De Gaulle's decision was also based upon his assessments that alliances were redundant in the nuclear age and that it was unrealistic to expect allies to come to one's defence when the cost might be their own nuclear destruction. The direction of French defence policy under the three *loi-programmes* from 1960 to 1975 certainly ran counter to both NATO strategy and American plans for allied military co-operation, neither of which had a place for the independent strategic nuclear force (SNF), which became the core of France's military posture. Furthermore, de Gaulle's policy of all-round defence, which characterised France as a citadel that would deter an attack from anywhere in the world, appeared to leave little scope for allied participation in the defence of France.

Yet even when de Gaulle asserted French independence most vociferously and condemned American domination and alliance 'integration' most thoroughly, he never lost sight of the necessity of co-operation between the states of the West. In 1966, soon after France's withdrawal from the NATO military structure, he charged General Ailleret with negotiating agreements for the continued stationing of French troops in Germany and for ties of practical military co-operation with the other allies, and these produced the Lemnitzer-Ailleret agreements, which came into force in 1967. These negotiations so bewildered one journalist that he remarked 'La France se retire de l'OTAN, mais reste dans le NATO'.[10]

After May 1968, pressure to increase spending on domestic programmes whilst holding down taxation, added to the unanticipated inflation in the cost of developing the SNF, began to cut the ground from beneath the independent foreign and defence policies of France. These pressures were reinforced by the political and strategic repercussions of the opening of the great-power dominated 'era of negotiations' in the 1970s. In these circumstances one has seen the theme of pragmatic and selective co-operation with allies, which formed the undercurrent of de Gaulle's policies, gradually emerge as the predominant feature of the defence and foreign policies of Pompidou and Giscard d'Estaing. It is true that Giscard has said that there 'can be no question' of France rejoining NATO, but his Chief of Staff has said that it is 'difficult to conceive of a European defence completely independent of an American alliance'.[11]

One must add too that France recognised that many important issues vital to France and to Europe were being discussed by the superpowers. One of the avenues for exerting influence on these détente discussions was the NATO Council, especially after 1968 when the Eurogroup began to present America with a united front and an agreed programme of demands. America's willingness to hear and act upon the special interests of the Europeans has been made conditional upon their being more co-operative in NATO, especially on the questions of accepting a greater part of the allied conventional defence burden and of rationalising, standardising and perhaps ultimately specialising the allied supply of weapons. France has refused to join the Eurogroup, which has discussed and made some progress on these problems within NATO, and in 1972 she flirted with the idea of revamping the WEU as an independent European defence forum. However, since 1976 France has been a member of the Independent European Programme Group (IEPG), which, despite the name, is the Eurogroup plus France. France's primary interest in IEPG is the possibility of involvement in European collaborative arms projects, but she recognises that her participation also increases the chance of resolving some of the issues that have strained Atlantic relations in recent years.

France's resistance to the leadership of the United States and to the concept of an Atlantic Community that includes France, has for political reasons been muted, but there have always been apparently independent French interests that are also the interests of America and that have served to unify the Western system. The deep, if troubled, commitment of France to the European Communities clearly entrenches her in the Western camp. The same may be said of the Franco-German bilateral link regularised in 1963. It reflects de Gaulle's awareness that the interests of France include the ability to restrain and counter the power of Germany, and when the bilateral relationship was not sufficient he was prepared to call upon the help of major allies, as in the monetary crisis of November 1968, when he enlisted the aid of America and the United Kingdom against pressure from Germany.[12] But, at the same time, machinery for the containment of Franco-German relations is vital for Western unity, and the 1963 treaty has been strongly supported and valued by America.

France has been the most important but not the only state to exploit the flexibility of the Atlantic ties to achieve independent foreign policy positions within the Western camp. Turkey and Greece temporarily broke off bilateral ties of military co-operation with America, and left the integrated military structure of NATO after the Cyprus war of 1975; but at the same time they were able to confirm their links with the West by retaining their seats on the NATO Council and by giving even more weight to their attempts to join the European Communities. This flexibility allows rifts within the alliance to be absorbed more easily and has prevented any Western European state making a complete break with, or being disowned by, the West; but the resilience of the Atlantic Community in its broadest sense has been bought at the price of making American leadership uncertain and Western solidarity variable.

American leadership in security affairs is least subject to challenge because of the obvious dependence of Europe on American protection. The position is reinforced by America's membership of NATO and by the fact that all the major NATO commands are in the hands of American generals and admirals. Even though NATO has been the scene of acrimonious debates about allied security policy, American proposals usually win out, and given the importance of the American nuclear guarantee allied defence policy must, in any event, adapt itself to the changes in strategic doctrine wrought in Washington and to changes in the strategic relationship negotiated by the great powers. NATO has been variously the 'trip-wire' for Dulles's massive retaliation; the shield for Norstad's nuclear sword; and is now part of the flexible response strategy originally devised by Robert McNamara. Added to this, NATO has, since the publication of the Harmel Report in 1967, the twin objectives of defence and détente. This development has allowed America to manifest its leadership less by the manipulation of the needs of security and more by the manipulation of the requirements of negotiating détente successfully. It seems clear that American leadership in security affairs can be effectively exercised through the institutional links of NATO.

For economic and diplomatic affairs, however, transatlantic links of the same kind do not exist. At times, the European Communities group of states have followed policies fundamentally at odds with America. This was particularly the case during the oil crisis that followed the October 1973 Middle East war. America sought to engineer a 'Western' response at the Washington Conference of oil consumers in February 1974, but met a direct challenge from France and the United Kingdom, which sought to organise an exclusively European Arab Conference designed to detach the Nine from the pro-Israel policies of America and ensure an uninterrupted supply of oil for Europe. But there have been many other issues that have caused a rift in Atlantic relations, and détente — which has extended the scope of possible inter-bloc agreement and settlement — has in turn widened the scope of intra-Western-bloc discord about how these settlements should be made and what they should contain.

In circumstances such as these, the United States seeks to win converts to its position through the usual channels of diplomacy and by exercising its considerable economic influence. But the 'management of interdependence' in the West, now the central concern of the United States, requires new diplomatic skills and techniques. The preferred method — especially in Kissinger's foreign policy — has been to link the major issue areas in allied diplomacy in an unusually explicit way,[13] in an attempt to hammer out a comprehensive Western global strategy, and the preferred device has been the major foreign policy speech or proclamation. Kissinger's Year of Europe speech set out an 'Agenda for the Future' based upon the premise that 'political, military and economic issues in Atlantic relations are linked in reality, not by our choice nor for the tactical purpose of trading one off against the other'. This initiative was described as 'not an American prescription but an appeal for a joint effort of creativity'.[14] However, it was a prescription and the United States not only attempted to trade off Europe's independence in political and economic affairs against its dependence in military matters, it also exercised all the levers of influence to ensure that the trade-off would succeed.

American statesmen have continued to set out the agenda of problems that face the West, and it is notable that the man upon whom Kissinger's mantle fell — Brzezinski — was himself a prominent member of the North American-Japanese-Western European Trilateral Commission set up in 1972 to identify areas of common interest and select issues that might be susceptible to great-power management. America has found no easy solution to the management of interdependence, but explicit issue-linkage and bargaining with allies has enabled her to add an additional commitment to her policy positions and to ensure that the West talks about the same things at the same time.

THE EAST

The links that bind the Eastern European states to the Soviet Union and that express and ensure Russian leadership within the bloc are less flexible and less diffuse than those in the West. Even so, 'the East' is no easier to define than its Western counterpart. When the Cominform was set up in September 1947 as a reply to the Marshall Plan, it contained the leaders of the Communist parties of the Soviet Union, Poland, Bulgaria, Czechoslovakia, Romania, Hungary and Yugoslavia, but also the Communist Party leaders of France, Italy and, later, The Netherlands. At the height of the Cold War, China and Albania were regarded as bloc members, but by 1960 they, along with Yugoslavia, had broken away and the German Democratic Republic (GDR) had become a prominent member. Unlike the United States, which developed the concept of the Atlantic Community early in its relationship with the Western European states, the Soviet Union was slow to develop a concept to express the corporate identity of the Eastern bloc. The idea of a 'Socialist Camp' fully developed only after Khrushchev's liberalisation started following the Hungarian Revolt in 1956, and was intended to set limits to the new independence allowed to the East European states by requiring allied solidarity on foreign policy issues and the non-export of national-roads-to-communism experiments to other bloc members. It remained, however, a poorly defined concept until Khrushchev's removal from power in 1964 and it lost all coherence in the period of rapid change that followed, which culminated in the Prague Spring of 1968. The 'Socialist Camp' underwent a substantial revision after the invasion of Czechoslovakia and re-emerged as the 'Socialist Commonwealth' which included the idea of 'limited sovereignty'.

The central feature of this policy was that Communist parties had a responsibility, not only to their own people, but to all other socialist countries and to the entire communist movement. It also carried the implication that the Soviet Union would both define the obligations that each party owed to the movement and ensure that the wider interest would prevail. The concept bears one similarity to the Atlantic Community idea in that it is intended to embrace not only those states that are core members of the bloc, but those that have enjoyed a degree of independence from great-power control. Here the similarity ends, because implicit in the idea of an Atlantic Community are the views that bloc solidarity will be the product of values spontaneously shared, and the achievement of bloc goals the product of joint but independent action by the states of the West. The 'Socialist Commonwealth', on the other hand, carries with it the notion of the ideological primacy of the CPSU and Russian responsibility for organising and directing concerted action against revisionism. Bloc goals are achieved by allied support of Soviet initiatives, with support resulting more from Soviet mobilisation than from East European participation.

The failure to develop a corporate identity for the Soviet bloc until after 1956 reflects the fact that, until the relaxation of the ties built up by Stalin, such a concept was both meaningless and superfluous. The unity of the Eastern bloc was established in the years up to 1956 through an elaborate web of bilateral state treaties focused upon the USSR, which covered most aspects of security, economic and political affairs. The use of Soviet 'experts' and 'advisers' throughout Eastern Europe was extensive, but the two most important instruments of control were provided by the contact between Communist parties, both within the Cominform and outside it, and through the agency of the Red Army units stationed in European states. The leisurely creation of CMEA in 1949 and of the Warsaw Pact (WTO) in May 1955 attests the fact that the Soviet Union had ample alternative channels through which it could exercise control.

Russia's development of Eastern Europe bloc institutions was as much a propaganda exercise within the Cold War as it was an attempt to enforce Soviet rule. This is especially the case with the WTO, which was established as a direct reply to the re-arming of West Germany and its membership of NATO. Military links in East Europe were nevertheless already well established before the creation of the Warsaw Pact. From 1948 onwards, each East European state entered into a mutual defence treaty with the Soviet Union, and, at the same time, the process of Stalinisation of East European political regimes was extended to national armed forces. Command structures, military doctrines and even uniforms were standardised on the Soviet model, and Communist Party members filled the most senior command positions. Indeed, in many cases ex-Red Army commanders formally resumed or took up East European citizenship and filled senior command positions in East European armies. Thus it was that Soviet Marshal

Konstantin Rokossovsky became Minister of Defence and Commander-in-Chief in Poland in 1949. The use of Soviet military advisers was also extensive at this time, and the rates of conscription, introduced into all East European states in 1949, with the exception of the GDR, and the defence budgets of each bloc member, were set by the Soviet Union.[15]

The Treaty of Friendship and Mutual Assistance and Co-operation signed at Warsaw by Russia, Albania, Bulgaria, Czechoslovakia, the GDR, Hungary, Poland, and Romania left the foundation of the Eastern European security system little altered. The Treaty provides for the establishment of a Political Consultative Committee, supported by a Joint Secretariat that is headed by a Soviet official, but the Committee was not intended to meet, nor has it met, on a regular basis. The Treaty further provides for a Joint High Command with a Soviet Commander-in-Chief, and this was set up in Moscow in early 1956 and has remained closely linked with the Soviet Ministry of Defence. Before the post-Czechoslovakia reorganisation of the Pact in 1969, the non-Soviet Ministers of Defence were directly subordinated to the Soviet Commander-in-Chief. Pact members were able to act collectively only when the Soviet Union called upon the bilateral obligations that each member owed her. Even if the non-Soviet Pact members had decided upon joint action, it would have been difficult, if not impossible, because the entire Pact communications system and most of its command system are the preserve of the Red Army.

The experience of CMEA is dealt with in chapter 11, but there are some notable parallels with the WTO in this period. The CMEA structure overlaid the fundamentally bilateral economic system of the Soviet bloc. Until 1955, resources flowed primarily from Eastern Europe to the Soviet Union. It is also notable that of the twenty-three Permanent Commissions of CMEA created by July 1963 none predates May 1956. Neither CMEA nor WTO did anything to disguise the strict regimentation of European economic and security forces by the Soviet Union and neither of them were of any help in syphoning off or containing the growing resentment that was felt in Eastern Europe and that was most vividly expressed by the Hungarian Uprising in 1956. After that date, Khrushchev sought to develop the institutions of both organisations in an attempt to find a method of consolidating Soviet rule while allowing a gradual process of de-Stalinisation to develop.

In the military sphere this attempt was to meet with little success, and the accomplishments of East European de-Stalinisation far outstripped the development of multilateral military institutions in the Warsaw Pact. The Soviet Union first signed status-of-forces agreements with Poland, the GDR, Romania and Hungary between December 1956 and May 1957, but was unable to negotiate a similar agreement with Czechoslovakia until October 1968. The agreement with Romania lapsed in June 1958 when Soviet troops withdrew. This, combined with the break of relations with Tirana in 1961 and the decision not to station Soviet troops in Bulgaria, meant that, by the early 1960s, the Pact had not united but had developed a two-tier structure. A Soviet presence and control remained in evidence in the North but was much reduced in the South. This was not simply the product of southern intransigence or strength, but reflected rather Russia's particular concern with the military readiness and dependability of those states in the North that are close to the central front in Europe. This helps explain Russia's greater concern about the demonstration of Czechoslovakian independence than about that of Romania, whose assertion of national autonomy persisted after Brezhnev came to power.

In November 1964 Romania reduced its term of military conscription from twenty-four to sixteen months in line with its policy demanding that the burden of Pact defence on East European states should be cut. By 1966 Ceausescu was calling for the withdrawal of Soviet troops from Eastern Europe and refused to have Warsaw Pact manoeuvres on Romanian soil. Romania was to show a remarkable independence in foreign and economic affairs too. In the early 1960s, Romania refused to accept economic direction from CMEA and successfully opposed a Soviet-sponsored CMEA plan that would have limited Romania's economic role to that of supplying raw materials to the Soviet Union. After this, Romania sought a more balanced trade with the West and took an important step in that direction when a West German trade mission was established in Bucharest in October 1963. Along with Czechoslovakia, Romania also introduced internal reforms, based not upon the Soviet but upon the Yugoslav model, which involved the introduction of the market mechanism, indicative planning and membership of, or co-operation with, the General Agreement on Tariffs and Trade, the World Bank and the International Monetary Fund. These were accompanied by the less spectacular but nevertheless important changes in Hungary, where the New Economic Mechanism was introduced, and in the GDR, which experimented with the New Economic System.

In political affairs, too, Romania led the way to greater East European independence. In 1963 support was publically announced for the principle of non-interference in the affairs of other states, and in 1964 it was declared that all Communist parties were equal. Differences with the Soviet Union in foreign policy emerged in 1964 with a dispute over China, and Ceausescu underlined his independent stand in June 1966 when he received the Chinese Prime Minister. One of the most important foreign policy 'deviations' occurred when Romania established diplomatic relations with West Germany in January 1967. A similar independence was not shown by Czechoslovakia until after January 1968, when Novotny was forced to resign as First Secretary of the Czechoslovak Communist Party and was replaced by Alexander Dubcek.

In the face of all this, Khrushchev and for some time Brezhnev made only desultory attempts to exert Soviet leadership. Indeed, Soviet reticence about resorting to Stalinist techniques before August 1968 are confirmed by reports that Brezhnev overruled Novotny's plan to purge the liberals in Czechoslovakia during 1967.[16] Some purely preventative measures were taken in the military sphere when the GDR agreed to abandon its tiny military aircraft industry, and Brezhnev was also able to persuade Poland to discontinue development of advanced combat aircraft in 1967. Brezhnev's attempt 'to set up within the framework of the Treaty [WTO] a permanent and prompt mechanism for considering pressing problems', which he announced in September 1965, came to nothing.[17] The major attempt to preserve what was left of Pact unity took the form of a return to the device of building bilateral links, and a series of twenty-year defence treaties were signed beginning with the Soviet Union-GDR Treaty in 1964. By October 1975 no less than twenty-two such defence treaties had been signed by the members of the Warsaw Pact, thirteen of them before the invasion of Czechoslovakia. The Soviet treaties with Romania and Czechoslovakia came after the invasion, as did all the treaties between Romania and non-Soviet Pact members.

Once the invasion of Czechoslovakia was over, the Soviet Union had two major tasks. The first was to reorganise the affairs of its Eastern bloc, which had begun to disintegrate under the impact of de-Stalinisation, but even more under the impact of the largely European-led détente of the 1960s. The second was to put the détente process itself on a new great-power-management basis. This was intended to resolve the great and outstanding issues of European politics — largely ignored in the détente of the 1960s — which could lead to inter-bloc crisis and which could be resolved only by the great powers. In short, Russia wanted great-power-imposed discipline at home and great-power-conducted dialogue abroad, and assumed that the success of the latter was dependent upon the effectiveness of the former.

In the attempt to restore order to the defence and foreign policy affairs of the whole of the Pact, the invasion of Czechoslovakia had an immediate and obvious effect. This was the transfer of some five Soviet divisions from Russia's Western military region into the European Pact area and the reinforcement and reinvigoration of the twenty-six Soviet divisions already there. The commitment of this quantity of manpower at a time when Soviet forces were building up on the Chinese border and the retention of the five additional divisions in Europe during their violent dispute on the Ussuri River in March 1969, were powerful indications of Russia's intention to regain a dominant position in the affairs of communist states. But, as in Khrushchev's day, the attempt was also made to use the Warsaw Pact as an additional and more legitimate instrument of bloc solidarity. In 1969 a Council of Defence Ministers was established, which is the supreme military body of the Pact and its task, it seems, is to advise the Political Consultative

Committee. In full session this Committee is made up of the First Secretaries of the Communist Party, heads of government and the foreign and defence ministers of the member countries. Its task is to consider general questions of defence and foreign policy but full sessions of the Committee meet very rarely. A second and more practical change is that a military council has been attached to the Joint High Command, and meets regularly under the chairmanship of the Soviet Commander-in-Chief. The Committee is composed of the Chiefs-of-Staff and a permanent military representative from each of the allied armed forces, and 'seems to be the channel through which the Pact's orders are transmitted to its forces in peacetime and through which the East European forces are able to put their view to the Commander-in-Chief'.[18] Whether these modifications were the culmination of the 1960s East European pressure for a greater voice in Pact affairs or an exclusively Soviet response to the post-Czechoslovakian situation remains unclear. What is certain is that the new institutions have allowed the Soviet leadership to engineer a 'directed consensus' on many major foreign and defence policy issues.[19]

Romania is still the country least in harmony with the Soviet Union's defence and foreign policy goals, and the visits of President Nixon to Bucharest in August 1969 and of Ceausescu to the United States in October 1970 were intended to underline Romania's continued independence. The Soviet response to this situation has been to use its improving relationship with the United States to isolate Romania and loosen its ties with the West, and, at the same time, to undermine Ceausescu's close links with the non-aligned movement. Even so, as late as the April 1974 WTO summit meeting, Romania was still asserting its independence. However, the Soviet Union supplies nearly 60 per cent of the Pact's combat and direct support troops,[20] its logistic and communications infrastructure, the majority of its conventional arms and its nuclear weapons, and Soviet domination of the Pact remains unquestioned.

In economic affairs, too, the Soviet Union has been quite successful in reducing the deviations that exist within East Europe, and once again a combination of bilateral and institutional links has been used. At the bilateral level, the Soviet Union has encouraged and sometimes assisted the reversal of economic techniques and policies that deviate from the Soviet model. Hungary's New Economic Mechanism (NEM) came under Soviet scrutiny from 1968, and Moscow's concern was made known from early 1972 onwards. Russia's tactic was simply to encourage the domestic criticism of NEM that already existed, and to set what limits it could put to the NEM's success by the manipulation of bilateral economic ties. This policy had some effect when, between March 1974 and May 1975, Rezsö Nyers — one of the architects of the NEM — and other reform leaders went out of public life. Success was also achieved in the GDR where the New Economic

System was wound up in 1971, and in Poland and Czechoslovakia where Gierek's reforms (partly a response to the December 1970 Riots) and Husak's normalisation policies reduced the difference between the economic policies of Russia and her allies.

The beginning of the Soviet attempt to revitalise CMEA as a device of bloc control was signalled by the decision of April 1969 to draw up an economic integration programme. It is interesting to note that it was to be an integration 'built upon coordination of [national] plans, not commonality of the market as found in the west'.[21] The programme of integration made little headway at first, but at the twenty-fifth meeting of the CMEA Council in July 1971 a document on integration was approved and published as the Comprehensive Programme, but it did not provide for a systematic reform of Pact economic relations. Such a reform has still not been achieved, but evidence that the Soviet notion of 'integration' is having some effect can be found in a CMEA decision of June 1975, which was supported by Romania and approved by a joint co-ordinated plan as well as the now routine harmonisation of national economic plans. The joint plan has a limited scope, but its major provision is for the construction or expansion of joint enterprises, mainly in the extractive industries and all involving the Soviet Union. The CMEA organisation is not simply a device for Soviet economic domination. Like the WTO, it provides a mechanism through which the East Europeans can express their views, but in the post-Czechoslovakian situation, in which Russia has reasserted its control, CMEA is another agency through which the Soviet Union can engineer a bloc consensus, in economic affairs. With economic relations playing a significant role in the modern détente, CMEA may well prove to be an extremely useful agency to prevent East-West trade getting out of hand. Russia's suggestion that East and West Europe should negotiate their growing trade relation on a CMEA/EEC basis demonstrates this.

One can detect, therefore, three quite clearly defined periods in the Soviet relationship with, and leadership of, Eastern Europe: the period under Stalin, in which the firmest Soviet control was exercised through bilateral links; the period under Khrushchev, in which the idea of the 'Socialist Camp' was developed to mark out the boundaries within which de-Stalinisation could be exercised in the bloc; and the period under Brezhnev in which the 'Socialist Commonwealth' linked to the concept of limited sovereignty, re-emphasised Russia's leadership role, this time employing multilateral and bilateral controls. The changes reflected in good measure the different personalities and the political visions of the three leaders, but in each case the decisive change in relations between Russia and East Europe followed major Soviet policing operations in the Pact. Khrushchev's de-Stalinisation gathered momentum some time after the Hungarian Uprising of November 1956, and Brezhnev's re-assertion of Russian leadership was signalled by the invasion of Czechoslovakia in August 1968; both crises coming some three to four years after a change of leader in the Soviet Union.

These periods also overlap and in part reflect significant changes in the relationship between the two superpowers. The relaxation of Soviet leadership in Khruschev's period caused less alarm in the Eastern bloc after 1962, when the introduction of the new technology of second-strike nuclear delivery systems made the strategic relationship between the great powers very stable and when the resolution of the Cuban missile crisis opened the first period of East-West détente. Brezhnev's resumption of control in Pact affairs was not only to prevent the virus of revisionism spreading within the Pact, but also to restrain further political changes in Europe. Such changes might have provoked a great-power crisis in a strategic environment that by 1968 had become very much less stable with the introduction of defensive missiles and MIRVs — the generation of strategic weapons that the SALT negotiations seek to control. The shared interest of the great powers in avoiding nuclear war became a central theme of the second, great-power-managed détente that emerged in the 1970s.

The joint Nixon-Brezhnev announcement in 1973 declared that America and the Soviet Union would 'act in such a manner as to prevent the development of situations capable of causing a dangerous exacerbation of relations, as to avoid military confrontation, and as to exclude the outbreak of nuclear war between them and between either of the parties and other countries'.[22] This was widely interpreted as a great-power agreement to restrain the activities and diplomatic initiatives of their allies, and to encourage support for foreign policy goals laid out by America and Russia. In order to settle the outstanding problems in Europe that could cause a crisis—Berlin, a divided Germany, and other border issues—both America and Russia has already acted to control their client states. One telling example of the different problems faced by each great power in resolving these problems is that America had to check and control the pace of Brandt's *Ostpolitik* by making the ratification of the Bonn—Moscow and Bonn—Warsaw treaties negotiated in 1970 conditional upon the outcome of the essentially great-power-dominated talks on the future status of Berlin. Russia, on the other hand, had to remove a reluctant Walter Ulbricht from the GDR to ensure that Brandt's *Ostpolitik* would be met by an equally positive *Westpolitik*. Both the United States and Russia exerted leadership quite successfully in the early 1970s, but problems have arisen for both great powers as the process and successes of détente itself begin to dissolve the framework of the postwar order in Europe.

Prospects

For nearly three decades American and Russian involvement in contemporary Europe has taken the form of leadership of rival blocs and their leadership has been most evident when relations between the camps have been most hostile. The effect of crisis between East and West has invariably been to produce solidarity in the two European blocs. The events of August 1968 confirmed this. However, in retrospect, the invasion of Czechoslovakia did not bring a return to a Stalinist form of leadership in the East, nor was it intended as a threat to the military security of NATO. What rapidly emerged after the invasion was a Soviet attempt to stimulate a managed détente, and the milestones of the great-power rapprochement are now a matter of record. But as détente progresses, so it changes the framework within which great-power leadership has been traditionally exercised. It is still unclear whether or not that leadership can survive these changes intact.

President Nixon spoke of a penta-polar world in the early 1970s at a time when superpower diplomacy was at its height, but it is now clear that we have witnessed the end of the postwar era, in the West at least. The economic strength of the Nine, now so powerful that they rather than America can determine the success or failure of attempts to control or liberalise trade, and their halting attempt to develop joint foreign positions, are revolutionary new developments, but in a world where Europe still lacks the military capacity needed to counterbalance the might of the Soviet Union. The West may still exist in the sense of a group of economically developed, free-enterprise, liberal-democratic states, but relations between them reflect the shifting coalition between North America, Western Europe and Japan. The West, as a unified bloc under American leadership, is increasingly difficult to discern.

Both Russia and America have expressed the view that the problems of the contemporary international system cannot be satisfactorily handled within the context of blocs. In a major speech in 1974, Kissinger said

> bloc diplomacy of any kind is anachronistic and self-defeating. We see a danger of new patterns of alignment that are as artificial, rigid and ritualistic as the old ones. The issues the world faces are so urgent that they must be considered on their merits, on the basis of their implications for Humanity and for world peace ... rather than on some abstract notion of ideological or bloc advantage. In a real sense the world is no longer divided between East and West, North and South ... We will solve our problems together or we will not solve them at all.[23]

The commitment to end the bloc structure in the Soviet Union is not nearly so pronounced, but comes through nevertheless in the WTO Prague Declaration on European Security made in October 1969, and in various statements made during the Conference on Security and Cooperation in Europe (CSCE) from 1973 to 1975. In both cases the Soviet Union hinted at its willingness to see pan-European solutions for security and an end to discriminatory economic relations between the blocs. But both great powers find themselves in the dilemma of transition from one type of international system to another. To negotiate the change effectively both great powers have to assert leadership, but just at the time when the centrifugal forces of the old system are collapsing and the centripetal forces of the new increasing.

In the West the threat of bloc conflict, for long the most effective producer of Western unity, is receding, and with it recedes the solidarity of the West. In difficult economic circumstances and with defence spending not substantially increasing the Europeans' security or their participation in the central decision-making process of détente, European defence budgets have continued to shrink in the 1970s. This has thrown up many problems. The declining military capabilities of NATO compared with the WTO undermined the West's capacity successfully to negotiate Mutual and Balanced Force Reductions (MBFR) in Europe. This not only increased American pressure on her European allies to take up more of NATO's burden; it threatened to revive the Congressional drive unilaterally to withdraw American troops from Europe. It also, ironically in the present circumstances, delays the departure of America's power from Europe and emphasises her leadership role.

This American-European discord on the security issues of détente also contains dangers for a Europe that is unable to organise its own defence or articulate a common foreign policy. The British government's *Statement on the Defence Estimates* for 1976 noted that

> The Russians may . . . be tempted to apply other forms of pressure designed, in particular, to influence the political and economic policies of Western European nations to wean them away from their alliance with the United States and to make them more susceptible to Soviet influence . . . It must be recognised therefore that the social and economic problems now facing the West could, if not satisfactorily resolved, have consequences for the external security of Western countries.[24]

Here the British government points to the potential 'Finlandisation' of Western Europe if the Western allies do not find a new *modus vivendi* for American leadership and protection or make preparations to define and to defend European interests themselves.

This problem was graphically illustrated in a discussion between members of Congress and members of the European Parliament concerning an Atlantic Convention on the establishment of institutionalised political links between the United States and Europe. A British Member of Parliament said: 'it is neither desirable nor feasible for the Nine to enter such a relationship until they are able to speak with one voice on terms of equality with the United States.'[25] Here the dilemmas of transition are clearly expressed.

In the East, problems have also arisen, and there the recession of the threat of bloc conflict has had important repercussions, but détente has had a rather different effect. The Helsinki Agreement of 1975 contains provisions dealing with the free exchange of ideas, freedom of movement of people and greater economic contact between East and West. The Soviet Union has been relatively successful in controlling the exchange of ideas and the movement of peoples, but even so the Helsinki Agreement revives echoes of the more liberal regime of the 1960s. President Carter's decision to make human rights central to his foreign policy and, further, to 'aggressively peacefully challenge the Russians in their own spheres' and to 'treat the countries of Eastern Europe as independent and sovereign entities',[26] entrenches this problem for the Soviet Union.

In its détente economic relations with the West, however, the Soviet Union has met with even more substantial problems. A Presidential report to the US Congress noted that 'during 1973-76, the USSR and Eastern Europe have run fairly consistent and relatively large trade deficits with the West. These countries which face fundamental problems in developing export supplies and in entering Western markets, have simply not been able to increase their exports as rapidly as they have increased their imports.' It went on to note that the great bulk of trade deficits have been made up by borrowing in the West to the sum of about 39 billion dollars at the end of 1976.

> West Germany and to a lesser extent the United Kingdom, France, Italy and Japan, are the largest creditor nations [and] it is evident that the continuing expansion of debt cannot indefinitely finance a continuing increase in Communist country imports from the West. At some point, Communist country exports to the West must increase so significantly as to achieve greater balance in East-West trade and restrain the growth in debt.[27]

This East-West economic relationship further compounds the problems of leadership for the great powers. For Russia, the growing debt of all the Soviet bloc nations to the West and her own reliance on American grain supplies compromises her freedom of action when dealing with the core Western European states and with America. Perhaps of more importance for the future is the fact that the new economic relationship with the West, including the prospect of wide-scale direct investment in the Soviet bloc, exposes East European states not only to temptation but also to economically sound reasons to deviate from the prescribed Soviet economic model. In the West, the new economic opportunities have tended to make America, the Europeans and Japan competitors rather than collaborators, thereby compounding their apparent inability to solve economic problems within the West and with the third world. For the forseeable future the leadership of America and the Soviet Union in Europe will remain, even though it is challenged and resented, but if détente progresses and the traditional style of 'adversary politics' between East and West diminishes, then the logic of a competitive bloc system for the management of the international system by the great powers will diminish too. It is too soon to say if détente will succeed, but if it does no one has yet offered a viable model of an international system that could accommodate it.

NOTES AND REFERENCES
1. Lionel W. Llyle, *A Geography of Europe*, London, Adam and Charles Black, 1914, p. 1.
2. The term was applied to Britain by W.T.R. Fox in 1944. See Hedley Bull, *The Anarchical Society: A Study of Order in World Politics*, London, Macmillan, 1977, p. 203.
3. See George Modelski, *Principles of World Politics*, New York, The Free Press, 1972, Chapter 8.
4. Bull, *op. cit.*, p. 203
5. Stanley Hoffmann, *Gulliver's Troubles, Or the Setting of American Foreign Policy*, New York, McGraw-Hill, 1968, p. 388.
6. Henry Kissinger, 'Address to the Associated Press annual luncheon in New York on April 23rd, 1973', *United States Information Service Official Text*, 24 April 1973, p. 2.
7. *ibid*, p. 3.
8. James R. Schlesinger, 'Press Conference in Munster November 5th, 1974', *United States Information Service Official Text*, 6 November 1974, p. 1.
9. See Johan Galtung, *The European Community: A Superpower in the Making*, London, Allen and Unwin, 1973.
10. Quoted in Jean Houssay (rapporteur), *La participation de la France à la défense de l'Europe dans le cadre de l'Alliance Atlantique*, Paris, Association Française pour la Communauté Atlantique, 1975, p. 7.
11. Quoted in John Baylis, 'French Defence Policy: Continuity or Change?', *Journal of the Royal United Services Institute for Defence Studies*, vol. 122, no. 1, 1977, p. 42.
12. See Edward L. Morse, *Foreign Policy and Interdependence in Gaullist France*, Princeton, N.J., Princeton University Press, 1973, Chapter 4.
13. See William Wallace, 'Issue Linkage among Atlantic Governments', *International Affairs*, vol. 52, no. 2, 1976, pp. 163-79.
14. Kissinger, *op. cit.*, p. 4.
15. See A. Ross Johnson, 'Has Eastern Europe become a liability to the Soviet Union?' in Charles Gati (ed.) *The International Politics of Eastern Europe*, New York, Praeger, 1976.
16. *The Sunday Times*, 19 June 1977.
17. Johnson, *op. cit.*, p. 43.
18. *The Military Balance, 1976-77*, London, The International Institute for Strategic Studies, p. 11.
19. See particularly J.F. Brown, *Relations Between the Soviet Union and its Eastern European Allies: A Survey*, Santa Monica, The Rand Corporation, 1975, R-1742-PR.
20. *The Military Balance, op. cit.*, p. 99.
21. James A. Kuhlman, 'Eastern Europe' in James N. Rosenau, *et al.* (eds), *World Politics: An Introduction*, London, Collier-Macmillan, p. 459.
22. 'Joint US-Soviet Declarations on the Avoidance of Nuclear War', *United States Information Service Official Text*, 23 June 1973.
23. Henry Kissinger, 'Speech to the Indian Council of World Affairs on October 28th, 1974', *United States Information Service Official Text*, 29 October 1974.

24. *Statement on the Defence Estimates, 1976,* Cmnd. 6432, London, HMSO, p. 9.
25. Committee on International Relations, House of Representatives, *The Ascendancy of Economic Goals in the World Order,* Washington, US Government Printing Office, 1975, p. 7.
26. See, 'Excerpts from President Carter's Conference, Washington, June 13th, 1977', *United States Information Service Official Text,* 14 June 1977, p. 5.
27. 'President Ford's International Economic Report transmitted to Congress on January 18th 1977', *United States Information Service Official Text,* 19 January 1977, p. 11.

SELECT BIBLIOGRAPHY

Buchan, Alastair, *The End of the Post War Era,* London, Weidenfeld and Nicolson, 1974.
Camps, Miriam, *The Management of Interdependence: A Preliminary View,* New York, Council on Foreign Relations, 1974.
Galtung, Johan, *The European Community: A Superpower in the Making,* London, Allen and Unwin, 1973.
Kohl, Wilfrid L., (ed), *Economic Foreign Policies of Industrial States,* Lexington, Mass., Lexington Books, 1977.
Kuhlman, James A. and Mensonides, Louis J., (eds), *Changes in European Relations,* Leyden, A.W. Sijthoff, 1976.

CHAPTER 10

The European Economic Community: Expectations and Realities of Integration

Jürgen Wohlfahrt

Every state, being an autonomous decision-making centre endowed with authority, has the task of seeking a compromise between the conflicting needs of various interest and pressure groups within its society. As the state and its society are inseparable from each other the term 'society' can thus refer only to the society that falls within the boundaries of a single state. Three provisions, however, must be fulfilled before the term 'state' can be applied: there must be a sovereign territory, a people and a public authority.

It is clear that the European Economic Community (EEC) does not fulfil these minimum requirements as a state, with the result that the terms 'state' and 'society' cannot strictly be applied to it. It is nevertheless rather interesting to examine this association of states to see if it is capable, in fact and in the legal sense, of confronting the centrifugal powers of both the member states and the national societies with stronger centripetal powers, and in the long term of integrating them. Only when it is possible to achieve a just compromise between the member states and to merge the societies of these states into a European Society will the classic source of integration, national consciousness, be augmented by the consciousness of common tasks and achievements. Whether, unlike traditional international organisations, the union of the members into a Community means more than merely the sum of the individual parts can be seen particularly clearly from the conception of the institutions and the structures of the Community.

The establishment of the three European Communities, the European Coal and Steel Community (ECSC), the European Economic Community (EEC) and the European Atomic Community (EAC) must be seen in the light of the institutional and military collapse of the European states after the Second World War, the subsequent world dominance of the continental superpowers, as well as Soviet claims to hegemony in Europe. The Western European Union (WEU) and the North Atlantic Treaty Organisation (NATO) were established for defence purposes, the Organisation for Economic Cooperation (OEEC) for economic purposes. The Council of Europe was to be the real political centre of a European union. As a result of deep-rooted differences of opinion about the aims, functions and methods of European integration as well as the role of the national states and as a result of differing political and economic interests, the original plan for a comprehensive European union was dropped in favour of a functional approach. Thus, the attempt was made to prepare for European federation by means of closer integration in selected economic fields.

With the treaty establishing the European Coal and Steel Community, which came into force in 1952, the six founding members relinquished their sovereignty over their coal and steel industries. These were then put under the administration of Community institutions, which were provided with sovereign powers. The supranational nature of this sectoral common market was particularly clear in the position of the High Authority, which was composed of independent members who were empowered to make general regulations equivalent to state norms. The interests of the member states were guaranteed only by the approval of the Council, which was usually required.

The Coal and Steel Treaty was supplemented by the signing of a treaty establishing the European Defence Community (EDC), which also provided for common institutions. Even before the treaty was adopted by the member states, the assembly of the ECSC set itself up as an ad hoc assembly and worked out a draft statute for the establishment of a European Political Community (EPC). The fate of this political community was sealed, however, when the French National Assembly failed to ratify the EDC Treaty.

After the realisation that even the Coal and Steel Treaty was not functioning properly, particularly that the High Authority could not assert itself against the national governments to the required degree and frequently had to seek the backing of the Council of Ministers, a new way forward had to be found. The interest in further progress towards economic co-operation finally led to the signing of the treaties establishing a European Economic Community and a European Atomic Community, which came into force in 1958. The most important treaty, establishing a European Economic Community, contains very precise economic and social aims and at the same time provides for the necessary institutions and procedures for putting them into practice.

It is the task of the Community to promote a harmonious development of economic activities, a continuous and balanced economic expansion, an increase in stability, an accelerated raising of the standard of living, as well as closer relations between the member states. These objectives are to be achieved by the establishment of a common market and the co-ordination of economic policies. The Common Market is based on the principle of liberalisation, that is to say the removal of barriers between the member nations for goods, persons, services and capital. The basis of free movement of goods is a customs union involving the abolition of customs duties and quantitative restrictions and measures having equivalent effect, and in addition establishes common customs tariffs for third countries. In order to provide for the abolition of customs duties and quantitative restrictions for agricultural products, a special arrangement was required in view of the fact that this branch of the economy was subject to state intervention in every member country. A European market organisation was established to replace the national laws, and consequently the intervention of the individual states was brought into line by a common policy with a complex price mechanism.

The free movement of persons entails a general freedom from discrimination based on nationality and is augmented by special elements such as equal treatment of workers from member states in employment, remuneration and other conditions of employment and work. Equally, nationals of other member countries who establish themselves as self-employed persons must not be subject to different conditions from nationals. Thus the regulations and qualifications for the self-employed were to be co-ordinated. The commitment to liberalisation, however, has not been fulfilled to the same extent in this field, as the movement of capital is only to be liberalised as far as possible and necessary. Apart from the basic principle of liberalisation, a further element, the harmonisation of laws, plays an important part in creating as similar conditions as possible for competition in the economic field.

Although the Economic Community was established by a multilateral international treaty like all international organisations of a conventional nature, internally the Community is different from such organisations. The member states have relinquished some of their sovereign rights in favour of an institution that, in its structure and the powers conferred on it, resembles more traditional states. This act of integration, with which original and autonomous laws have been created, can be regarded as the basis of Community laws. The Community constitutes a new legal order between international law, for whose benefit the states have limited their sovereign rights, albeit within limited fields, and national law, the subjects of which comprise not only the member states but also their nationals.[1] By incorporation of the treaty into the municipal law of the member states, Community Law became part of the internal legal system of the member states. In particular, the treaty permits the creation of binding general norms and individual acts. This new legal order sets out to create in the short term a customs union, in the medium term an economic union and in the long term a political union and thus a qualitative change in the member states. This is clear from the outset, the possession of legal personality permitting the Community gradually to assume the same rights as the member states in international organisations. For instance, the Community is a subject of international law and as such is able to conclude treaties as well as to send and receive ambassadors.

A survey of the acts of the institutions shows that the regulations have general application, are binding in their entirety and directly applicable in all member states. These are the 'laws of the Community', as they are equally valid in all member states. Unlike other international acts, they require no internal acts of ratification. Unlike the general norms, the decisions are the individual acts of the Community having direct effect and are as such comparable to any national administrative acts. The third instrument of Community legislation, the directive, concerns only the member states and is binding only for the result to be achieved. It leaves the choice of form and methods to the national authorities. These acts are typical of the technique employed under international law, which does not create a unified law but promotes the harmonisation of the laws of various national legal systems. Finally, recommendations and opinions are acts with no binding force and thus correspond to the classic forms common in international organisations.[2] The gradual, phased execution of the plan for the Common Market and the prescribed nature of the maintenance of its function implies also the setting up of programmes that are binding only for the institutions of the Community and are simply for the information of the subjects of the member states.

The separation of powers along the classical Montesquieu lines does not operate in the Community. Instead there is an institutional balance that stems from a system of division of functions. Particularly in the field of legislation, the Community could not be satisfied with transferring national decision-making procedures to the Community. For this reason a new method was developed for the specific requirements of nations growing together in a community, which differs from traditional legislation in that it distinguishes, in its institutions and procedures, between two essential aspects: the decision-making process itself and legislation. The definition of the common functional interest is basically a matter for the Commission, which has a right of initiative, while the important act of political decision itself is given to the Council. This solution was reached because the EEC Treaty, unlike the ECSC Treaty, applies to the whole economy; it therefore cannot contain detailed regulations and consequently provides the institutions with a wide latitude in interpretation. The institutions of the Community have therefore to make real political decisions, which the governments of the member states, as the holders of power in the Community, wished to reserve for the Council.

The representatives of the governments of the member states meet in the Council. This procedure involves the government representatives who have the power to take decisions to the European process of decision-making. However, a close co-ordination of national ministries is required, otherwise a further conflict, for example between the foreign ministers and the ministers for agriculture, might result.

In negotiations and voting, the representatives of the member states are bound by the mandatory instructions of their governments and normally can be supervised by the national parliaments according to the relevant clauses in the national constitutions. There is a link with national policy in as much as they are empowered to represent national interests and are also called upon to seek compromises in the interests of the integration of the Community. National supervision, however, is restricted in as much as the Council sessions are not public and the national institutions cannot, by supervising their ministers, control the Council as a whole. As a result of the closed sessions the representatives can, for instance, claim that they had to sacrifice the national interest for a 'package deal'. Because of the lack of openness, control of the Council by the national parliaments is curtailed and the governments are provided with an opportunity of making a wide range of binding decisions at European level without referring to their own parliaments.

Apart from its legislative function the Council also concludes the treaties negotiated by the Commission with third countries and international organisations, although member states mostly sign as parties to these treaties and always do so in the case of budgetary matters. When the Rome Treaty contains no other stipulations, the Council makes decisions by an absolute majority of its members. Generally, however, the Treaty demands a qualified majority while unanimity was only envisaged for the transitional period. After this period, unanimity is only required for decisions of fundamental political importance or decisions with far-reaching effect on national interests, particularly when the Council wishes to depart from a decision of the Commission. Unlike other political organisations of states, differentiated forms of equal treatment were developed for the voting mechanism of the Council. In votes with a qualified majority, economic and political importance has determined the distribution of votes so that the members do not always have the same voting rights. This procedure is to prevent the larger member states from dominating and to give the smaller states minority rights.

The Commission consists of independent members who are bound only by the common interests embodied in the Treaty. Its members are appointed by common accord of the governments of the member states and the practice has been for the larger states to propose two, the smaller states one member of their nationality. Their independence is characterised by the fact that after their appointment the members of the Commission are responsible not to the Council but only to the European Parliament and their term of office can be ended only by a motion of censure by this institution.

It is the task of the Commission 'to ensure the proper functioning and development of the Common Market' by preventing and prosecuting treaty breaches by member states and individuals as well as initiating decisions. Besides making recommendations and expressing opinions without binding force, it can only make decisions when these are expressly provided for in the Treaty, for example in matters of implementation and the introduction of protective measures. In order to set the decision-making and legislative procedures in motion, there must be a detailed analysis and consultation by the Commission, which alone can define the European interest and on this basis present its policy proposals or a bill. In this way its function is both to control and stimulate.

As the twenty-year history of the EEC shows, there has been a continuation of the tendency, already visible in the development from the ECSC to the Treaty of Rome, to strengthen the position of the Council as an institution of national interests. The Council has only rarely used its power to delegate legislative jurisdiction to the Commission. In addition to the institutions provided for in the Treaty, numerous bodies were created that can act either without the initiative of the Commission or in relation to which the Commission has merely an advisory function. The most important committee is the Committee of Permanent Representatives of the member states, which became part of Community law with the Merger Treaty of 1965 and which has led to increased emphasis upon national interests in the preparation of Council sessions. This committee is made up of national civil servants who cannot take independent decisions and who have their decisions prepared by their ministries, as well as representatives of the Commission. Besides promoting the exchange of information between the national administrations and the institutions of the Community, it serves primarily to articulate and co-ordinate national points of view, which results in package deal negotiations.

The most marked shift of power between the Commission and the Council was initiated by the crisis of 1965-66 and its settlement by the Luxembourg Compromise in 1966, which postulated — against the terms of the Treaty — that decisions should not be made by majority vote when the vital interests of members were at stake. Since then even decisions of minor importance are no longer taken without unanimity. The majority rule depriving the member states of their veto was, as a result, undermined. It was the Commission's right of initiative, as one of the institutions representing the European interest alone, that was to ensure that the Council could negotiate and take decisions only on proposals that arose as a result of an objective analysis of European problems without harming the vital interests of the member states. Thus it is logical that provision should be made in the Treaty for the Council of Ministers to amend a proposal of the Commission only by a unanimous decision and otherwise to decide by a majority. This mechanism, however, is suspended when the Council prefers to take no decision. In order to avoid this situation, the Commission is forced to reduce its proposals to the lowest common denominator to achieve a compromise between the member states. This means that it is not possible for the Commission to take further initiatives without being certain beforehand that all members are interested in the project. It can no longer ally itself with the majority of the governments to prevent the amendment of its proposals, and has thus been forced into the role of a mediator. Consequently, it resembles a technical administrative authority more than a political authority. As the functional interests that, on a European level, should be safeguarded primarily by the Commission, are no longer adequately represented, interest groups exert pressure mainly through their national decision-making mechanism. This attitude makes even minor technical questions into political issues that must then be discussed in the Council.

Compared with the share of the Council and the Commission in Community decision-making processes, the position of the Assembly, known as the European Parliament since 1962, seems to be of subordinate importance, having the advisory and controlling function given to it in the Treaty. Its composition is determined by the weighting of the states and not by the size of their populations. To prevent the supremacy of single states, there has been an over-representation of the smaller and an under-representation of the larger states. Until 1979 the delegates were appointed from and by the national parliaments using a procedure determined by each member state. Thus the party-political composition is also determined by this process and reflects the fluctuations of the spectrum of national parties and factions, with all its negative implications for the continuity of parliamentary work. Delegates have united in transnational factions, according to their party leanings, which could overcome insular ways of thinking and behaviour.

The Council often voluntarily requests the opinion of the Parliament on the conclusion of international agreements, to guarantee[3] a certain co-operation in the shaping of foreign relations. When there is no consultation on important matters, the Parliament has reserved the right in its rules of procedure to report on the matters in question without being asked. The weakness of the system, however, lies in the fact that no ruling authority is obliged to consider the contribution of the European Parliament to Community legislation or its opinion in fundamental questions of European policy.

There is, however, a true controlling function over the Commission, carried out by the discussion of the annual report on activities, which includes the presentation of a programme of action for the coming year, as well as by oral and written questions from parliamentarians, which must receive a reply from the Commission. Potentially the most far-reaching method of control is the motion of censure, which forces the Commission to resign if it is passed with the qualified majority required. The system of putting questions could also be extended to the Council, which, however, has not committed itself to giving replies. Even the Foreign Ministers have expressed willingness to provide a certain amount of information in matters of European political co-operation, which takes place outside the actual Community framework.

Like other sovereign organisations the Communities have their own financial arrangements, which are a particularly good indicator of the degree of integration achieved. The original financing of the Community by resources of the member states was increasingly replaced by a limited financial autonomy, which has culminated in a financial independence through the collection of external tariffs and a percentage of Value Added Tax. The budget is controlled by an independent European Court of Audit. After the Community was provided with its own financial basis, the Parliament was granted substantial budgetary powers for part of its expenditure. For most of its expenditure, the so-called obligatory expenditure, the Council retains, however, the last word.[4] Although the Parliament has still no right to reject the budget totally, these budgetary powers can be seen as a step on the road to a modern parliamentary democracy.

Like the Parliament, the Economic and Social Committee has merely an advisory function in the process of legislation in the Community. The Committee is made up of representatives of various groups from economic and social life, particularly producers, farmers, workers, traders, craftsmen, liberal professions and the general public. Its members are appointed by the Council from a list of candidates submitted by the member states which strive to enforce a party ratio. Thus the representation of interests is weakened by the application of both nationality and party membership criteria. Although the Committee's advice is not legally binding, it has a certain importance in shaping Community opinion that goes beyond the informal participation of interest groups. By submitting reports and opinions, the Committee can counteract national endeavours in the Council, and this affects national interest groups. On the other hand, organisations that are not represented often turn to the Economic and Social Committee and not to the European bureaucracy, so that the former has come to represent interests outside its framework.

Apart from the Economic and Social Committee and its sub-divisions, there are of course a number of other bodies, some of which have been provided for in the Treaty, some not, and which are consulted by the institutions of the Community. Here the procedure is partly formalised with the consequence that meetings similar to Committee sessions take place between European civil servants and representatives of the special interest groups. Recently, more and more attention has been given to the large pressure group of consumers in the programme of action for consumer protection initiated by the Council. In addition to the department for environmental and consumer protection within the Commission, an advisory Consumer Committee has been established that is made up of acknowledged representatives of consumer interests.

As this complex decision-making process shows, the stages from the initial discussion about the guidelines of policy or about the solution of a single problem to the passing of an act are often long and difficult. The Commission cannot begin to prepare a proposal based on the common interest before it has consulted all concerned, such as government representatives, private and public organisations, employers, workers and other interest groups, as well as independent experts. The other institutions involved in the decision-making process also always have a chance to receive representations from interest groups, mostly farmers, workers and consumers, who provide them with background information and often use this opportunity. The integration of national policies has led to a European union within these groups. It is, however, difficult to estimate the real influence of these pressure groups on the decision-making processes of the Community. Their practical influence has increased since the establishment of the Community because, unlike the Economic and Social Committee, their activities are based on homogeneous interests.[5]

In the relations between the Community, the member states and their subjects, an important role is played not only by the institutions involved in the legislative process but also, finally, by the Court of Justice as guardian of the law of the Community. Its existence means that at least one element of the classic division of powers is fulfilled in the laws of the Community. The Court of Justice has many spheres of jurisdiction, which can be divided into the following main groups: proceedings against member states for failing to observe the Treaties, preliminary rulings on questions of interpretation of Community law that have come before the national courts, questions about the compatibility of acts of the institutions with original Community law, and finally labour disputes between the Community and its servants. The preliminary rulings are an excellent example of an instrument of legal integration by guaranteeing that Community law is interpreted and applied in the same way by all the institutions of the member states.

This survey of the constitution of the Community proves that the basic ideas behind the Community come from state laws rather than from international law. Community law, however, leads to a concept of order that is complete in itself and that modifies the legal systems of the member states. The most important elements of such an *ordre public communautaire* are the principles of supranationality, constitutionality, democracy and the welfare state.

Supranationality, as understood here, is not concerned with the existence or non-existence of a hierarchy in the relation between the Community and its member states, but simply expresses their real and legal interdependence in the sense that various sovereign groups share common tasks.[6] This sharing of tasks can be seen particularly in the principles of direct applicability and the precedence of Community law. The direct effect of Community law is that the norms of the Treaty, even when their wording is addressed to the states, can still have direct application within the states in that individuals can appeal to them in cases coming before national courts. In this way the Court of Justice has extended the poorly developed right of legal redress for the individual beyond the framework drawn up for the Commission in the complaints procedure of the EEC Treaty, which has its roots in international law. Through this jurisdiction, the member states become an 'automatic switchboard' as certain Treaty norms may be enforced immediately, even against the will of the member states.

After it established that the member states were not always prepared to make the directives, which were basically aimed at the states, into national law within a prescribed period of time, the Court of Justice employed the same technique by declaring these acts of secondary Community law immediately applicable under certain circumstances, although their procedural rules are otherwise governed by international law.[7] In cases where Community law is at variance with national law, the Court of Justice has reasoned that no national laws, in whatever form, can have precedence without the character of the Community being denied and the very legal basis of the Community being questioned.[8] To protect the sovereignty of the member states, however, the national law that is in conflict with Community laws need not be repealed. It is sufficient if the latter is given precedence. Although this precedence is postulated by Community law and does not require the separate approval of the member states who have relinquished their claim to exercise exclusive supremacy, it has in fact been recognised by most of the national courts.

The protection of fundamental rights developed by the Court of Justice is worthy of particular note. Through the enforcement of Community law, areas of friction can arise between the individual freedom of the subjects of the Community and the activities of the Community institutions. The Community Treaties themselves give only a fragmentary guarantee of basic rights. The precedence and the uniform application of Community law still forbid any appeal to national basic law. In its basic law jurisdiction, the Court of Justice (making at first only cautious reference, later an unequivocal declaration) chose those general legal principles common to the laws of the member states as a way of filling the gaps in the Treaties and thus creating a Community protection of basic law.[9] An additional source for the determination of the content of these general legal principles is taken from international treaties to which the member states are parties. As the Court stated, restrictions that can also be made by acts of secondary Community law must comply with the structure and aims of the Community with regard to the social function of the protected interests and activities and be justified by aims serving the general interest of the Community. Furthermore, they must not infringe on the substance of the interests.

The idea of the constitutional state is very close to that of the principle of democracy, as both serve to protect the freedom of the individual. The essential features of the principle of democracy, which forms the basis of the constitutions of all the member states, are reflected in the Vedel Report:

> The citizens of the country are the sole source of power; they possess rights and liberties valid as against the State and its organs; those who wield power are designated by genuine and meaningful elections; the political parties are free; the right of opposition is a fundamental fact of political and social life; the status and role of the parliament with regard to the executive are an essential part of democracy; in relation to law-making, the parliament is vested with the highest power; in one form or another, it exercises supervision over the government.[10]

The European Communities were established on this common basis of representative parliamentary democracy, even if the European Parliament suffered from a double congenital defect: the lack of direct legitimation (until 1979) and restricted legislative powers.

Finally, the principle of the welfare state is part of the basis of the Community order. It must be seen as supplementary to the principle of the constitutional state, despite the undeniable tension between them. In comparison with the security deriving from the freedoms of movement of workers, of establishment and to provide services as laid down in the Treaty, the extent of unification in the internally and financially critical area of a common social policy as envisaged in the Treaty provisions is very modest. This is due to the fact that, when the Community was founded, the idea was prevalent that social progress would automatically result from economic growth in the Community and the quality of the goods would almost necessarily mean an improvement in the quality of life. Thus the social sphere was seen merely as a corrective element that was to smooth difficulties arising during the process of economic integration. Community relief measures, according to the creators of the Treaty, were only to guarantee that changes of structure resulting from the pressure of competition would not lead to social hardship. Practice has shown, however, that the Economic Community has indeed led to greater prosperity, but that instead of solving the social problems of the Community it has increased them. The removal of trade barriers has meant that the individual economies began to influence each other. Thus there was a transfer of resources beyond the borders of the individual states to the detriment of the poorer regions and the weaker branches of industry. The political instability of some member states led in particular to a transfer of workers instead of the desired transfer of capital and producer goods. This in turn meant that already overcrowded areas had to absorb an even larger population, with all the subsequent urban and environmental problems.

The growing realisation that these social problems can no longer be treated effectively from a national angle alone, was the first step to a change in the attitudes of the member governments towards social policy, which was expressed in the declaration by the heads of government at the Summit Conference of 1972. It gave an energetic development in the social sphere the same priority as the realisation of the planned economic and monetary union. In this way social policy was raised to the level of policy in its own right and was no longer simply a means of smoothing out the undesirable social consequences of economic policy. However, it was not intended to replace national social policies or merge them into a single policy. Rather it sought to contribute to the solution of problems that went beyond national capabilities. In order to fulfil the allotted task, a common social policy required the support of systematic Community policies in other fields, particularly in the economy, currency, industry, agriculture, competition and regional policy fields. However, ambitious plans for a social union have faded in the face of limitations on economic growth. The reasons for this derive from internal developments in the Community as well as changes in the world political environment.[11]

The working of the Community in practice does not present a uniform picture. It is well known that the implementation of the measures that were clearly laid down in the Treaty was relatively simple. The customs union — with the freedom of movement of factors of production and a common code for competition as its logical accompaniment — and a common trade policy could be set up in their essentials. A common agricultural market and a Community agricultural policy were created and first steps were taken towards a common transport policy. These measures have led to economic expansion and a general increase in the standard of living. The harmonisation of laws, which is often underestimated by the public, has also proved to be a driving-force of social progress in fields such as the enforcement of equal pay for men and women, of social conditions, safety regulations at work and consumer and environmental protection.

Apart from these achievements, the Community has not succeeded in effectively combating the basic manifestations of the present economic crisis such as unemployment, inflation and monetary disparity as the expressions of the widening gap between economic performance and the real standard of living in the member states. The reason for this failure is not that the creators of the Rome Treaty did not foresee the necessity in a Common Market for an integrated monetary system and economic policy, but rather that as a result of national sensibilities and structural differences it was not possible to reach agreement beyond the laboriously negotiated terms of the Treaty. As a result of the changes in the political environment since the Treaty, the willingness of the member states to integrate has constantly diminished. It is symptomatic that, in order not to jeopardise what has already been achieved and at the same time only to take steps required by new situations, the necessary competence was created not by amending or adding to the Treaty but by extending powers, within the framework of the objectives set by the Common Market.[12] Yet the scope for such extension in the Treaties of Rome is almost exhausted. A further consequence has been the resort to Summit Conferences for the solution of current problems.

Fundamental changes in the world economy and the gap between structural conditions and economic preferences have, for instance, resulted in the recognition that the rationalisation of trade that follows from a customs union must be given firm support by a monetary foundation combined with a gradual integration of economic policy. In 1971, therefore, the member states decided to complete the transition from customs union to economic and monetary union by the end of 1980, the Werner Plan providing the basis of discussion.[13] But this would have meant the end of the tradition of national autonomy in the field of economic policy. Such a considerable step would have led to a redistribution of responsibilities between the Community and its member states and taken the Community beyond the threshold of political union.[14] A greater transfer of funds from the Community budget to compensate for regional differences would have been the inevitable consequence of this plan. The heads of government of the member states, however, at a number of Summit Conferences, could not commit themselves to this change in structure, which was anyway dominated by conflicts of interest. It remains to be seen whether the 1977 proposals for the creation of a European Monetary Authority as the centre of an economic and monetary union will prove to be more successful.[15]

The failure to co-ordinate political planning can also be seen in the energy sector. The reduction in energy supplies to the countries of the Community that resulted from the Middle East crisis of 1973 quickly demonstrated the conflicts of interest and proved that the integration achieved so far was not sufficient to mean effective solidarity. A start has been made on a Community energy policy; but, this is rendered more difficult by the distribution of energy sources within the Community. By contrast, agricultural expenditure accounts for three-quarters of the EEC budget and blocks potential developments in other areas such as regional policy or development aid. In this way the Community spends a totally disproportionate percentage of its budgetary revenue on a mere 8 per cent of the population. Moreover, agricultural policy promotes the better-off regions, as the largest part of agricultural expenditure goes on subsidies that increase agricultural overproduction and only a small part is spent on necessary improvements in structure.

The development of external relations, on the other hand, provides a more encouraging picture. The EEC plays a major role in international trade, and in questions of trade all nine Members speak substantially with one voice. Trade agreements have been made with over thirty states. The Community is to negotiate a trade agreement with the People's Republic of China and relations with the COMECON states have developed in such a way that trade agreements can now be made between the EEC and COMECON's member states. In the Mediterranean area the Community is developing a comprehensive policy, and over fifty states from Africa, the Caribbean and the Pacific have been associated with the Community by a preferential agreement whereby they have been guaranteed a more stable income from exports.[16] However, one should note that certain international organisations such as the United Nations only recognise states as members.

The asymmetry between an underdeveloped internal policy and the requirement of a common policy towards the outside world is particularly clear in the case of fisheries policy. Here the Community must negotiate with third countries without being able to fall back on a common basis within the Community. There is also a continuing danger of slipping back into protectionism through an increased number of sectoral agreements of a restrictive nature, particularly in the steel and textile industries. This damages the trading image of the Community in the eyes of the developing countries.

An important problem for the future is the further enlargement of the Community to include three Mediterranean countries, Greece, Spain and Portugal. There can be very little doubt that from a defence point of view it is expedient to incorporate these states on the southern edge of the Community in the Western world and to reinforce their democratic institutions by bringing them into contact with the democratic institutions of the Community. The structural disparities can only be resolved by an expanded transfer of resources.[17] Working out a common policy with twelve states must be prevented from becoming even more laborious than it is at present and exceptions and transitional periods must be prevented from jeopardising the Community system. It is therefore clear that the powers of decision of the Community must be strengthened if it is not to be reduced to a mere free trade area. It would, however, be dangerous to couple the negotiations for enlargement with the revision demands required for the survival of the Community, as this would delay the increase in membership unduly and would harm the credibility of the Community in the states applying to join.

NOTES AND REFERENCES

1. Van Gend and Loos Case, 5.2.1963, 26/62 Rec. IX, 23; Costa-ENEL Case, 15.7.1964, 6/64 Rec. X, 1167.
2. Art. 189, EEC Treaty.
3. Common Statement of the European Parliament, the Council and the Commission, Official Journal, 1975, no. C 89/1
4. Erwin Reister, *Haushalt und Finanzen der Europäischen Gemeinschaften*, Baden-Baden, Nomos, 1975.
5. See the study of Mary T. W. Robinson, 'La participation du citoyen dans le processus de prise de décision au niveau de la Communauté Européenne', Brussels, 1975, Seventh FIDE-Congress.
6. See Ernst Wohlfarth, 'Elemente einer Europäischen Verfassung' in *Miscellanea W. J. Ganshof van der Meersch*, Brussels, Bruyland, 1972, p. 585.
7. Grad Case, 6.10.1970, 9/70 Rec. XVI, 825; SACE Case, 17.12.1970, 33/70 Rec. XVI, 1213; Van Duyn Case, 4.12.1974, 41/74 Rec. 1974, 1337; Rutili Case, 28.10.1975, 36/75 Rec. 1975, 1219.
8. Internationale Handelsgesellschaft Case, 17.12.1970, 11/70 Rec. XVI, 1125.
9. Ernst-Werner Fuss, *Der Grundrechtsschutz in den Europäischen Gemeinschaften aus deutscher Sicht*, Heule, UGA, 1975; see Ernst-Werner Fuss, *Die Europäischen Gemeinschaften und der Rechtsstaatsgedanke*, Heule, UGA, 1968.
10. Report of the Working Party examining the problem of the enlargement of the powers of the European Parliament, *Bulletin of the European Communities*, Supplement, no. 4, 1972, p. 11.
11. Heinrich Schneider, 'Integration — gestern, heute und morgen', *Integration*, vol. 1, no. 3, 1978.
12. Art. 235, EEC Treaty.
13. *Bulletin of the European Communities*, Supplement, no. 11, 1970.
14. Tindemans Report, 'The European Union', *Bulletin of the European Communities*, Supplement, no. 1, 1976.
15. See Roy Jenkins, 'Die Integration der Europäischen Gemeinschaft angesichts der Erweiterung', *Europa Archiv*, 1978, no. 1
16. Lomé Convention, *Official Journal*, 30 January 1976, no. L25/1
17. Wilhelm Haferkamp 'Chancen und Risken der zweiten EG-Erweiterung', *Europa Archiv*, 1977, p. 617.

SELECT BIBLIOGRAPHY

Constantinesco, Léontin-Jean, *Das Recht der Europäischen Gemeinschaften*, vol. I, Baden-Baden, Nomos, 1977.
Herman, Valentine and Lodge, Juliet, (eds), *The European Parliament and the European Community*, London, Macmillan, 1978.
Ipsen, Hans Peter, *Europäisches Gemeinschaftrecht*, Tübingen, Mohr, 1972.
Robertson, A.H., *European Institutions*, London-New York, Stevens, 1973.
Sasse, Christoph, *Regierungen, Parlamente, Ministerrat*, Bonn, Europaunion, 1975.
Schneider, Heinrich, *Leitbilder der Europapolitik*, Bonn, Europaunion, 1977.
Wallace, Helen, Wallace, William and Webb, Carole (eds.), *Policy-Making in the European Communities*, London, J. Wiley & Sons, 1977.

CHAPTER 11

COMECON: Inter-State Economic Co-operation in Eastern Europe

Alexander Uschakow

Any examination of the question of the origins and history of Eastern European integration cannot ignore the military, political and economic state of affairs that existed in these countries after the Second World War. Only against this background is it possible to understand the forces that have become active in Eastern Europe and the motives that have inspired the actors since then. There are various views on the phases of development within COMECON, depending on which discipline the individual authors come from and which criteria they take as the basis of their judgements.

For a long time Soviet literature[1] looked upon 1956 as a turning-point in the development of COMECON, since in May of that year it was decided at the Berlin Conference to extend existing co-operation to particular branches of production and to set about establishing international specialisation by co-ordinating the various national economic plans. Others, however, use as their criterion for delineating phases the type of co-operation involved; while from 1949 to 1953 co-operation was restricted exclusively to the exchange of goods, the subsequent period has been characterised by specialisation in production. Among economists,[2] further, there is a prevailing tendency to assess developments within COMECON solely in terms of the 'extensive' (co-ordination in certain areas of trade and production) phase up to 1970 and that of 'intensive' co-operation since 1971, the latter phase being equated in COMECON with the concept of socialist economic integration. Experience has shown that its economic activities are closely connected with the way COMECON is organised and legally regulated. Economic co-operation is, in fact, reflected in the basic legal instruments of COMECON. The law is based on the economic processes, which constitute one aspect of its function, but at the same time it points the way forward by creating appropriate legal regulatory mechanisms. The economic content of the legal norms prevailing in COMECON had hitherto more of a national than an international character since, for a long time, the tempo was determined by the need to adapt the national planning apparatus to the demands of co-operation and not vice versa. From the legal point of view,[3] which involves the legal basis of COMECON, its organisation, its sphere of jurisdiction and inter-state instruments, two main phases can be discerned in the development of the organisation. The period from the setting-up of COMECON until 1971 can furthermore be sub-divided into the phases 1949-1953, 1954-1956, 1957-1962 and 1963-1970. However, there is one criterion available to lend unity to categorisation in terms of economics and structure. It is the basic concept of integration in Eastern Europe, which is controlled by Moscow and manifests itself in the degree to which the individual countries are interlocked with the economy of the USSR. It is in the bloc that the phenomenon of military-political integration in the Warsaw Pact and economic integration in COMECON becomes visible. In contrast to the USA, which only co-operates with Western Europe in NATO and sometimes finds itself in direct confrontation with the EEC, COMECON forms the economic basis for the Warsaw Pact. In both organisations the Soviet Union plays the dominating and decisive role.

The Creation of COMECON

The date of the setting-up of COMECON is generally given as 25 January 1949. But there is something mysterious about the proceedings surrounding the setting-up of this first international organisation in Eastern Europe because a treaty and a set of statutes usually mark the beginning of such an organisation. In the case of COMECON there is no document of this kind, or at least such a memorandum of association was never published. Since no details were given about the foundation conference that took place in Moscow at the beginning of January 1949, there was considerable speculation about a 'secret treaty' between the Eastern bloc countries. Only today do we know that this conference took place from 5 to 8 January 1949 in Moscow and accepted a rudimentary statute for the organisation.[4] Between this conference and the announcement of the decision to found COMECON, a tussle took place between the Soviet Union and the other Eastern bloc countries against the background of Yugoslavia's withdrawal from the Eastern bloc over the expediency of establishing such a body in general and the form COMECON should take in particular. The Soviet side looked upon COMECON as being primarily of political importance, serving as an instrument to strengthen the Eastern European countries and to bind them to Moscow. The meagre communiqué[5] on the setting-up of COMECON states that the representatives of Bulgaria, Hungary, Romania, Czechoslovakia and the

USSR consider the establishment of a Council for Mutual Economic Assistance (COMECON) to be necessary. It was meant to serve as a counterweight to the Western European Marshall Plan and to constitute at the same time a further step along the path towards economic co-operation.

The first stage of this economic co-operation falls within the period immediately prior to the setting-up of COMECON, i.e. in the years 1945 to 1949. It was a direct result of political events and is closely tied up with the formation of a system of communist states in Eastern Europe under the leadership of the Soviet Union. As can so often be observed in history, the start of such a process of integration was brought about by the need to protect a group of states by means of a military alliance against an enemy. Thus immediately after the Second World War the USSR built up a network of bilateral pacts to form a front against Germany and gradually also against the Western powers. Very early on, the duty of the partners to engage in economic co-operation was laid down in these bilateral pacts and in this way these pacts came to assume an economic function in addition to their military one. The claim of a threat from outside was often reason enough to make increased economic efforts and to modernise a state. In this way the threat from Sweden at the time forced Russia under Peter the Great to accept Western culture in the face of the military struggle, and Japan adopted the forms of modern life in order to stand up against the fleets of the USA, Britain and France.

After the Second World War both an upheaval in the internal social conditions and a revolution in the international economic relations of Eastern Europe took place. Industries were nationalised, the planned economy was introduced, and trade, which before 1939 had been oriented towards the West, was switched to the Soviet Union. Whilst trade with the Soviet Union amounted to about 2 per cent of the foreign trade of the smaller countries before 1939, it rose after 1945 to 90 per cent. This sudden and radical change in the whole economy and trade was accompanied by the adoption of the Soviet economic model, which had been primarily not so much geared towards economic co-operation as towards warding off external influences during the interwar period. They copied the self-sufficient economy of the Soviet Union. By 1950 the Eastern European countries had attained an economic level that, broadly speaking, was comparable in its volume and structure with that of the prewar period. The difference between the national income per head of population in the individual countries involved a spread between 1 and 5. For political reasons, the Soviet Union was the most important trading partner, supplying in the first phase after 1945 mainly machines and equipment for industries that had largely been destroyed. At the same time, reciprocal trade between the other Eastern bloc countries accounted for only 10 per cent of their total trade.

The organisational basis for the rapprochement that was emerging was to be formed by the bilateral commissions that were set up after 1947 with the first three-year plans. However, for political reasons, they were unable to exploit all the possibilities that this bilateral system presented. The point was that there were already agreements, particularly those between Poland and Czechoslovakia, which also provided for the co-ordination of production and trade between the two countries. Similar plans in the Balkans had gone down in history as attempts to form a Danube federation between Yugoslavia, Bulgaria, Romania, Hungary, Poland and Czechoslovakia. These plans evoked a harsh reaction on the part of Stalin and contributed to the break between Moscow and Belgrade. At the same time, there was no lack of plans by the Soviet leadership to enter into federal ties with the Eastern bloc countries, with a view to halting centrifugal forces at the beginning of the East-West conflict. Many factors were responsible for the failure of bilateral co-operation, started before 1949, to make progress. The setting-up of COMECON can therefore be regarded as a break in these developments, which were not continued until much later in the 1960s and 1970s.

Economic literature places considerable stress on the close commitment to the Soviet economic model, referring to it as the autarchic or statist planning model of the co-ordination phase of Eastern European economies. This was brought about by external and internal developments. Among the external influences, the Cold War and the embargo imposed by Western countries on the Eastern bloc during the Korean War may be cited. The internal factors include Moscow's directive concerning the all-round development of the national economies. The individual countries were supposed to develop their production reserves and consumption self-sufficiently. The tempo and extent of nationalisation in the people's democracies of Eastern Europe, analogously to the Soviet Revolution after 1917, did proceed very quickly and embraced not only basic industries but the private sector as well. The state became the sole master of industry and the sole employer. The planning system taken over from the USSR of the 1930s concentrated almost all decisions at the centre, the few exceptions being those concerning consumption and the choice of work. This system did not make use of economic levers, but rather drew on administrative orders, which resulted in the importance of money for the whole of the national economy being secondary. The centralised management of the national economy ruled out the possibility of genuine economic democracy in the plants, although, according to the ideology, the workshop should be the basic unit of a socialist state. In short, only the nationalisation and not the socialisation of the economy took place.

As a result of the political change-over, another development ensued. Immediately after the war the Eastern European countries had large labour reserves, which, in turn, seemed to guarantee that these countries could develop along their own lines. Also, following nationalisation, the governments had considerable capital at their disposal, which allowed immediate measures to be taken. In the predominantly agricultural countries (Bulgaria and Romania) and in the agricultural-industrial countries (Poland and Hungary) the nationalisation of the banks, industry, trade and other branches resulted in this financial basis being too small to guarantee long-term dynamic development. Although supplies from the USSR to the Eastern European countries helped to overcome immediate bottlenecks, they also constituted one of the reasons why for a long time the national economies of the COMECON system pursued policies of self-sufficiency.

Strict economic centralism was reinforced still further by Stalin's political dictatorship. As no sessions of the Central Committee were called in the USSR between 1947 and 1953, no meeting of the COMECON Council occurred between 1950 and 1953 either. There is a difference of opinion between experts in the East and West as to whether this statist phase of COMECON was necessary and of positive value, or whether it had a damaging effect on the expansion of industries that was dictated more by questions of national prestige than by economic considerations. One view defends this model by arguing that, on account of the backwardness of these countries, this centralist system was necessary in order to eliminate the difference in their respective levels of development by planned concentration on a number of main areas. At all events, this approach did not produce only positive results, otherwise reforms would not have been embarked upon following the death of Stalin. As has already been remarked, economic co-operation during the initial period following the setting-up of COMECON took the form of one-sided dependence on the USSR and was even directed by Soviet experts in the people's democracies. In the plants and works there were special departments that had the task of co-ordinating their activities so as to tie up with the Soviet economy. COMECON formed a passive platform for consultations about economic plans, which were largely drawn up and executed by the Soviet planning office. COMECON still has the character of a consultative body, because it lacks authority of its own. On the other hand, the significance of such technical organisations should not be under-rated. The member states depend more and more on their work. The economic potential of the individual COMECON countries differed considerably and still does, whilst the participation of the USSR creates additional problems. The USSR produces twice as much as the other countries, but its involvement in foreign trade is only a quarter of that of the other partners. In other words, the USSR is economically self-sufficient and so integration does not have the same importance for it as it does for the other states.

Economic Reforms in Eastern Europe

In the first period of the existence of COMECON the individual economies of the smaller countries developed along self-sufficient lines in accordance with the Soviet prewar model. But what was feasible for the Soviet Union with its space and potential proved to be unworkable for the smaller countries in the long run. Moreover, co-operation within COMECON took place exclusively along the axis Moscow-other COMECON countries.

Although the term 'economic integration' was only formally accepted in general usage after 1969 — until then it was only used in a negative sense to characterise the EEC — a certain reversal can be detected in recent Eastern European ligerature, since it is now maintained that by uniting practical and institutional elements, economic co-operation between Eastern European countries since 1945 has always been aimed at promoting integration, irrespective of the various terminologies used. As was the case with the setting-up of COMECON, both external and internal factors were responsible for reforms after Stalin's death. The example of COMECON, in particular, puts a very different complexion on the Marxist assertion of the primacy of domestic policy. Very strong trends towards effective international co-operation have made it necessary to examine the mechanisms that regulate inter-state economics. With the COMECON conference of March 1954 a halting start was made in correlating the economic plans of the individual countries in the field of production. The so-called co-ordination stage of COMECON began. It was also decided to end the one-sided exchange of goods with the Soviet Union by first of all co-ordinating production plans among the individual countries and only then making trade agreements with the USSR. This step presupposed a common economic policy, which up to that time had not existed. The search for new models for international co-operation was a direct consequence of the previous pursuit of self-sufficient economic policies, which had resulted in both labour and raw materials shortages between 1950 and 1970, except in the Soviet Union.

Although the discussion about economic reforms began in 1953 in Eastern Europe, this first phase was not given legislative expression until the decision of the Soviet government of 9 August 1977 to extend the authority of works directors. Similar measures ensued in all the COMECON countries. In 1955 a dispute broke out in the USSR about the role of the market in a centralised economy and the decentralisation of economic management with the publication of Liberman's articles, economists in Hungary, Poland and East Germany following suit. This movement influenced cooperation within COMECON. The COMECON conferences from 1954 to 1956 were devoted to this complicated problem. In May 1956 COMECON recommended its members to specialise production in mechanical engineering. To arrive at a criterion for these measures, the absolute costs of production were taken as the basis in the context of the discussion about how to increase the effectiveness of economic control. The result was that those countries that were already highly developed, namely East Germany and Czechoslovakia, gained a dominant position under this international division of labour within COMECON, whilst the predominantly agricultural countries, Bulgaria and Romania, were reduced to the role of supplying the industrial nations in COMECON with raw materials. It is therefore not surprising that during the 1950s the governments of East Germany and Czechoslovakia were among the strongest supporters of integration within COMECON. This also explains why Romania succeeded in emerging as the 'opposition' spokesman in the Eastern bloc. Poland and Hungary were basically sympathetic towards the standpoint of their weaker partners but, following the revolutionary events of 1956, avoided provoking Moscow.

Towards the end of the 1950s the whole concept of COMECON entered a critical phase. It has been shown that neither simple cooperation in exchanging goods with the USSR nor the splitting up of production according to the principle of profitability was an answer, because the latter approach encouraged the division of countries into two classes, namely industrial and agricultural states. If the political consequences of this situation were not to lead to a far-reaching crisis, the Soviet Union, for better or worse, would have to assume the role of supplying raw materials for a long time to come.

Both in the Soviet Union and in the other Eastern bloc countries there were political and economic reasons for the reforms that were introduced after Stalin's death. The intention was to give the population a greater share of consumer goods. But this could only be achieved by taking effective measures to limit the powers of the central authorities vis à vis the production plants. Towards the end of the 1950s, the call for economic reforms changed very quickly into demands for the transformation of the whole political system. Consequently, the reforms that had been initiated were revoked one after the other, with the result that the first spate of economic reforms collapsed at the beginning of the sixties.

The termination of the reforms, together with Khruschev's attempt in 1962 to establish a central planning body for COMECON in Moscow in order to resolve the difficulties regarding co-operation within COMECON, was unsuccessful. In the mid-1960s East Germany, Czechoslovakia and Hungary experienced a drop in their growth rates. In the case of Czechoslovakia from 1961 to 1964, this almost assumed the proportions of an economic collapse. The three countries had no labour reserves to sustain highly extended economies, they lacked raw materials and were all dependent on foreign trade. An additional factor was the need felt by these countries to adapt themselves to the technological revolution that had taken place in Western Europe. Thus these countries switched to the integrated economic model, whilst the Soviet Union, Poland, Romania and Bulgaria recorded considerable growth rates on account of their labour reserves, raw materials, and (in the case of Romania and Bulgaria) their receipts from tourism.

In East Germany a comprehensive reform was carried out in 1963 with the transfer of extensive powers to the Association of State-Owned Industries, although the centralistic model was still adhered to. In Czechoslovakia economic reforms had already been implemented under Novotny but they did not produce the desired results; instead they brought on the democratisation of the political system during the 'Prague Spring' of 1968. During the 1960s the uniform picture presented by the COMECON countries changed and became more differentiated. Three groups can be distinguished. The first group comprises only Romania, which, although recording considerable growth, still adheres to a centralised planning system, stemming from the co-ordination phase. The autonomy of the production plants has remained at its former level. On the other hand, Romania, along with Yugoslavia, has taken the lead in opening its doors to Western capital. By taking the way the economy is regulated as a criterion, East Germany, Czechoslovakia and Bulgaria can be placed in the second group of countries. Here the economy is regulated from above through directives concerning matters of both quantity and quality of production. In these countries the production plants are accorded a certain financial interest, but investments still remain under central control. Poland and Hungary fall into the third category. Here, the central plan only determines the general direction in which the whole economy is to develop. When, however, one looks at the level of development that the various countries have attained, a different picture emerges. One finds that East Germany and Czechoslovakia are among the most developed, since their lack of raw materials and labour forced them at an early stage to specialise in particular fields.

All in all, however, it may be said that the economic reforms in Eastern Europe did not produce conditions favourable to promoting integration within COMECON since, although they brought the economies of the individual countries closer together, they revealed considerable differences as to the methods to be employed in economic organisation, planning and administration. Such differences included the precision of plans and directives and the fixing of prices and of wages. The reforms gave rise to various methods of fixing prices. It may be said that whilst all governments recognised the need for reforms in the sixties, with the exception of Hungary they did not attain their prescribed goal of efficient production. The basic features of a political and economic dictatorship were not eliminated. In particular, the process of decentralisation was not carried out consistently. In the course of the economic reforms a certain degree of liberalisation emerged. However, at the inter-state level in COMECON, where the countries are particularly concerned about their sovereignty since no other means of control existed, the role of the Communist parties increased. As long as co-operation at the international level confined itself to declamations directed towards co-operation rather than towards effective integration, the matter was left to the so-called technocrats. The Communist parties not only control political life; they also play an active part in making economic decisions. They met for this purpose in May 1958 in Moscow, where they discussed organisational measures. As the first step towards reorganising COMECON, a number of specialist commissions were established. A new Commission for Economic Questions was instructed to draw up an economic programme. After a revision of the draft had been completed, the first programme for an international division of labour was accepted by party and government leaders in the summer of 1962.

The Organisation of COMECON

In the past, the strengthening of the organisational structure of COMECON has been accompanied by increasing co-operation, but this process has stopped short of the threshold of a supranational organisation, since COMECON decisions are not allowed to interfere with national planning. As has already been mentioned, the first step in this direction was taken at the fourth session of the COMECON Council in March 1954. Many authors maintain that it was not until then that the idea of integration arose. In place of the COMECON Bureau, the Conference of the Representatives of the Countries in the Council was established as the standing executive organ of COMECON. A Secretariat was set up, and it was agreed to hold meetings twice a year. As far as the organisation of COMECON is concerned, the twelfth session of the Council in December 1959 in Sofia was of great significance, since the delegates embodied the structure of COMECON as it had developed in practice in a constitutional document. The new Charter confirmed existing practice. The thirteenth session of the Council in July 1960 extended the duration of the long-term plan to 1980 and passed a set of procedural rules and a model statute for the standing commissions. Serious attempts to reform COMECON were embarked upon at the special session of April 1969, following the completion of economic reforms in the individual communist countries and the intervention in Czechoslovakia. According to the communiqué, the delegates decided to create 'a system of strong and durable ties'. As a first move in this direction, the authority and powers of COMECON together with its basic constitution were to be improved. Since 1969, the term 'economic integration' has been officially recognised. In December 1969, the Executive Board established a COMECON organ for legal questions, which, in co-operation with a newly founded legal department of the Secretariat, was to draw up a programmatic document on co-operation. In July

1971, this document entitled 'A Comprehensive Programme for the Further Deepening and Perfecting of Co-operation and Development of Socialist Economic Integration of Member Countries of COMECON' was passed by the party and government leaders.[6] According to the 'Comprehensive Programme', socialist economic integration is to be achieved without creating supranational institutions and is planned to take between fifteen and twenty years. It also considers the most important precondition for the achievement of such integration to lie in the Communist parties exerting greater influence on co-operation.

COMECON lacks any authority to make decisions, merely constituting a forum for discussing agreements on economic co-operation. This advisory capacity is ascribed to COMECON occasionally even by Eastern observers. Thus, since 1971, the organs of COMECON have not applied community law, as is the case in the EEC, but have merely assisted in the preparation and conclusion of agreements. Also there is no court to decide how the law should be applied or to specify and interpret the common law. COMECON's Charter contains a wide range of aims and principles governing the community. The reference made in Article 1 to the transformation of economic and social conditions in the member countries in order to build socialism and communism may be regarded as an empty formula that says little about the practical steps to be taken to make it a reality.

According to the Charter, COMECON assists its members in promoting the international division of labour. Formally, its powers are weak. Although it is comprehensive in the sense that practically all areas fall within its sphere of competence, according to Articles 3 and 4 its executive power lies only in the making of recommendations rather than decisions. As far as the effectiveness of the organisation is concerned, one principle is particularly important, namely that of consensus, which implies that all member countries have the same rights and that all the organs of COMECON must be made up of representatives from all member countries on the same footing. These rights are not specified in detail, as is the case in the EEC, but they apply to all the organs of COMECON in the same way, from the highest organs down to the technical ones. Recommendations that accord with international law are not binding but require the assent of the national authorities to be put into effect and must be transformed into national laws. Recommendations are made on material questions, whilst decisions are made on organisational questions and became legally binding after the protocol has been signed by the representatives of the member countries. Acceptance of a recommendation is at the discretion of the member countries; it is not applicable to those countries that have declared that they are not 'interested' in the matter concerned. Within sixty days the Secretary of COMECON must be informed of the decision of those governments whose representatives have previously accepted a COMECON recommendation. Since the representatives in COMECON are also leading functionaries who wield power at the national level, it has significantly hardly ever occurred that a country that has given its consent to a matter in the COMECON Council has afterwards refused to give it national ratification.

The COMECON Charter of 1974 cites the main organs to be the Council, the Executive Board, the Standing Commissions and the Secretariat. There is no mention of the Conferences of the Communist Parties, although they have repeatedly made basic recommendations to COMECON. They are able to give directives and to take organisational measures on account of the position they enjoy in the member countries.

From the formal point of view, the Council is the highest organ in COMECON. It is empowered to deal with all questions falling within the competence of COMECON. In practice, it has decreased in significance since 1962 on account of the growing importance of the Communist parties. Instead of meeting twice a year as earlier, it now holds sessions only once a year. The delegations are led by the deputy chairmen of the Councils of Ministers, who, as a rule, are also their countries' representatives on the Executive Board. This personal union between the Council and the Executive Board is suspended when the party leaders attend the Council.

The Executive Board replaced the Conference of the Representatives of the Countries in the Council following the reorganisation of COMECON in 1962. It is composed of the deputy prime ministers, who are also their countries' permanent delegates in Moscow, where the Board has its headquarters. As a rule, they lead their countries' delegations to the Council sessions. The Executive Board meets three times a year and is responsible for co-ordinating the economic plans and for specialisation and co-operation in production. It issues directives concerning economic co-operation and trade, and the Secretariat and the Standing Commissions are responsible to it.

The Standing Commissions were set up in a resolution passed by the seventh session of the Council in 1956 in East Berlin. Their creation was tied up with the internal economic reforms of the COMECON states and with the reorganisation of COMECON. They can be divided up into general and specialised commissions. The former include the commissions for foreign trade, standardisation, and finance; the latter comprise the commissions for engineering, building, transport, etc. It is the commissions that do the actual work in COMECON. There are twenty-one such commissions at the moment. The agenda of the commissions is drawn up by the corresponding departments in the Secretariat. In the commissions, specialist ministers or their deputies work together. Like all other COMECON organs, they can make recommendations and decisions. They also form working parties to deal with special questions, as the need arises.

The key position among the COMECON organs is occupied by the Secretariat. It participates in the making of all COMECON agreements; it supervises the implementation of recommendations, gathers information, compiles expert reports, administers the affairs of COMECON and deals with an abundance of other technical matters.

The organisation of COMECON is based on functional principles. When the creation of additional organs for special tasks have become necessary, they can be set up by drawing on the authorisation contained in the Charter. COMECON has made considerable use of this authorisation since 1971. The former Standing Commission for Economic Co-operation has been transformed into an International Institute for Economic Problems of the Socialist System. Other subsidiary organs are: the Conference of the Chiefs of Water Resources Authorities, the Institute for Inventions, the Institute for Standardisation, the Conference of Ministers for Internal Trade, the Conference of Representatives of Shipping Organisations, the Conference of Member Countries of COMECON for Legal Problems (1970), the Committee for Co-operation in the Field of Planning (1972), the Committee for Scientific and Technical Co-operation (1972), and the Committee for Co-operation in the Field of Technical and Material Supplies (1974). The Planning Committee, which replaced the Planning Bureau of the Executive Board in 1962, has the most important tasks.

A multitude of international organisations and agencies do not constitute organs within COMECON, but nevertheless may be regarded as an attempt to make it more effective. The specialised agencies date back to the decisions of the Conference of Communist Party and Government Leaders of 1962. The Comprehensive Programme of 1971 devoted a special section to them, stating that they were to direct economic co-operation in certain selected areas of industry and technology and within individual branches and types of production. They are established by agreements between governments and their legal structure is therefore determined solely by such agreements and certain passages in the Comprehensive Programme. Such specialised agencies include the International Bank for Economic Co-operation, the International Investment Bank and the Organisation of the Joint Power Grid. They do not themselves engage in economic activity, but co-ordinate the work of the undertakings and ministries placed under them. They can be called the international cartels of COMECON.

An interesting new phenomenon is the emergence of common agencies within COMECON established on a bilateral or multilateral basis. Among such bilateral organisations, special mention must be made of the trading organisations, which include such joint Soviet-East German organisations as Domkhim for the production of chemicals, Assfoto for the production of film material, and Interport for the administration of docks and ports. There is also the collaboration between East Germany and Poland in the field of cotton production. All these organisations have particular production tasks to perform; they engage in trade and co-ordinate economic co-operation between their countries in the area assigned to them. Since 1971, the number of these multilateral organisations has increased considerably: Intersputnik, Interelectrotest, Interatominstrument, etc. These organisations are production associations and trading agencies within COMECON.

Economic integration results in a new system of ties, whereby certain areas of the national economies come to form part of COMECON. There is, however, no common plan. Such integration therefore demands that the plans agreed upon in the Planning Committee should be put into effect in the national economies. As a result, the Soviet Union demanded as early as 1971 in COMECON that a special section on integration should be adopted in all the national economic plans. Finally, in June 1973, the twenty-seventh session of the Council passed a resolution calling for the immediate implementation of the Comprehensive Programme. In accordance with this decision, particular sections on integration within COMECON were incorporated into the one- and five-year plans. Thus, in June 1975, the twenty-ninth session of the Council approved an integration plan for the period 1976-1980. Similarly, the law pertaining to the East German economic plan for 1976 states that 'the coordination plans based on bilateral or multilateral agreements approved by COMECON form a firm part of the economic plan for 1976'. The laws devoted to the economic plans of the other COMECON states contain similar passages. In this way, foreign trade obligations become part of the national economic measures adopted by these countries. In all the countries of the Eastern bloc, the highest organs were given the authority to carry out integration.

The agreements reached at the international level are to be put into effect by the agencies. To this end, a body of inter-socialist commercial law has been created and this is applied directly to the exchange of goods. In addition, these international norms and standards serve as the basis for production plants that produce goods for the special foreign trade organisations of COMECON. The same COMECON standards apply to the production of quality goods by national industries.

Whilst COMECON was initially conceived of as a planning community, it is now expected to develop gradually into a market community. Since the acceptance of the integration programme of 1971, the first signs of the emergence of an international production community have become discernible. Here we are concerned with the setting-up of common agencies, which pose difficult economic and legal problems. Even if the state participates in such an agency, it does not forfeit its sovereignty in COMECON, a fact that is demonstrated by the member states having equal voting rights.

Since co-operation is expected to be transferred more and more to such agencies, it is imperative for the achievement of integration in COMECON that the agreements should be strictly adhered to. This is all the more important since this process, involving governments, ministries, authorities, and economic organisations, is to be extended. For a planned economy, which is cut off from the outside world, breaches of agreements have an immediate effect on the equilibrium of the economy, since a chronic shortage of foreign exchange precludes the possibility of turning to outside markets. However, so long as there is no solution to the problem of liability and guarantees, which arises when a country agrees to embark on specialisation, the COMECON countries continue to endeavour to make themselves as independent of their partners as possible. This is one of the reasons why East European countries still tend to be autarchic. For this reason, too, they refuse to transfer powers to the COMECON agencies until these economic problems have been settled.

The whole question of liability in economic co-operation is becoming more and more pressing. The COMECON countries are becoming increasingly involved at the international level on account of their economic ties. The communist state as such is producer, trading partner and competitor at one and the same time. But international law has had no experience in dealing with the question of liability when co-operation agreements are violated. This stems from the fact that in the case of a planned state, the international level cannot be separated from that of civil law. The joint agencies have hitherto been bilateral and the part played by the partners is absolutely equal, with the result that the principle of consensus prevails in all important matters. Neither of the two partners has sole authority. Experts admit that this phenomenon of joint agencies, which stems from the sovereignty of the COMECON states, poses many unsolved problems. Since there is no fixed level to prices, it is impossible to assess the profits due to the partners when they perform different services for the agency. Similarly, when the agencies are given a free hand, it is impossible to calculate the cost of the work performed, since the various countries employ different methods of calculation. Each country is eager to fix a proportionately higher price for its contribution. Since a free labour market does not exist, workers are simply 'detailed', and so complicated problems of calculation arise.

A Comparison of Integration in COMECON and the EEC

One difference between the two communities lies in the fact that in COMECON the type of integration aimed at was not legally laid down, whereas the Common Market was to be established within a definite period of time stated in the Treaty itself. Both the COMECON Charter and the Comprehensive Programme of 1971 construe 'socialist integration' as a process of rapprochement between the various national economies. The final goal is not legally defined, since complete integration would amount to the surrender of the political independence of the East European countries. For the East European countries, the Soviet economic model was and remains the example to be followed. In its totality it embraces investments, production, distribution and foreign trade. With such an economic conception, only the central authorities have the right to represent the interests of society. Thus COMECON is based solely on the will of the member states, which represent particular national interests. Their commercial interests are identical with their political interests.

In Western Europe, Common Market law forms the economic and legal nucleus; in Eastern Europe this role belongs to the planned economy. The Western integration model was rooted in a supranational organisation; COMECON, on the other hand, depends on the ability of its member states to engage in international integration. Both models are a direct consequence of the differing constitutional principles of their member states. Whereas the European Community adheres in principle to the postulates of the constitutional state by dividing up the powers of government into legislature, executive and judiciary, COMECON is based on the unitary principle of government. In addition, the state is not only the owner of the means of production, but also the planning agent. The economic activity of a COMECON state forms the basis of its sovereignty. The Charter only defines the limits of economic integration in a negative way. Socialist integration on the other hand is not bound up with the creation of supranational agencies; it does not impinge upon the internal authority of the member countries in questions of planning. COMECON therefore has no effect on the national sovereignty of the member countries.

Thus whilst the countries of the European Community have partly relinquished their sovereignty, developments in Eastern Europe have gone in the other direction. In the course of inter-state involvement, the states have acquired increasingly more powers for themselves, and their planning autonomy has become increasingly more complete. The member states are intent on accentuating their national interests, and this gives rise to a contradiction. According to COMECON law, direct dealings between authorities and undertakings across national frontiers are to be encouraged in future, i.e. they are to be deconcentrated. But this development presupposes that the undertakings will gain a greater degree of self-sufficiency.

The formal structure of the European Community appears in part to be that of a federation of states, with its institutions of Parliament, Council, Commission and Court. A consideration of the functions of these organs, however, produces a different picture. It is not Parliament but the Council that primarily decides how the treaties are to be put into effect. The representatives in the Council, who are bound by the instructions of their governments, assert national interests. Whilst the Council is an organ of the Community, it can also serve, in accordance with international law, as a conference of the governments that are party to the Treaty. It co-ordinates the economic policies of the member states. The position of the Commission also deviates from the pattern of international organisations and federal states. Together with the Council, it is designed as the executive organ of the Community. But it is only accorded the right to administer and execute policies in specific areas, whilst it also possesses legislative powers. The members of the Commission are totally independent of their governments. It is the Court that evinces the clearest features of a federal structure. Although it does not function as a court of appeal to which the judgments of national courts are referred, it does possess comprehensive and sole powers to interpret and apply the treaties. It is considered by many to be the motor of integration.

In COMECON the goal of integration is to be achieved with the help of treaties in accordance with international law. In keeping with its weak organisational structure, the lines between federal and unitary interests are not very clearly delineated. There is the highest organ, the Council, then the Executive Board, the Standing Commissions and the Secretariat. There is no Parliament or Court. The Standing Commissions are not comparable with the Commission of the EEC. They are technical work-groups. Both in the Council and the Executive Board, the representatives of the national governments are not independent. These bodies are community organs, but the process of decision-making takes place in accordance with international law. They can thus also be termed government conferences.

Relations Between COMECON and the EEC

It was in the summer of 1962 that the Soviet Union first raised the question of a trade agreement between COMECON and the EEC. This was received very coolly in Brussels. It was not until ten years later, on 20 March 1972, that Brezhnev made the first overtures to the EEC in a speech to the XV Congress of Soviet Trade Unions in Moscow. He remarked:

> The Soviet Union is in no way ignorant of the current situation in Western Europe, including the existence of an economic grouping of capitalist countries known as the Common Market. We are following its activities and development most closely. Our relations with the members of this group will understandably depend on the degree to which they, for their part, are prepared to accept the realities which have arisen in the socialist part of Europe, including the interests of the COMECON countries. We are in favour of equality in economic relations and against discrimination.

The Soviet party leader spoke here of the 'de facto situation' and of the 'recognition of realities', phrases that were inserted deliberately in the wording of Bonn's *Ostverträge* (Eastern Treaties) of 1970. The relations between COMECON and the EEC are also part of the overall political discussions about a *modus vivendi* in Europe. Brezhnev went a step further when he spoke about European security at the Central Committee of the Supreme Soviet on 12 December 1972:

> In our opinion, the time has come for a programme of European economic and cultural co-operation to be drawn up. This raises the question: 'Can a basis be found for any realistic ties between the inter-state economic and trading organisations which exist in Europe, between COMECON and the Common Market?' Probably, yes, if the EEC countries refrain from all attempts to discriminate against the other side and if they contribute to the development of bilateral connections and co-operation in the whole of Europe.

Following the conclusion of the Conference on Security and Cooperation in Europe on 1 August 1975 in Helsinki, COMECON prepared to make a counter-move. The decisive step was taken by the COMECON headquarters in Moscow when, on 16 February 1976, it instructed the Chairman of the Executive Board of COMECON to hand over to the President of the EEC Council of Ministers a note together with the draft of a treaty between the two organisations. This draft, which was in Russian, was to be treated confidentially and was not to be published. The timing of this initiative was chosen so as to allow Brezhnev to comment on it in public immediately afterwards at the XXV Congress of the Soviet Communist Party:

> Our foreign trade is co-ordinated with our fraternal states. In keeping with the spirit of the final act of the Conference on European Security and Cooperation, the Council for Mutual Economic Assistance has, on behalf of the governments of the COMECON countries, extended an offer to the European Economic Community to establish official relations. The EEC Council of Ministers has been handed the draft of a treaty concerning the basis of such relations which provides for the creation of favourable conditions to establish co-operation between the two organisations and their member countries. We are willing to go ahead with this.

There are many difficult problems lurking in the background concerning the establishment of official relations between the EEC and COMECON. On 25 April 1976, Radio Moscow addressed itself to one of the most tricky problems, namely the German question and the status of Berlin:

> As is well-known, the final goal of the European Community is the political integration of all its members. If West Berlin were to participate in such integration, it would be drawn via the European Community into the political system of the Federal Republic. It is clear that this would completely undermine the present status of Berlin as laid down in the Four-Power Agreement of 3 September 1971 . . .

The West Germans indicated to the EEC that as long as the position of inter-German trade in relation to EEC-COMECON trade was not clarified, the

Federal Republic would not commit itself. The outline draft treaty was also criticised for being a hybrid treaty, since it contained provisions both for agreements between the two organisations as such and for agreements with individual EEC countries. This, however, would constitute a retrograde step in view of the degree of integration already achieved in Western Europe. The EEC was of the opinion that, in this way, COMECON would obtain all the demands that the Eastern bloc countries had unsuccessfully made at Helsinki. The draft treaty contains the following provisions: the application of the most-favoured nation principle; the prohibition of all forms of discrimination such as are employed against third-party countries; the renunciation of unilateral actions in the case of market disturbances; the elimination of EEC agricultural restrictions. In addition, the EEC should grant general customs preferences to the COMECON countries. The EEC replied that the question of customs tariffs played an insignificant role in trading nations that are state controlled.

In the middle of November 1976, the President of the EEC Council of Ministers handed over a reply from the Brussels headquarters to the Chairman of the Executive Board of COMECON. Whilst, in this reply, contacts were not broken off, on account of the forthcoming review conference in Belgrade in the summer of 1977, the EEC confined itself for the time being to matters concerning working relations and technical problems regarding mutual relations (information, conservation, reciprocal visits, etc.). In the EEC special stress is placed on the inadequate definition of the legal status of COMECON. In Western eyes, COMECON lacks the ability to act as an agent under international law. In particular, it lacks the power to make agreements to establish common trading policies, which according to Article 113 of the Treaty of Rome the EEC is empowered to do. COMECON has no will of its own. However, it was not legal but political arguments — notably over the application of the treaty to West Berlin — that were mainly responsible for the negative answer from Brussels to the COMECON initiative of February 1976.

Nevertheless, the Soviet Union continues to strive to improve its bargaining position vis à vis the EEC. The new version of the COMECON Charter of 21 June 1974 also serves this purpose. COMECON is empowered to make treaties with states and international organisations; but to do this, the General Secretary still requires a special mandate from the COMECON countries. The reference made in the Comprehensive Programme of 1971 to the military importance of integration may also be regarded as an attempt on the part of the USSR to get on equal terms with or even surpass the EEC. Socialist integration is meant to bring about 'a strengthening of the ability of the member countries to defend themselves'. This official pronouncement of a tie-up with the Warsaw Pact is entirely new.

It is unlikely that rapid progress will be made in promoting links between

COMECON and the EEC. There are too many political and economic problems to be solved. The objection of the EEC that the structure of the two organisations is too disparate is undoubtedly based on the realisation that the two superpowers occupy entirely different positions in the two organisations. The EEC would conclude a treaty with a group dominated by the USSR, whilst the USA would remain outside the EEC.

NOTES AND REFERENCES

1. On the development of COMECON in the 1960s, see the study by the Soviet specialist E.T. Usenko, *Sozialistische internationale Arbeitsteilung und ihre rechtliche Regelung*, East Berlin, 1966, pp. 26-37.
2. Cf. P. Knirsch, 'Bemühungen um eine Wirtschaftsintegration', *Europa Archiv*, no. 1/1972, pp. 21-32. See, in particular, the book by the Director of the International Institute for Economic Problems of the Socialist System, M.W. Senin, *Sozialistische Integration*, East Berlin, Dietz-Verlag, 1972.
3. Cf. A. Uschakow, *Der Ostmarkt im COMECON*, Baden-Baden, Nomos Verlagsgesellschaft, 1972, p. 15.
4. See the work by the Secretary of COMECON, N.V. Faddeev, *Sovet Ekonomicheskoi Vzaimopomoshchi* (The Council for Mutual Economic Assistance), Moscow, Izdatel'stvo 'Ekonomika', 1974, p. 34.
5. For text, see A. Uschakow, *Der Rat für Gegenseitige Wirtschaftshilfe (COMECON)*, Cologne, Verlag Wissenschaft und Politik, 1962, p. 86.
6. For the English text, see *Soviet and East European Foreign Trade*, 1972, pp. 187-305.
7. German translation in A. Uschakow, *Europa Archiv*, no. 11, 1975, pp. D 281-92.

SELECT BIBLIOGRAPHY

Agoston, I., *Le Marché Commun communiste. Principes et pratique du COMECON*, Geneva, Droz, 1964.
Amerongen, Otto Wolff v. (ed.), *Rechtsfragen der Integration und Kooperation in Ost und West*, Berlin, Duncker & Humblot, 1976.
Kaser, M., *COMECON. Integration Problems of Planned Economies*, 2nd ed., Oxford, Oxford University Press, 1967.
Lavigne, M., *Le programme du COMECON et l'intégration socialiste*, Paris, Editions Cujas, 1973.
Lebahn, A., *Sozialistische Wirtschaftsintegration und Ost—West—Handel im sowjetischen internationalen Recht*, Berlin, Duncker & Humblot, 1976.
Schulz, E., *Moskau und die europäische Integration*, München-Wien, R. Oldenbourg Verlag, 1975.
Seiffert, W. (ed.), *Das System rechtlicher Regelung der sozialistischen ökonomischen Integration*, East Berlin, Staatsuerlag der DDR, 1976.
Szawlowski, R., *The System of the International Organizations of the Communist Countries*, Leyden, A.W. Sijthoff, 1976.
Uschakow, A., *Der Ostmarkt im COMECON*, Baden-Baden, Nomos, 1972.
Usenko, E.T. (ed.), *Sovet Ekonomicheskoi Vzaimopomoshchi* (The Council for Mutual Economic Assistance), Moscow, Izdatel'stvo "Nauka", 1975.

CHAPTER 12

The Multinational Enterprise: A 1977 Perspective

Roger Williams

It fiddles its accounts. It avoids or evades its taxes. It rigs its intra-company transfer prices. It is run by foreigners, from decision centres thousands of miles away. It imports foreign labour practices. It doesn't import foreign labour practices. It overpays. It underpays. It competes unfairly with local firms. It exports jobs from rich countries. It is an instrument of rich countries' imperialism. The technologies it brings to the third world are old-fashioned. No, they are too modern. It meddles. It bribes. It overturns economic policies. It plays off governments against each other to get the biggest investment incentives. Won't it please come and invest? Let it bloody well go home.
[The Economist, *24 January 1976*]

Multinational enterprises (MNEs) are the very essence of the age. Made organisationally possible by the modern technologies of computation, communication and transportation, they have come to seem commercially inevitable in the context of highly interdependent, growth-oriented economies. Even superficial investigation convinces one that they deserve to be taken seriously, though not, as they so often have been, hysterically. It is a distortion to speak of them as 'states within (or between) states', and though they are by no means neutral servants of the current economic order, neither, at least as yet, are they unchallengably its masters. Kindleberger's view that the nation-state is 'just about through' as an economic entity remains an extreme assessment.[1] It is, unfortunately, part of the problem they pose that many of their activities are extremely difficult to document and research. A further complication is that they are not a problem apart. Thus, for example, to the European mind the American MNE is symbolic of the larger 'American Challenge', whereas to a third world country all MNEs are ultimately agents of neo-colonialism. From the Marxist viewpoint, the MNE phenomenon is part of a larger international imperialism embracing all other capital flows as well, and indeed international economic activity quite generally. These issues clearly transcend the question of the MNE itself. There are also many other still more general topics, the overall control of technology, for instance, or the special political economy of South Africa, on which the phenomenon of the MNE has a significant impact.

There is an initial difficulty with the multinational concept that is substantive as well as semantic. Several qualifying adjectives and several different nouns are in common use: multinational/transnational/international — company/corporation/enterprise/firm. These can have meanings that differ in important respects. This paper employs the term multinational enterprise (MNE) as being the most useful, essentially because most general, for its purpose. An MNE is, then, any commercial undertaking with a headquarters in one country and at least one subsidiary in a different country. Narrower definitions are, of course, necessary for specific regulatory purposes. All such multinational enterprises are in any case to be distinguished from more traditional import/export organisations, and from simple types of overseas licensing arrangements.

The MNE can be regarded as a dynamic compendium of specialised knowledge. The part of this knowledge more or less common to all MNEs centres on the mechanisms of international commerce and is concerned with how to organise, finance, produce (in the sense of manufacture, provide or extract) and market. In addition to this there is a conceptual core, of variable size, comprising specialised technical know-how, and this is commonly backed by a research and development capability.

It is when one thinks of an MNE in these terms that one realises why nationalisation of MNE assets is so often an irrelevance, even in those cases where it is politically and legally feasible. Certainly assets can be nationalised, but knowledge cannot. Nor is there even much point in nationalising assets if the MNE can easily compensate by substitution elsewhere for those nationalised.

MNEs are hardly new, certainly not in the resource industries. What is striking is their postwar expansion in the manufacturing sector. In 1971, excluding the socialist economies, the aggregate value added of MNE activity, at approximately 500 billion dollars, was some 20 per cent of the world GNP.[2] Three quarters of this MNE activity is in the developed economies, but it looms larger in the less developed countries, since they have only about a sixth of the world's GNP. It must be noted that MNEs are also now to be found in the service industries. Furthermore, a capability in advanced technology is not now a necessary identifying qualification. It should also be appreciated that from the point of view of political analysis the three categories of MNE (extraction, manufacturing, service-operations) need to be treated somewhat differently. An MNE in an extraction industry is obviously more limited in its freedom of deployment than one in the manufacturing category. In particular, because the former may be 'no match for the sovereignty of the nation state',[3] which in this case *may* be able to use nationalisation as an effective weapon, it does not necessarily follow that the latter cannot be either. It has been fairly said that 'In one sense, the emergence of the multinational corporation reflects a differential pace in the evolution of political institutions relative to business organisations',[4] the implication for other authors being that political structures will have to adapt to the economic realities of technological change if they are to remain functional.[5]

What then are the practical problems posed by the MNEs? Everything one has read and everything one could write has probably been true of some multinational enterprise, somewhere, at some time. The OECD code of practice for multinationals, drawn up in the mid-1970s, in that it sets out what MNEs should and should not do may be taken as an indicative guide to what at least some of them do, have done, or are thought capable of doing.[6]

The guide-lines in this code fall under seven headings. The first of these is a catch-all: MNEs should behave as good corporate citizens wherever they operate, complying fully with all relevant government policies, allowing subsidiaries as much freedom as possible, and avoiding improper political involvement. Second, they should publish as much information as possible about their activities, and third, they should never act so as to reduce competition. The fourth and fifth headings cover financial matters: MNEs should pay due regard to the balance of payments and credit policies of affected governments, and they should adopt an honest position on taxation, avoiding unfair transfer-pricing and other dubious financial manipulations. The sixth heading is concerned with labour and industrial practices: MNEs should respect union activity, aim to improve the local labour force, consult adequately, avoid threats and generally negotiate in good faith. Finally, MNEs are urged to assist the local capacity to innovate in countries where they operate, simultaneously facilitating the diffusion of technology.

Very broadly, the main problems may be said to centre on control in relation to ownership, balance of payments issues, employment and labour practices, transfer prices and taxation, consequences for the performance of research and development and the diffusion of technology, and effect on competition. And because governments cannot control what they do not understand, disclosure of timely, relevant and adequate information is basic to all these problems.

Implicitly at least, the existence of these OECD guidelines signifies an acceptance that MNEs constitute a potential political threat. But it is well to recognise that these bodies have their defence counsel and a number of arguments have been put in their favour. Perhaps chief among these is the view that MNEs are more in tune with the contemporary reality of world politics than either national governments or national corporations. Those who hold this belief may see the MNE as simply more efficient generally than traditional organisational forms, or they may claim specifically that it is a more effective instrument of technological innovation and world development than any alternative. They may justify the political involvement of MNEs by asserting that they encourage political responsibility and stability, and excuse those of the MNEs' shortcomings that cannot be explained away by suggesting that MNEs are even now relatively new economic forms still developing their socio-political sensitivity. Such positive defence of the MNE apart, there are many detailed refutations of most of the specific charges that have been made against MNEs. Indeed, there is an enormous economic and managerial literature on the MNEs that scarcely manages to acknowledge that these bodies have had an unusually bad political press. Nevertheless, on whichever side of the argument one comes down, there can be no denying that MNEs generally, even the best-behaved of them, are an easy target for frustration and a powerful catalyst of nationalism.

It is certainly important to realise that many of the complaints levelled against multinationals arise from a more general fear of corporate power. A little reflection shows that many charges, if they can be made to stick against multinationals, can be made to stick just as well against the larger national corporations. It must also be remembered that by no means all MNEs are corporate giants. There are probably upwards of 10,000 MNEs, upwards of 100,000 subsidiaries, but political concern centres on only a few hundred of these, mostly those whose turnover is greater than or comparable with states the size of, say, Belgium. The real point is that the relationship between government and big, and especially technologically advanced, companies is too often long on dependence and short on accountability. To recognise this is not necessarily to believe uncritically in what Galbraith has called the 'technological imperatives'. No doubt the imperatives he has identified have their place, but so perhaps do other factors. In particular, there is the general background pressure of public opinion, less formally 'imperative' but just as likely to lead indirectly to the increasing concentration of industrial power that has become such a dominant referent of the 'new industrial states'. In any case, we have become schooled to accept that oligopoly, accompanied very often by state-company symbiosis, is not only compatible with competition, efficiency and a measure of social responsibility, but may even be, in certain fields, the single arrangement that can preserve these virtues. Yet if one does accept this, it is probably with reservations. What more natural then that the MNE, conceived as an alien epitome of corporate power, should become the focus for transferred suspicions, both soundly based and specious.

If we are able to understand the challenges and the opportunities that the MNEs present, we must have a clear idea of the main elements in the system of which they are part, and also of the potential relationships between these elements. There are four types of main element: the MNE's HQ and its subsidiaries, the responsible authorities, the base and host governments. Beyond these is a large supporting cast of national and international interests. But it is with the four prime elements that one must begin.

In some analyses only three elements are recognised and an identity of interest, perception and action is assumed as between the MNE HQ and its subsidiaries. There are occasions when this proves an adequate simplification, but there are also others when it can lead to error. A second common fallacy is to suppose that every action by a business organisation is consistent, calculated and clever. It is salutary to observe how often analysts who would not think to attribute more than approximate rationality to governments see behind every move of a multinational the machinations of a Machiavelli or a Metternich. Certainly the objectives of business organisations, including MNEs, are capable of being formulated more precisely than those of governments. But because they can be, it does not mean that they always are; or when they are, that the formulation is matched by execution.

In principle, governments have political, economic and social objectives, whereas MNEs have only economic ones. In practice, such companies also turn out to have political and social objectives, though these are normally adjuncts to their economic aims. It becomes therefore a matter of sorting out the various ways in which governments and MNEs can behave in their relationships with each other.

In the first place, the *base government* will wish to regulate the activities of the MNE just as it does the activities of purely domestic corporations. It is immediately apparent that control in this case cannot be as complete, and that base as well as host governments are therefore deserving of some sympathy. On the other hand, base governments can also attempt to use MNEs as vehicles of foreign policy. Since it was as a rule not designed for this purpose, the exact utility of a particular MNE will naturally depend critically on the context and on the actual individuals, officials and company personnel involved. Some obvious questions arise. Is it a pliant or an unwilling instrument? What are the consequences for its own, to it presumably paramount, economic goals? A third dimension of base government involvement can result from concern that MNE subsidiaries should act as good corporate citizens sensitive to local political and social circumstances, at the least refraining from damaging the image and foreign policy objectives of the base government. This dimension of base government interest seems to be missing more often than one would expect.

The most fundamental aim of the *MNE HQ* is the successful orchestration of what may be a far-flung international empire. The HQ organisation is subject to three relatively distinct pressures: it needs to demonstrate that it is a responsible entity in its own domestic environment; it is the focus for the reactions and demands of its subsidiaries; and it must strive for a global economic efficiency. Its perspective is essentially economic but, in its own right, it cannot afford to ignore political developments, both at home and abroad, that might threaten that perspective. It can indeed easily become a directly political actor. Some MNEs appear more reluctant than others to accept this role, but probably none fails to recognise that the requirement can arise. What MNEs often do fail to recognise is that their very existence, and even the most innocuous of their managerial practices, can constitute important, if subtle, social forces. They are, in fact, capable of changing the political balance indirectly and gradually as well as directly and dramatically. Despite the well-known *causes célèbres,* it would hardly be surprising, in the long term, if this were to prove their major international effect.

As a political actor on its own behalf the MNE is, if anything, at an even greater disadvantage than when it acts as an agent of government. If it conducts its affairs openly it will not be believed when it claims sometimes to be furthering more noble ends than its own. And if it proceeds in a undercover fashion, only one hint need emerge — and often not even that — for the worst to be suspected. Nevertheless, MNEs have a wide range of techniques, and normally quite sufficient resources, available. Furthermore, as Nye says, 'governments are sometimes alliances of competing bureaucracies pulling in different directions [so that] one can conceive of policy coalitions composed of parts of different governments and corporations'.[7]

When one turns to *host governments* one confronts an immediate and huge divide between the cases of the developed and the underdeveloped economies. Not all countries fit this dichotomy equally well so far as MNEs are concerned. One at least, Canada, fits it very badly, but the overall distinction remains a perfectly sound one. At its most basic, the relationship between the MNE and the host government is a trade-off between efficiency and equity and between effectiveness and accountability. We may say quite generally that very many developing countries lack the economic flexibility, the bureaucratic competence and the legal discipline adequately to address these issues. Not all developed economies by any means can be given a clean bill of health under each of these three headings. Some economies are weaker and some bureaucracies less technocratic than others. Ethical standards can vary very widely. Nevertheless, it is the developing countries that one expects to be deficient in respect of one or more of these three parameters. Political shortcomings in these countries, if they do not discourage the MNE in the first place, paradoxically may well subsequently strengthen its hand.

On the other hand, host governments and their policies, even in the developing countries, rarely provide a quiescent environment for the MNE.

It is indeed easy to underestimate the capability that many states, including some of the less developed ones, have developed to cope with and exploit their situation vis à vis these organisations. The literature on the MNE in the context of specific countries is now large, and Robock and Simmonds have provided an interesting conceptual framework for thinking about the risks that MNE subsidiaries may run.[8] As sources of risk these authors include competing political philosophies, general social unrest, the vested interest of local business groups, consequences of recent or impending independence, specific armed conflicts and new international alliances. As effects of risk, they identify confiscation, expropriation with compensation, a wide range of detailed operational restrictions, outright breaches or unilateral revisions of agreements, discrimination and physical intimidation or damage. These sources and effects are relevant both when the host is aiming at the MNE itself and when it is acting indirectly against the base government. Actions quite unrelated in any calculating sense to the presence of MNEs can also have a significant effect. One notes this framework — and there are many similar categorisations — only to redress a little the imbalance in the general appreciation of the state-MNE interaction. There is no wish to set aside the common understanding of imbalance in that interaction in the reverse direction. The MNE as hostage has become less uncommon than one might think, but this still tends to be noticed only when the safety of its individual servants is involved.

And so one comes to the *MNE's subsidiaries*. These are partly satellites and partly suns, and the mix can vary enormously as between MNEs, and even as between different subsidiaries of a particular MNE, though naturally this is less usual. Their thrust is economic, but to survive, and still more to thrive, they too in their own right must develop political antennae. It is here that the individual manager can come into his own. He must monitor two power balances, that within the host government and that within his own MNE. Bertin has made the point that the interests of the host/base government are likely to be ignored depending upon whether the subsidiary is closely supervised by or independent of its HQ.[9] Beyond this again, individuals within subsidiaries can evidently have their own special leverage and vulnerability.

The existence of MNEs has understandably stimulated the expression of countervailing private power. National trades unions have for the most part found themselves at a considerable disadvantage and they have therefore sought to evolve multinationally as well. As compared with MNEs, the resulting multinational trades union groupings have many weaknesses and, as yet, few strengths. Not the least of their problems is that, to use a military analogy, the MNE can fight on interior lines: it is compact and integrated as they are not. In addition, up to the present, MNEs have been able both to act and to react; multinational unions mostly only to react. As a third point, differences of culture, language and practices are far more constraining on a multinational union than they are on a multinational enterprise. Finally, the normal disparity in financial resources appears even more of a limitation when operations are spread over continents than when they are spread only over countries.

The United States is not the only industrial state to spawn MNEs, yet American MNEs are indubitably different, precisely because in the community of industrial states the place of the United States is different. Gilpin makes this point very forcefully: 'In conjunction with the international position of the dollar and with nuclear supremacy, the multinational corporation became one of the cornerstones of American hegemony. These three elements of American power interacted with and reinforced one another.'[10] Some in fact regard the very term 'multinational' as little more than an evasive euphemism for 'American national'. Gilpin identifies several particularly important political aspects of American MNEs, including their role in 'the creation of a liberal international economic and political order', in guaranteeing the West a 'secure supply of relatively cheap energy' to complete the circle of economic growth and interdependence, and in financing America's global hegemony by means of 'technological and monopolistic rents extracted from abroad'. They exercise, he says 'a strong influence over the locus of manufacturing . . . and . . . determine in large measure the distribution of gains in the world economy'. He sees US corporate expansionism as having been used rather than planned by American officials. He also argues that:

> In general . . . corporate interest and the 'national interest', as the latter has been defined by succeeding American administrations, have coincided. Corporate and political elites have shared the American vision of a liberal world economic order.

Despite this, Gilpin points out many instances in which the two interests have 'sharply diverged', and he says that in such cases 'the tendency has been for the larger interests of foreign policy to prevail'. His thesis, as he acknowledges, 'runs directly counter to both the prevailing liberal defence and the radical critique' of the MNEs. It is very relevant in this connection that European direct investment in the United States at the end of 1974 was only about a third that in the reverse direction (approximately 17 as compared with 44.5 billion dollars). US government agencies, specifically the Federal Trade Commission, have scarcely helped over the years to redress this imbalance.

Certainly as regards the 'high' technology industries, the international relationship of greatest interest continues to be that between the United States and Western Europe. Here the three 'highest' technology industries, computers, nuclear energy and aerospace, while having much in common, are also distinctly different with respect to their susceptibility to American advances. The case of computers, with the worldwide strength of IBM, comes closest to the multinational behemoth/juggernaut scenario, while aerospace, though still American dominated, has been furthest away. In aerospace, straight purchase, especially by governments and national airlines, has been the characteristic business mode, though sometimes with European engines or avionics being fitted. Commercially, the products of Boeing and McDonnel Douglas, and latterly of Lockheed, mostly powered by the engines of General Electric or Pratt and Whitney, have achieved decisive positions, but with Britain and France retaining important independent capabilities in the airframe sector, and Britain also in aeroengines. The same two countries have similarly prevented the United States from sweeping the board in the military field. In the military case there has also been considerable production under US licence in Europe.

The nuclear industry seems to belong in an intermediate category. Britain has to date retained a wholly independent technological capability, but in reactor development both West Germany (early) and France (late) opted for American reactors under licence, both going on to establish their own technological competence, largely on the basis provided by their licences. Elsewhere in Europe, American reactors have also, like aircraft, been sold in a more straightforward way.

In a discussion embracing multinationals, Europe and advanced technology, there are in fact some important and intriguing conclusions that one can draw. First, on the evidence (and there is plenty of it) it is categorically not technological inadequacy that Europe has to fear. When the European nations want to, which above all means when they are prepared to spend enough, they can usually match and occasionally even surpass the American best. Second, in the advanced technology sectors this is exactly what European governments have wanted, Britain first and largely by reflex, France second and more distinctly by policy, and West Germany third and perhaps partly by imitation. If the governments of these countries had not decided or been persuaded, whether from wisdom, folly or because they thought they had no choice, to continue in computers, nuclear energy and aerospace, then it would simply not have been possible for their national companies to sustain a vanguard capability in these fields. Yet despite these governmental commitments, each involving at different times a significant exchequer burden, a third observation that must be made is that the European governments concerned have made only piecemeal progress towards a rationalisation, still less integration, of their respective industries. There have been, and are, some major European co-operative projects in advanced technology, but a European industrial or technological policy is still absent.

Furthermore, it is reasonable to suggest that the calculus of costs and benefits in supporting particular high technology projects should in each

European country have been considered more determinedly and discussed much more publicly. All too often rational debate has had to be suspended, or has never even started, because national prestige, or national security, was held by key lobbies to be at stake. Several European countries have, as a result, had to learn the hard way that bad decisions and unwise projects can undermine rather than enhance national prestige.

With regard more generally to the future of MNEs in Europe, Schmitthoff's remarks deserve to be noted.[11] Schmitthoff distinguishes between national multinationals (Ford, ICI) and international multinationals (Unilever, VFW-Fokker), and he suggests that the trend in Europe is firmly towards an increase in the number of national multinationals rather than towards more cross-national mergers. He also feels that the utilisation of a European company form will not significantly change this state of affairs. This is in line with the long-standing preference registered by the various European governments for a 'national champion' whenever possible, especially as evidenced in their support for national-level take-overs, mergers and rationalisation. Schmitthoff thinks that MNEs will eventually come to occupy 'the same prominent position in business as does the joint stock company today', and he expects that relations between MNEs and European hosts will remain amicable out of mutual interest.

MNE penetration of the communist states has been very thoroughly documented by Wilczynski.[12] He finds that there has been an 'amazing reversal of attitudes' especially since 1970, MNEs as well as communist governments now believing that they stand to gain from the relationship. Of the 500 Western MNEs with 1973 sales in excess of 500 million dollars and five or more foreign subsidiaries, Wilczynski found that at least 140 had had 'significant dealings' with the socialist countries, more than a third of them with at least five such countries. Wilczynski ends his book with what he calls 'some intriguing paradoxes': similarities between MNEs and socialist states; strange partnerships between socialist states and pillars of the Western 'military industrial complex'; ironical alliances between Western MNEs and socialist partners, the former even sometimes preferring to do business in the socialist countries; socialist orders supporting MNE shares; MNEs competing to sell to socialist countries, then being confronted with competition from socialist countries in the West; mutual favoured treatment as regards interest rates and the like; damaging effects on Western employment and trade unions; co-operation with Western cartels; and socialist investment in capitalist countries. Wilczynski quotes with approval Perlmutter's[13] theory of trans-ideological collaboration, namely that technological revolution will so transform the industrial world that neither 'submergence', 'divergence' nor 'convergence' will be adequate to describe the new social order of new/super/post industrialism, though he recognises that the socialist regimes, at least formally, continue to believe in the struggle between communism and capitalism.

Technology transfer to the communist countries remains an especially sensitive subject, but, quite generally, the performance of research and the transfer of technology by MNEs do, it is apparent, present fundamental problems. The less developed countries for example spend perhaps 4 billion dollars each year on technology transfer, around twice what they spend on arms imports. In recent years they have made very plain their dissatisfaction with the amount of technology that is transferred to them, with the nature of much of it, with the costs to themselves and with the conditions under which it is made available. Technology transfer is clearly highly complex; all four of these criteria are obviously important, and generalisation in respect of each of them is evidently dangerous. Nevertheless, one point demands to be made in regard to the one factor that is usually most under the control of the recipient government, the nature of the technology. As a general rule, it may be said that governments want only the best, by which they mean the most modern/advanced technology. This is usually more capital intensive than older, though not necessarily old, alternatives. A more enlightened view would sometimes lead them to settle for the older options, which are usually cheaper. More labour-intensive technologies could even be defended as being to the long-term advantage of the multinationals themselves, since they must have an interest in political stability and in economic development, and it is hard to see how unemployment, part caused and part correctable by appropriate international technology transfers, can be other than politically destabilising.[14] MNEs in this regard and in others, like all organisations and individuals, are sometimes quite capable of being their own worst enemies.

The issue of technology transfer is an especially sensitive one for developing countries but it may have more political relevance to transfer between developed states than it is given credit for, and not only because of the high level of unemployment that so many of these states currently have. In any case, the location of the multinationals' research certainly is a problem for both developed and developing countries, though for rather different reasons. Sir Michael Clapham, in an intelligent apologia for MNEs, underlines this point where the MNE is pursuing what he calls an 'extreme strategy'.[15] This is a strategy that 'allows subsidiaries no research potential and therefore deprives the host country of the very ability to produce technology and develop technical staff which is a multinational's greatest value to it. It perpetuates the division of the world into nobles and peasants. ...' The essence of the problem is the ownership of, and tax revenue on, research results, the latter making it in Sir Michael's view 'not a conflict between multinational and native state, but rather a conflict between nation states catalysed by a multinational'. Sir Michael, however, also notes that 'alarm bells rang at a time when IBM, a company with a particularly enlightened policy of multinational research and development, and probably because of that, seemed likely by sheer superiority of technology to be left without serious competitors in a field of enormous economic importance'. The point would seem to be that the concentration of research in a country, and even more in a single firm, is threatening. Some devices are available to attack this problem, and example has shown that others can on occasion be devised, as need arises. The issue is still far from a light one, nor is it clear that a plateau of research concentration will eventually be reached in respect of any given MNE.

There is one unhappy fact of international political and commercial life, which multinationals certainly did not create but which they have equally certainly significantly worsened: corruption. Unethical practices such as bribery, industrial espionage, receipt of improper information, arrangements that restrict competition, and so on, because of the motivation behind them and because they are mostly difficult to police, will never be eradicated. We have learned since the 1976 Lockheed affair, if we believed differently before, that bribery in particular is a serious problem for developed as well as for developing countries. We can be confident as well that this same case sensitised those whose responsibility it is to monitor such things. And we may expect that it caused those who actually do them to proceed with more circumspection. With regard to many unethical practices, boards as well as governments have an interest in at least limiting the worst excesses, if only because they can be expensive, uncertain and self-corrupting. This interest was borne out, for example, in the draft code worked out in 1977 by a commission of the International Chamber of Commerce. The more cynical would, of course, say that this itself was only an attempt to prevent, delay or pre-empt governmental action.[16] But while no ethical transformation should be expected from a voluntary commercial code of this kind, neither should inter-governmental agreement be thought likely, or if likely, enforceable.

There are, in theory, several different methods through which MNEs can be regulated: unilateral action by governments, bilateral initiatives between governments or between MNEs and governments, multilateral agreements between governments, usually on a regional basis, and thoroughgoing international action.[17] Again in theory, there are a number of possible bases of enforcement authority: international law, community law as in the EEC, national law and conventions and codes of practice. As things stand, the regulatory methods constitute an untidy and uncertain framework and the strength of the enforcement authority cannot always be relied upon to be appropriate to the need. Much international economic activity is already subject to international or supranational regulation, via the International Monetary Fund, the General Agreement on Tariffs and Trade, and bodies such as the International Civil Aviation Organisation or International Telecommunication Union. With the 'eruption into the public consciousness' of the MNE phenomenon, these earlier arrangements seemed to many inadequate, and a multiplicity of proposals have since been made; 'possibly the most profound difficulty' with all of them, it has been said, being the need to combine a political (and symbolic) approach with a technical (and substantive) one.[18] In particular, in recent years the UN has sponsored a report by a Group of Eminent Persons, has established a Commission on Transnational Corporations, and has been working towards a code of behaviour for MNEs as an interim step towards a new international legal order for them. The OECD has, meanwhile, produced the set of guide-lines referred to earlier, as a follow-on to its Codes on the Liberalisation of Capital Movements and of Current Invisible Operations. Other international bodies have also been active in this field, e.g. the Organisation of American States, International Labour Organisation and International Chamber of Commerce.

Just as the substance of the OECD code is a useful introduction to the challenge posed by MNEs, so also is the context in which it was drawn up a good measure of the inherent regulatory problems involved. The main points to be noted in this regard are: first, that the conventional wisdom dictated by the mid-1970s that something along these lines be produced; second, that this was a code and not in any sense a law; third, that it was directed only at operations within OECD countries; and fourth, that the toughness of earlier drafts was progressively reduced under pressure from the multinationals. Naturally, there could be no enforcement machinery for this code, but an inter-governmental committee of review was established. This was to be allowed to take evidence from companies and unions, but at the outset a specific criticism made of the arrangement was that it was not formally tripartite. Despite the intrinsic weaknesses in the code, there was some evidence by mid-1977 that it could provide a degree of leverage to determined unions, at least when these were backed by governments.[19]

One is so used to thinking of the regulation of MNEs in terms of economics and politics that one can easily overlook the quite separate problems of technological regulation. Essentially there are three such problems, relating respectively to occupational health and safety, environmental impact and product safety. The hard fact is that comparative national standards and practices in respect of all three differ, often by orders of magnitude. This being so, the MNE has a temptation to locate its most polluting and hazardous activities where standards are lowest. Unhappily, poorer countries can even be found advertising, in the columns of national newspapers for instance, their relaxed attitudes towards technological regulation. Relocation abroad of the most environmentally damaging activities has also been something of a Japanese national policy in recent years. As regards the occupational context, conditions in the asbestos mines of South Africa, to take the obvious example, have long been a devastating indictment of multinational commercial activity. The accidents in recent years at

Flixborough in England and Seveso in Italy, both involving multinational enterprises, only underline the fact that it is often a very thin line that separates the occupational and general environments.

Technological regulation is likely long to remain the poor relation; after all, even in developed economies, unions have shown themselves more concerned about employment and remuneration than about such issues. Third world countries can hardly be expected to be different. When we add that technological regulation calls for its own brand of expertise, we only underline the weakness of these countries. Cases involving product safety, the third category mentioned above, though probably rarer, also occur, as for instance in the test marketing of new drugs in third world countries.

That MNEs represent a significant challenge to the sovereignty of all nation-states can scarcely be doubted, especially if these challenges are defined, as they must be, to include gradual socio-economic evolution as well as more immediate confrontations on political objectives. It is in respect of socio-economic evolution that MNEs are most relevant to the theme of this book. The values, expectations and practices that attach to MNE activity are of fundamental and growing importance in shaping the societies over which governments preside. It is because of this above all that the MNE is such a potent instrument of socio-economic change. The resulting flux in society, even those aspects of it unintended by MNEs and unrecognised by analysts, must eventually find reflection in the character and response of the state. We can think of the MNE as having managed to establish itself 'between' society and state in a deeper sense than purely national corporations could ever do, even when state-owned, precisely because it can legitimately claim to be 'outside' both state and society. The fact is that MNEs just are large vessels, and they needs must leave large wakes. It may be argued that governments, or at least the strongest of them, have always possessed, and may always possess, in their own right, all the powers they needed to assert their authority. It remains the case that in the last three decades governments have seen irresistible advantages in an economic interdependence that has led to the apotheosis of the multinational. Those advantages have lain in the contribution of the postwar economic order to those traditional twin concerns of the nation-state, national security and national prosperity. But this economic order was itself independent upon the new political order ushered in by the Second World War, and the latter has for some time shown signs of potential change. The relative decline of the United States and the rise of Western Europe and Japan, the coming end of simple military bipolarity, oil power and the crises attaching to unemployment, recession and inflation: these seem more than mere transient fluctuations and adjustments. They could nevertheless prove misleading indications. In particular, it is all too easy to underestimate the resilience of the United States. Such indeed has been the inherent stability and performance of the postwar order that one easily finds oneself believing that it will survive indefinitely, at any rate in its main features. If it does, one must expect that the governments of nation-states will continue to see advantage in encouraging multinational industry, doubtless with some of the trappings of improved administrative regulation. Unfortunately, where MNEs and states are concerned, only in theory is it easy to distinguish between a parasitic and a symbiotic relationship. Failure to so distinguish will not necessarily mean selling yet more sovereignty for only a mess of potage, but it will mean forfeiting, to a greater extent than nation-states already have, more of the true kernel of that sovereignty, the right to full national self-determination and the right to set the objects and the myths by which men live. Wider equity participation, advocated as a means of avoiding polarised conflict between MNEs and governments,[20] even if successful in that limited objective, would still continue the underlying trend. If this should be the shape of the future, then the world will presumably become still more of a global village, though with the rich and their tertiary industries continuing to live at one end, and the poor with their primary and secondary industries at the other. It is, however, not self-evident that a world economy, increasingly dominated by MNEs, is the best antidote to strident nationalism. Nor is there any solid reason to suppose that MNEs can ultimately succeed where nation-states have largely failed in establishing dynamic global co-operation. The interest that they represent, however they present it, is in the end inferior to the resultant sum of national interests.

If the existing order should not persist and prediction becomes difficult, this is mainly because there appear then to be a variety of different routes forward. One disturbingly unpredictable possibility would entail a retreat at least to such defensive nationalism as the security situation permitted, and perhaps, by miscalculation, even beyond this point. There are also a number of other scenarios that would involve some re-assertion of political over economic values. Some alternatives could actually be distinctly attractive if, as they might, they led to a new emphasis on the quality rather than the quantity of life, and to a genuine redistribution of economic power internationally. Virtually all possibilities amount more to revolution than to evolution and, like all prospective revolutions, must be judged uncertain in their potential consequences. In any case, MNEs in some form would surely persist, for their strengths lie somewhat deeper than a simple congruence with the existing economic order, even if it was that order that originally nurtured them.

NOTES AND REFERENCES
1. C. P. Kindleberger, *American Business Abroad,* New Haven, Conn., Yale University Press, 1969, p. 207.
2. As a general source, see *Multinational Corporations in World Development* (ST/ECA/190), United Nations, 1973 (UN Dept. of Economic and Social Affairs).
3. Geoffrey Chandler, 'The Myth of Oil Power: International Groups and National Sovereignty', *International Affairs,* London, vol. 46, October 1970, pp. 710-18.
4. Stefan H. Robock and Kenneth Simmonds, *International Business and Multinational Enterprise,* London, Irwin-Dorsey International, 1973.
5. Sidney E. Rolfe, 'The International Corporation in Perspective', *The Atlantic Community Quarterly,* vol. 7, Summer 1969, pp. 255-70; also Sidney E. Rolfe and Walter Damm, *The Multinational Corporation in the World Economy,* New York, Praeger, 1970.
6. OECD, *International Investment and Multinational Enterprises,* Paris, 1976.
7. Joseph S. Nye, Jr, 'Multinational Corporations in World Politics', *Foreign Affairs,* vol. 53, October 1974, pp. 153-75.
8. Robock and Simmonds, *op. cit.,* p. 358.
9. Gilles Bertin, 'Les enterprises multinationales et les états nationaux ... zones de tension et recherche de solutions', *Analyse & Prevision,* vol. 10, November 1976, pp. 669-74.
10. R. Gilpin, *US Power and the Multinational Corporation: The Political Economy of Foreign Direct Investment,* London, Macmillan, 1975, Chapter 6.
11. C. M. Schmitthoff, 'The Multinational Enterprise in the United Kingdom' in H. R. Hahlo, J. G. Smith and R. W. Wright (eds), *Nationalism and the Multinational Enterprise,* Leyden, A. W. Sijthoff, 1973, Chapter 2.
12. J. Wilczynski, *The Multinationals and East-West Relations,* London, Macmillan, 1976.
13. H. V. Perlmutter, 'Emerging East-West Ventures: The Transideological Enterprise', *Columbia Journal of World Business,* September-October 1969, pp. 39-50.
14. Douglas Hellinger, *Unemployment and the Multinationals: A Strategy for Technological Changes in Latin America,* Port Washington, New York, Kennitate Press, 1976.
15. Michael Clapham, *Multinational Enterprises and Nation States,* London, Athlone Press, University of London, 1975 (The Stamp Memorial Lecture, 1974).
16. *Economist,* 19 March, 1977, pp. 88-9.
17. *Economist,* 28 May, 1977, p. 18.
18. Don J. Wallace, *International Regulation of Multinational Corporations,* New York, Praeger, 1976.
19. *Economist,* 4 June, 1977, pp. 93-4.
20. William R. Hoskins, 'The LDC and the MNC: Will they Develop Together?', *Columbia Journal of World Business,* vol. 6, September-October 1971, pp. 61-70.

SELECT BIBLIOGRAPHY
Barnet, R. J. and Müller, R. E., *Global Reach,* London, Cape, 1975.
Behrman, J.N., *National Interests and the Multinational Enterprise,* Englewood Cliffs, N.J., Prentice-Hall, 1970.
Dunning, John H. (ed), *The Multinational Enterprise,* London, Allen and Unwin, 1971.
Gilpin, Robert, *US Power and the Multinational Corporation: The Political Economy of Foreign Direct Investment,* London, Macmillan, 1975.
Keohane, R.O. and Nye, J.S., *Transnational Relations and World Politics,* Cambridge, Mass., Harvard University Press, 1972.
Keohane, R.O. and Nye, J.S., *Power and Interdependence,* Boston, Little Brown, 1977.
Kindleberger, Charles P. (ed), *The International Corporation,* Cambridge, Mass., MIT Press, 1970.
Vernon, R., *Sovereignty at Bay,* New York, Basic Books, 1971.
Vernon, R. (ed), *Big Business and the State: Changing Relations in Western Europe,* London, Macmillan, 1974.

CONCLUSION

The State of European Society

R. N. Berki and Jack Hayward

While not in the least wishing to belittle the efforts of our collaborators, whose researches and arguments are convincingly set out in the preceding chapters, we feel that it behoves us to conclude the volume with a few explicit — and possibly provocative — remarks concerning our subject matter as a whole. That such an endeavour is fraught with danger is quite obvious. We believe that it has nevertheless some uses. To begin with it is as well to establish the point, amply demonstrated by the foregoing discussion, that the relations of 'state' and 'society' in both halves of Europe present us with an exceedingly complex picture, one that is amenable to a generalised academic explanation only with a number of provisos and qualifications. Broadly speaking, one can and ought to acknowledge the presence of two distinct types of socio-political order in the area, to be loosely designated 'liberal-democratic' and 'socialist' or 'communist', each with its own typical configurations, political cultures and processes. It is, however, not simply the case that these broadly defined units themselves display certain problems regarding the relationship of state and society. In addition, we can detect a considerable amount of variation within our larger units, mainly but by no means exclusively along the lines of national and state frontiers. In a number of minor respects, that is, some Western liberal-democratic states can be seen to resemble more closely some representatives of the Eastern stereotype than states belonging to the same unit. We shall below have an opportunity to comment on some interesting instances of this deviation from the norm, in conjunction with our attempt to draw general substantive conclusions concerning the outstanding features of the major units themselves.

Before launching into this task, however, we propose briefly to remark upon the state of Europe viewed in a global context. Here it is necessary to employ an historical perspective, contrasting the Europe of the present with the Europe of the — not so distant — past. The simple but significant point to make here is that Europe is a small continent, its geographical proportions being today more in harmony with its demographic, political, cultural and economic importance than they were at any time in the past two hundred years. The days have long since gone when Europe was the undisputed centre of civilisation and power, the area with the most 'advanced' states and societies. What remains from this epoch of triumphant European imperialism (in the broadest sense of the term) is a feeling, probably well justified, that in sheer sophistication or complexity European politics and society still surpass those of other regions. Europe contains in a condensed miniature almost the whole spectrum of the widely differing social experiences to be found in the world today, some explicitly, some by way of latent (in certain cases atavistic) tendencies and aspirations. For the academic observer it thus presents the most delectable object of enquiry, even though the same observer would soon come to realise that the European laboratory drastically reduces the magnitude of the contending global forces that it seeks to reproduce and represent. Europe may indeed still be the centre (or one of the centres) of the stage, but it neither alone attracts all the highlights nor provides the main actors, producers and choreographers. In terms of area, Europe barely surpasses Australasia. In terms of population, it lags far behind Asia and the Americas. Its existing wealth, in terms of output per capita, is second only to the United States, but on the level of individual states European countries are being fast outstripped by such non-European rivals as Japan or Kuwait. As regards natural resources, which constitute the bases of wealth-creation, Europe is increasingly dependent on the outside world, a fact that has very obvious bearing not only on the standard of living, but on the political independence as well as military security of European states. Thus while Europe is a worthy prize in the global conflict of great powers, as well as being the foremost cultural 'workshop' and educational centre, especially for third world countries, its relative poverty of manpower and natural wealth makes it into hardly more than a client or junior partner of one or another of the superpowers. In this perspective, of course, the Soviet Union is rightly seen as at least in part an extra-European power. This is on account of its size and military-economic potential, and notwithstanding its culture and geographical location. The continuing division of Europe into two halves, the still important institutional and ideological cleavage between East and West, cannot, we feel, even begin to be comprehended without an adequate understanding of this global situation. Europe's shrunken status in the world is thus the inescapable starting-point for any analysis and evaluation of the present character of European states and societies.

The relative decline of European dominance in the world has been accompanied by a change in the relative balance of wealth and power within Europe. The great imperial countries of the nineteenth century, Britain and France, have suffered a serious decline in their standing in terms of power.

However, whereas an old industrialised society like Britain has, owing to a low rate of economic growth suffered a catastrophic fall in its relative wealth that has circumscribed its political independence, rapid development in a newly industrialised society like France has given it the economic capacity to sustain a relatively independent position in world affairs and a powerful place within the EEC. In terms of wealth, the German Federal Republic has attained a position of economic influence that it has not as yet been able to convert into a comparably dominant political standing. The same is largely true of the GDR within the East European system, where neither the countries that in various ways have successfully resisted Soviet political domination, notably Yugoslavia and Albania, nor the countries that have acquiesced in it, have made a significant impact upon the relative balance of power and wealth.

It will be convenient to present the main part of our concluding survey under five different headings, each representing a distinct area of enquiry into Europe's socio-political order. With this five-fold division we shall sometimes be cutting across the subject matter of the preceding chapters and occasionally we shall conflate the conclusions reached by two or more authors. We also, here and there, diverge to some extent from the judgements of one or another of our contributors.

Our first concern is the current nature of the European state and of authority-relations in general. Starting with the West, the point of utmost importance is the enormous extent of interpenetration of economic and political power, of industrial management and public authority. The economically neutral state, the governmental structure whose sole concern is to maintain an impartial system of law, is today nowhere to be found outside the pages of nostalgic treatises on political philosophy or the speeches of hopeful, but eccentric, politicians — for better or worse. It seems to have been established beyond any reasonable doubt that the welfare and managerial state as a political institution is compatible with the traditional features of liberal democracy, such as the public accountability of government departments and nationalised industrial enterprises, pluralism, free press and the like. It appears, furthermore, that this state of affairs has come about, if not exactly as an effect of 'inexorable laws' of economic development, relatively smoothly and naturally, without major social dislocations or the alienation of large interests, and without governmental authority drastically changing its character. As industry, in its present advanced state (size of operations, high technology, investment), needs the aid of government for its proper functioning, so do the requirements of government include the necessity of regulating economic activity and direct involvement in the production of essential goods and services. It is no longer a matter merely of providing basic welfare services for the needy but of actively participating in the production of wealth to be shared out to all sections of society. Here it is of considerable interest to note that nationalisation or direct public ownership is usually not the favoured method used by the state in its effort to control the economy. After the successes of French public entrepreneurship and planning and the relative loss of momentum in the British drive towards nationalisation, the emphasis has shifted towards 'concerted action', the latter process having in the 1960s been accorded legal status in the doctrinally anti-interventionist Federal Republic of Germany. Such developments have resulted in a vast increase in the number of people who have to carry on the state's business. Governmental bureaucracy is contiguous and often continuous with industrial bureaucracy; there is an overlap of roles and functions. The state then, to put it succinctly, had descended from its erstwhile olympian heights, without, however, relinquishing its supreme authority.

In the East we have to start from a different assumption. Here, under communist systems, the state as a definite institutional structure has always had a different position from its counterpart in the West. It has been, that is to say, fully subordinated to the direction of the Communist Party, which, in turn, has arrogated to itself the most important authority-functions. It appears that there has been no fundamental change in any East European country in this respect. The party is everywhere still firmly in the saddle and the state acts as its executive organ. This is true, basically, even in the special case of Yugoslavia. However, there have been significant changes in the way in which the party, mainly but not exclusively through the state, has been transmitting its authority and enforcing its decisions. In some communist countries at least, the era of Stalinism, of pure personal dictatorship, seems to be over, and with it also the arbitrary, terroristic regime of the political police. In Romania and Bulgaria, personal dictatorship has paradoxically become accentuated in the post-Stalinist period. In most countries, the party, or more precisely its highest executive organs, have established their collective, oligarchic ascendancy. This process has been accompanied by a definite change in the style of governing. There is a great deal more emphasis on persuasion and on the need to observe legality, as though the party, from an initial position of supra-legal authority, has been moving towards a situation where its role, in certain respects, comes to resemble more that of the traditional European state. There is, of course, a considerable amount of variation within Eastern Europe, but since the failure of the Czech experiment in 1968 no individual Communist Party has shown any signs of wanting to go further in the direction of diluting, let alone sharing, its authority, although, as has been said, the implementation of this authority has a markedly different character from what it was twenty years ago. In the spectrum of East European communist countries, it is the parties and governments of Yugoslavia, Hungary and Poland that stand nearest to this emerging model of a more consultative, semi-legal type of authority, whereas the Soviet Union, Bulgaria and Romania display a greater resemblance to the former situation.

We turn next to the position of European society, which illuminates, from the reverse side as it were, the nature of prevailing authority-relations. In the West we must note first of all the conspicuous presence, and increasing political importance, of organised interest groups, which have come to supplant traditional forms of representation. Political parties are still prospering, of course, and continue to fulfil an important role in recruiting for the executive and aggregating broad strands of opinion. The tendency has been in Sweden, Italy and France for hegemonic parties or coalitions to emerge that dominate for decades, although there has been a counter-tendency in these countries and in the home of the two-party system, Britain, towards a fragmentation of party support. Furthermore, parties are now being increasingly bypassed in day-to-day and even long-term governmental decision-making by groups that represent functional interests. The latter are now in close and direct contact with the executive. This development is the inevitable concomitant of the increase in the state's role in directing the economy, though it would be hazardous to assign causal priority either to secular economic changes, to the efficiency of societal agencies (pressure groups) in asserting their point of view, or to the initiatives of governments. An important question here concerns the prevailing position of social classes in respect of their share of political power and economic benefits. All in all, one might be justified in concluding that there has been no basic alteration in the power position of classes; that interest-group pluralism has not gone very far in eliminating inherited differences of wealth and status, although again one should not overlook the effect of the increase in total wealth of Western societies or the legal as well as practical extension of welfare benefits. Working-class interest organisations, like the trades union movement, have had their spectacular successes, but for the present they have proved too diffuse and badly organised to assert and sustain a unified sectional point of view. The experience of the various countries shows marked differences. Whereas a high degree of integration and consensus of conflicting social classes and their organised representatives exists in Sweden, Holland and West Germany, conflict and dissensus have been more prominent in France, Italy and the United Kingdom.

The changes in the nature of East European society have been no less significant. The relative loosening of the Communist Party's control over all aspects of life is to be correlated with the appearance of several pluralistic tendencies, with the general result that there is now a surprising extent of economic, cultural and political diversity in some, though not all, East European countries. At the same time, fresh problems of social organisation and integration have protruded onto the surface. Of greatest significance here is the introduction of changes in economic management. The process, to some extent, has been the exact reverse of the Western development mentioned in the preceding paragraph. Monolithic direction and fully centralised management have been considerably modified so as to make allowances for productivity and the profitability of single state-owned enterprises. This change has accompanied the shift away from heavy industrial production towards consumer goods, being no doubt to some extent occasioned by the demonstrable inefficiency of centralisation in certain sectors and by the increasing need for participation in world trade. Related social changes in a more general sense are also noticeable. Overall there is a higher and increasing material standard of living, and also a marked growth in income differentials, though one might hesitate to equate this process with the emergence of classes in the traditional sense. In terms of power position, social groups in the countries of Eastern Europe appear in some respects to be even more sharply stratified than in the countries of Western Europe. But again we have to be mindful of the amount of variety within the area. Self-management and decentralisation have existed in a fully-fledged form only in Yugoslavia, and here it is important to note the corresponding spread of social, even political, diversity, illustrated by the country's federal structure and the relatively free flow and exchange of ideas as well as relations with the West. Of the other East European countries, Hungary has gone farthest in the direction of integrating a novel kind of market mechanism into its state-socialist system. Again, this is accompanied by an extension of civil liberties, cultural diversity and last but not least the appearance of a form of 'apparatus pluralism', exemplified in the role being played by trades unions. It is worthy of notice in this connection that the problem of national diversity within single states is again dealt with in a remarkably pluralistic and tolerant manner in Yugoslavia, whereas the position of national minorities in the economically orthodox, centralistic state of Romania is one of oppression and continuing forced integration.

The third question concerns the manner in which and the extent to which the socio-political order in both halves of Europe has been able to reach its objectives, its stated goals and aspirations. Here of necessity the situation of the West presents greater problems, since there are no easily definable ends on which contending opinions would readily converge. Nevertheless, it may be possible at least to approximate the issue at hand if we were to relate efficiency to the admittedly vague and general goals of stability and prosperity. In very broad terms the verdict must surely be a positive one: West European countries are almost without exception among the most stable and prosperous in the world, and until the late 1960s it was assumed that wealth and a stable socio-political order were integrally (perhaps even causally) connected. The active managerial state, in other words, aided by the close co-operation of highly organised industry and economic interest groups, had been able both to increase production to a generally acceptable level and to effect a distribution of goods and services that was broadly equitable, though certainly not egalitarian. However, quite apart from the 1970s decline in growth rates and the increase in unemployment, one should guard against the error of self-congratulatory complacency. Attention should be paid to existing (and in some cases growing) pockets of destitution, instances of long-term and structural unemployment, the withering of certain basic industries, the often unsatisfactory level of investment and a preoccupation with the preservation of the natural environment from industrial inroads. Co-ordinated state and entrepreneurial bureaucracies facilitate, but can just as well hinder, the efficacy of economic performance and therewith political stability. It is only fair, though hardly encouraging, to acknowledge here the relatively poor performance of the state-aided economies of Britain and Italy in recent years, in contrast to the smooth-running efficiency of France and Sweden. However, the quality of life has not become necessarily worse in countries that were becoming or remained economically backward.

East European communism, in its contemporary phase of development, has also been showing signs of success measured in terms of stability and prosperity. In this case, however, since we are dealing with purposeful social organisation on a large scale, these general notions hardly suffice as criteria of evaluation. Granted that communist countries are by and large stable and prosperous (and here one should not forget such chronically inefficient industries as agriculture and the numerous instances of shortages, maldistribution and discontinuities in the transmission of economic decisions), the question still arises as to what, precisely, these developments signify. Stability and prosperity are not, as such, the goals that Communist parties have set out to achieve, and in the name of which they have exacted sacrifices from the mass of their populations in past decades. If we take their aim to be communism, not merely in the sense of material abundance but the complete elimination of social conflict, inequality and political power, then it will be somewhat difficult to grant that their recent socio-political development has been unmistakably moving in this direction. At best it could be said that they display the features (and not necessarily in a pejorative sense) of bureaucratic, 'statist' societies, with clearly delineated command structures and political hierarchies. Without necessarily going as far as detecting a significant degree of convergence, one would be entitled to argue that in many respects the East European development serves as a pointer to what the West itself might be moving towards, the primary reference here being to the merging of economic and political power. Freed from the straitjacket of ideological messianism, East European systems might well develop into noteworthy models of efficient economic organisation, suited to the secular requirements of the age. Freed from the effects of inegalitarian distribution (which might mean, in fact, the injection of a certain amount of messianism), Western systems could further enhance their attractions as models of efficient political organisation, to be noted and perhaps emulated by others. But the preconditions might well be too formidable in both cases to allow us to make more than bare statements of abstract, hypothetical possibilities.

This leads us directly to the fourth question, which concerns the legitimacy of the Western and Eastern systems of state and society. In the former case, concerned as we are with 'open' systems, with formalised pluralistic procedures of political choice, at first glance the answer might appear easy enough. Since Western governments and parties enjoy their authority by virtue of popular mandates (vote by majorities of electorates comprising all sane adult citizens), their legitimacy is taken for granted — almost by definition. But this is not the whole picture, and it would be irresponsible to pass over certain blemishes and disturbing tendencies. It may indeed be the case that the recent evolution of the Western state towards economic management and of Western society towards functional representation itself demands supplementation of the traditional procedures of liberal democracy. The erosion of the role of the traditional legislature *eo ipso* means the decrease of the political significance of the individual territorial vote. The danger of 'neo-corporatism', still hidden behind the façade of conventional representative institutions, looms large. Its presence, in the form of sophisticated 'negotiations' between governments and economic super-organisations behind closed doors and couched in a technical jargon hardly comprehensible to the average voter, can be gauged by the amount of apathy detectable in all Western countries. Beyond the traditionally accepted level of passive indifference, there are today many signs of disillusionment and cynicism, not to mention the active alienation of sizable segments of the population, particularly national minorities and the younger generation. Shop-floor militancy, ethnic conflict, corruption, the polarisation of political forces, urban terrorism, violent crime, hooliganism, all tend further to undermine the traditional respect paid to the law and government. Again, the experience of the various countries differs rather widely. At one end of the spectrum we could locate the Scandinavian countries, which enjoy a high degree of legitimacy, while among major European countries, Italy, France and in some respects Britain stand nearest to the other end.

In Eastern Europe also, there are many, though in the nature of the case less easily ascertainable, signs of popular dissatisfaction with the regimes holding power, rendering the legitimacy of the latter highly questionable. Of course the very question of legitimacy involves entirely different assumptions in the communist context, since communist political theory (except on the lowest level of propaganda) does not equate legitimacy with electoral popularity. Thus, strictly speaking, even a hypothetical free multi-party election involving the decisive defeat of the Communist Party, would not by itself impair the legitimacy of this party in its own eyes to lead society and state as the vanguard of the working class. We can take it as read that a multi-party election in most East European countries would in fact show up the lack of popularity of the ruling parties. It is, however, by no means certain that the voters' choice would favour parties advocating full-scale capitalist restoration. But perhaps we ought not to engage in speculation that envisages eventualities that are, to put it mildly, light-years away from the realm of probability. At the same time it is relevant to call attention here to such phenomena as the survival and even flourishing of organised religion and intellectual dissent, which is suppressed in some, though willy-nilly tolerated in other, communist countries. The West, with its avowed pluralism, can more easily accommodate these and similar features of social dissatisfaction, but for the East they indicate serious problems below the surface. In addition, one must note that the gradual process of Westernisation, in the sense of greater prosperity and a certain amount of free cultural exchange, has brought with it definite symptoms of Western-type social maladies of the kind we have referred to above, such as the cynicism and alienation of the young, drug-taking, and so on, added to the customary East European vices of alcoholism, personal violence and utter disrespect for social property. All these occurrences would tend to suggest that the legitimacy of communist systems, not in liberal-democratic but in expressly Marxist terms, is also open to some doubt. As in the West, these disturbing, dysfunctional tendencies seem to be on the increase.

Fifth and last, we must take a brief look again at the international context and ask if fresh developments here have brought about significant changes in the position of European states and societies. We shall consider this question under three sub-headings, namely superpower involvement, political and economic integration. As regards the first, there is no doubt at all that European countries in both East and West rest under the shadows, respectively, of the Soviet Union and of the United States. National sovereignty thus, though still proclaimed in legal terms, is being circumscribed by regional solidarity. This is unlikely to mean open military aggression on the part of the great powers. Despite the Brezhnev doctrine, the case of Czechoslovakia in 1968 is likely to remain an exception. Neither does it normally mean the assertion of great-power interest, in the form of political pressure or economic sanctions, against the expressed wishes of national governments, though again there are examples of this in both West and East. Basically it means the awareness on the part of national states and societies that they belong to a given socio-political order, the global fortunes of which have a direct bearing on their own interests and survival. But, to go further, this recognition of their dependence, economic, political and military, does not preclude European states from becoming restive and attempting, perhaps in an increasing measure, to define in their own way the interests of the global systems of which they form a part. Thus within the Western system we find such deviant foreign policies as those of France, Sweden, Finland and Austria. Correspondingly in the East there are the cases of Romania, Yugoslavia and Albania. In spite of this diversity and polycentrism, however, the overall pattern is still that of regional confrontation of states and societies.

By political integration we refer primarily to the European Economic Community. Its effect so far on the character of its members appears to have been limited. No doubt there has been an increase in the level and diversity of production directly attributable to the free internal market, accompanied by greater all-round prosperity, although it is taking rather a long time to materialise in certain member countries. Also the legal and institutional unification processes have made themselves felt in a variety of economic practices, with long-term implications for political configurations and patterns of living. No doubt, given present tendencies, these changes and their sundry effects will grow in magnitude and importance. It is, on the other hand, to be noted that the original hope of the fathers of European integration has not so far shown signs of being fulfilled in the foreseeable future. There has been, in other words, no dramatic transformation of national into European consciousness. Primary allegiance is still paid to the nation-state, with its evolved politico-legal institutions, rather than to their embryo equivalents in Brussels and Strasbourg.

In the field of societal or economic integration three phenomena should be afforded special mention, though here again our conclusion must be that the overall effects of this kind of integration on the European state and society have likewise been limited. Firstly there is the intrusive presence of the multinational enterprise. Although its operation from time to time understandably provokes criticism from various quarters, its importance is frequently overrated. Governments, it seems, are quite capable on the whole of dealing with the problems their presence creates. In most cases their presence is deemed desirable and their operations fit in with the prevailing pattern of state-aided or state-led economic activity. In the second place, the overt purpose of the East European Council of Mutual Economic Assistance has been to streamline the production of communist countries according to greatest comparative advantage and to facilitate the flow of credit and raw materials. It has doubtless contributed to the economic successes and prosperity of the region, although some countries have drawn much greater benefits than others. However, its operations have not materially altered either the relationship of the Soviet Union to its clients and allies or the internal political, social and economic balance of the several communist states themselves. Thirdly, we should note the marked increase in the volume of East-West trade, a phenomenon that holds out interesting implications for the future. While Eastern Europe, including the Soviet Union, has always needed to import Western technology and refined industrial products, the recent upsurge in the importation of Western capital and the spread of co-productive ventures seem to have opened a new chapter in the relationship of the two halves of Europe. The present détente could well be regarded as the political manifestation of this process.

This summary survey of the state of contemporary European society should not be concluded without a few cautious remarks of practical intent, at least as far as the West is concerned. With regard to the East we must be content with adopting the 'observer's point of view'. The substantive chapters dealing with Eastern Europe have not established the claim that communist political and social development leads towards convergence with the Western pattern of governmental and industrial organisation. However, it is undeniable that there are detectable tendencies in this development that suggest that convergence in some respects at least and at some future time is a distinct possibility. We think that these tendencies should be welcomed. Polycentrism within the bloc as a whole and pluralism within the several East European states, together with economic reforms and freer cultural exchange, are bound to create an atmosphere that could gradually bring the two halves of Europe closer to each other. This hypothetical rapprochement, in its turn, might be expected to lead to greater prosperity and the stability of the entire continent.

As far as the situation in the West is concerned, we are participants and not merely observers. Explicit or implicit value-judgements here become even less avoidable. Two points need emphasis. In the first place, it seems to us that the active economic role of the state, accompanied as it is by a certain amount of bureaucratisation and the interpenetration of political and industrial power, is an inevitable consequence of the secular process of economic development, and it cannot be undone. One should not try to undo it either. The extended state has substantially contributed to the growth in most West European economies and the measure of prosperity and stability achieved by most West European societies. Although some sections of the population resent a loss of their independence as producers, it is idle to think of turning the clock back and dismantling the state's managerial and welfare functions. If this increase in statism is seen as the Western expression of a hypothetical process of convergence with the East, the discovery should not be a disconcerting one.

On the other hand, we ought to stress the undesirability of neo-corporatist excesses. The state, in other words, while it rightly takes an active role in economic direction and organisation, ought to beware the dangers of becoming embroiled in the myriad social conflicts. It should not become a captive of entrenched interests, merely a 'partner' in high-level industrial consultation processes or even a weak, neutral umpire. In the wrangle of contending social forces the voice and interest of the individual citizen is hardly noticed. He would have most to gain from an organisation whose most important concern is to strive towards the formulation and implementation of the common or public interest of the whole society whenever this can be ascertained. The state could fulfil this function in former times by the relatively simple processes of legislation in popular assemblies and the enforcement of the law. In today's extremely complicated network of societal interest-group relationships, these instruments are no longer adequate. We definitely need new ones, though the problem of exactly what shape they should assume and what precise function they should fulfil is a difficult one, not to be prejudged in the present discussion. To devise these new instrumentalities will be the principal task of the generations that will prepare Europe to face the impending problems of the twenty-first century.

Index

Adenauer, Konrad, 79
aerospace, and multinational enterprise, 244, 245
agriculture, and state, 26
Agriculture, Ministry of, 27
Albania, 105, 190, 192, 255, 262
Almond, Gabriel, 17
Austria, 38, 43, 186; foreign policy, 262; political parties in, 49

Belgium, 44; political parties in, 48
Bentham, Jeremy, 9, 34, 38
Blanc, Louis, 160
Brezhnev, Leonid, 110, 113, 193, 194, 196, 197, 233, 234
Brzezinski, Zbigniew, 12, 14, 190
Bulgaria, 105, 106, 190, 256, 257; COMECON, 219, 221, 222, 224, 225; economy, 144; and USSR, 192, 193
Bundesverband der Deutschen Industrie, 28
bureaucracy, professionalism in, 62–6
Burke, Edmund, 8

Canada, 242
cartel, 72
Carter, Jimmy, 200
Catholic Church, 43
Ceausescu, Nicolae, 137, 193, 195
Cenić, Dimitrije, 160
Central Policy Review Staff, 66, 78
China, 190, 193
Christian Democracy, 43, 46; in Italy, 47; in Netherlands, 49
Christian Democratic Party, Germany, 47, 48–9, 79, 80; Italy, 43, 47, 50, 55
Civil Aviation Organisation, International, 248
Clapham, Sir Michael, 247

class, as Marxist paradigm, 25; and politics, 44
Cold War, 12, 13
Cole, G.D.H., 9
collective bargaining, 70, 71, 77, 78, 81
communism, as ideal, 11; and nationality, 118
Communist Manifesto, 10, 160
Communist Party, elections, 104–6; interest groups, 108–15; in Italy, 44; leading role of, 96–100; monistic power structure, 107; nationality issues, 119ff; Politburo, 101, 102, 107, 111, 114, 121; Presidium of Council of Ministers, 101, 102, 107, 111; Secretariat of Central Committee, 101, 102, 107, 111
computer industry, and multinational enterprise, 244, 245; *see also* under individual countries
Confederation of British Industry (CBI), 28, 77
Confédération Française Démocratique du Travail, (CFDT), 27, 80
Confédération Générale du Travail (CGT), 27, 80, 87
Confederazione Generale Italiana del Lavoro (CGIL), 80, 81, 82, 87
Confindustria, 28, 33, 55, 81
Conseil National du Patronat Français, 28, 81
conservatism, dynamic, 35
constitutional provision, effect on political parties, 45
consultative bodies, 36–7; *see also* interest group, pressure group
corporatism, 5, 39
corruption, and multinational enterprise, 248
Council for Mutual Economic Assistance

(CMEA, COMECON), 181, 192, 196; economic reform, 223–6; and EEC, 233–6; establishing, 219–22; integration, 231–3; organisation of, 226–31
culture, and political party, 44
Czechoslovak Communist Party (CCP), 130, 131
Czechoslovakia, 103, 105, 106, 113, 190; and COMECON, 219, 221, 224, 225, 226; economy in, 142, 144, 146, 150; interest groups in, 110; nationality issues, 130–34; and USSR, 192, 193, 194, 196, 197, 198

defence, expenditure on, 61; *see also* NATO
'demand input overload', 38, 39
Denmark, 70
Donovan Report (1968), 77
Dubcek, Alexander, 193

Easton, David, 16
Ecole Nationale d'Administration, 63
economy, in E. Europe, 141; reform, 144–56, 223–6; traditional planning system, 143–4; *see also* COMECON, EEC
education, expenditure on, 68
employer organisations, 28, 31
Engineering Workers, Amalgamated Union of (AUEW), 83
environmental issues, pressure groups and, 29
Eurocommunism, 27; *see also* communism, Communist Party
European Atomic Community (EAC), 203, 204
European Coal and Steel Community (ECSC), 87, 203, 204
European Defence Community (EDC), 204
European Economic Community (EEC), 27, 71, 87, 184, 203, 204; and COMECON, 233–6; Court of Justice, 211–13; economy of, 214–16; European Parliament, 209–10; integration within, 231–3; organisation, 205–9; and welfare state, 213–14
expenditure, public, 38, 58, 59, 60, 61; and economic planning, 70–73; *see also* economy

federalism, 9
Fichte, Johann, 7
Finland, 55, 262
Fourier, Charles, 160
France, 6, 17, 26, 27, 29, 31, 38, 257; aerospace industry, 245; bureaucracy, 62, 64, 65, 66, 67, 69; Communist Party in, 190; dissatisfaction in, 260; Economic Council in, 33–4; economy in, 70, 71, 259; foreign policy, 262; as great power, 182, 185, 254; and NATO, 186–7, 188; political parties, 42, 43, 44, 45, 46, 47, 52; pressure groups, 54; public expenditure, 59; trade unions, 78, 80–82, 87
Frederick William I of Prussia, 63
Fulton Committee, 65, 66

Gaulle, Charles de, 34, 182, 186–7
German Democratic Republic (GDR), and COMECON, 223, 224, 225, 229; economy, 144, 145, 150, 255; mass media, 111; party structure, 102, 105, 106, 113; trade unions, 114; and USSR, 190, 192, 194, 195
German Federal Republic, administration, 63, 65, 68; Economic Council in, 33; economy, 70, 71, 72, 255; as great power, 185; multinational enterprise, 245; political parties, 43, 45, 46, 47, 48, 49, 52, 257; pressure groups, 54; public expenditure, 59, 60; trade unions, 75, 77, 79–80, 84–6
German industrial workers union (DGB), 79, 80, 84, 85, 86
Gestioni e Partecipazione Industriale (GEPI), 60
Gilpin, Robert, 244
Gorter, Herman, 160
Gramsci, Antonio, 13, 160
Great Britain, 6, 26, 30, 31, 38, 254, 255; administration, 63–4, 65, 66, 67; aerospace industry, 245; decentralisation, 69; dissatisfaction, 260; economy, 70, 71, 259; as great power, 182, 185, 186; political parties, 45, 257; public expenditure, 59, 60, 61,

62; trade unions, 75, 77, 78—9, 82—4
Greece, 184, 188, 216
guild socialism, 9

Habsburg Empire, 6
Harmel Report (1967), 189
Hegel, Georg, 8, 11
Helsinki Agreement (1975), 200
Hungary, 98, 99, 102—6, 113, 114, 190, 256; and COMECON, 219, 221, 222, 223, 224, 225; economy, 144, 146—8; mass media, 112; trade unions, 109; and USSR, 192, 193, 195
Huntington, Samuel, 12, 14

Iceland, 184, 186
In Place of Strife (1969), 83
industrial relations, *see* multinational enterprises, trade union
Industrial Relations Act (1971), 83
industrialization, and regional inequality, 127; and state intervention, 58
inflation, 38
instrumentalism, 2, 3—4; extreme, 5; one-sidedness, 14; predominance in W. Europe, 6, 16; views on, 8—9
interest groups, attitudes to, 30—32; in E. Europe, 107—15; *see also* consultative bodies, pressure group
International Civil Aviation Organisation, *see* Civil Aviation Organisation
International Confederation of Free Trade Unions (ICFTU), 87
International Monetary Fund, 248
Istituto per la Ricostruzione Industriale (IRI), 60
Italian Ministry of Industry and Commerce, 33
Italian National Council of Economy and Labour, 34
Italy, 17, 26, 27, 33, 38, 190, 257; administration, 64, 65; dissatisfaction in, 260; economy, 71, 259; political parties, 42, 43, 44, 45, 47, 52; pressure groups, 55; public expenditure, 60; regional policy, 69; trade unions, 78, 80—82, 88

Japan, 200, 254

Kennedy, John, 183

Khruschev, Nikita, 97, 100, 112, 190, 192, 193, 196, 197
Kirchheimer, Otto, 51, 55
Kissinger, Henry, 183, 189, 198
Korsch, Karl, 160

Labour Party (GB), 27; and trade unions, 78—9
Lama, Luciano, 82
language, and political party, 44
LaPalombara, Joseph, 47, 55
Laski, Harold, 9
law, 3, 9, 260; in E. Europe, 99; lack of adaptation, 36
Lenin, Vladimir, 11, 12
liberal-democracy, 14, 25
Lijphart, Arendt, 53
Lindblom, Charles, 17
List, Friedrich, 8
local government, policy making in, 66—70
Local Government Officers, National Association of (NALGO), 75

Maistre, Joseph, de 7
Marković, Svetozar, 160
Marx, Karl, 10, 159
Marxism, 10, 13, 15
Mazzini, Giuseppe, 8, 11
McNamara, Robert, 189
Miliband, Ralph, 15
Mill, James, 9
Mouvement Républican Populaire (MRP), 43, 46
multinational corporation (MNC), 87—90
multinational enterprise (MNE), 237—8; and base government, 240—42; and communist states, 246—8; and high technology industry, 244—6; and host government, 242—3; problems posed by, 239—40; regulation of, 248—51; and subsidiaries, 243—4
Munich Agreement (1938), 182
mutualism, 9

National Economic Development Council (NEDC), 34, 82
National Enterprise Board, 72
National Farmers Union, 27

nationality, in Czechoslovakia, 130–34; and economic reform, 151–2; in Romania, 134–9; in USSR, 118–25; in Yugoslavia, 125–30, 159
neo-feudalism, 5
Netherlands, 27, 31, 38, 190; political parties, 43, 45, 48, 49, 52, 53, 55, 56, 257
Nixon, Richard, 195, 198
North Atlantic Treaty Organisation (NATO), 181, 184–8, 199, 204
Norway, 49
Novotný, Antonín, 132, 194
Nuclear Disarmament, Campaign for (CND), 29
nuclear industry, and multinational enterprise, 244, 245
Nyers, Rezsö, 195

Opposition in Western Democracies (Dahl), 51
Organisation of Associated Work (OAW Yugoslavia), 161, 162, 163, 169, 172
Owen, Robert, 160

Pannekoek, Anton, 160
paternalism, in politics, 34
Pauker, Ana, 135
Plowden Report, (1961), 65
pluralism, 23, 24, 25, 39
Poland, 105, 106, 190, 192, 256; and COMECON, 221, 222, 223, 224, 225, 229; economy, 144; and USSR, 194, 196
Political Parties (Duverger), 45
political party, 17; balanced, 48; coalition, 49–50; consociational model, 52–3; constitutional provisions, 45; hegemonic, 47; and interest groups, 54–5; linguistic differences, 44; in opposition, 50–52; and religion, 42–4, 46; role of, 42; and rural development, 44; and social class, 44–5
Popular Party (Italy), 43
Portugal, 184, 186, 216
Poulantzas, Nicos, 15, 25
power, political, in E. Europe, 101–12
pressure groups, attitudes to, 32, 33, 37; and political parties, 54–5; *see also* consultative body, interest group
proletariat, Lenin on, 11

proportional representation, 45
Protestantism, 43
Proudhon, Pierre-Joseph, 9

Quesnay, François, 8

Rassemblement Wallon (Belgium), 44
religion, and politics, 42–4, 46, 53
Rokossovsky, Konstantin, 192
Romania, 99, 100, 103, 105, 106, 190, 256, 257; and COMECON, 219, 221, 222, 224, 225; economy, 144; foreign policy, 262; interest groups, 110; nationality issues, 134–9, 258; USSR, 192, 193, 194, 195, 196
Rousseau, Jean-Jacques, 7, 11
rural development, and political parties, 44

Saltsjöbaden Agreement (Sweden 1936), 71
Sartori, Giovanni, 48
Schiller, Karl, 80
Schlesinger, James, 185
Schmitthoff, Clive, on multinational enterprise, 246
Shonfield, Andrew, 18
Slovak National Council (SNC), 130
Smith, Adam, 8
'social contract', 38, 83
social democracy, 46; in Sweden, 47, 61
Social Democratic Party (SPD Germany) 79, 80
social market economy, 71
social rights, principle of, 29–30
social security, in Germany, 71
sovereignty, and transcendentalism, 4, 8
Soviet Union (USSR), 6, 13; and Cold War, 12; and COMECON, 218–22; economic reform, 223–6; economy, 144, 145, 148–55; elections, 105; future role, 198–201; as great power, 181, 190–98; interest groups in, 110, 113, 114; leading role of Party, 96–9, 102; nationality issues, 118–25; and Yugoslavia, 159
Spain, 6, 27, 44, 185, 186, 216
Spencer, Herbert, 35, 38
Stalin, Joseph, 96

State and Revolution, (Lenin), 11, 159
statism, 12
subordination, in state/society relationship, 5
suffrage, 29
Suleiman, Ezra, 32
Svenska Arbetsgivareföreningen, 28
Sweden, 26, 27, 30, 31, 39, 186, 257; administration, 65, 66, 67, 68, 69, 70; economy, 71, 259; foreign policy, 262; political parties in, 47, 49, 51; pressure groups in, 54; public expenditure, 59, 60, 61, 62; trade unions in, 75, 77, 79
Swedish Employers Association, 77
Swedish industrial workers' union (LO), 79
Swedish Social Democrats (SAP), 79
Switzerland, 44, 186; political parties in, 52

Tariffs and Trade, General Agreement on, 248
taxation, 38, 61
technology, high, and communist countries, 247; and multinational enterprise, 244–6
Telecommunication Union, International, 248
Tito, Josip, 125, 128, 129
totalitarianism, 16–17, 101–3
trade, increase in East/West, 263
trade union, 25, 27, 31, 36, 54, 75–8; in E. Europe, 98, 106, 109, 111, 112, 114; integrated system, 82–6; international perspective, 86–90; and multinational enterprise, 243–4; and political party, 78–82; in Yugoslavia, 164
Trades Union Congress (TUC), 27, 78

World Federation of Trade Unions (WFTU), 87
transcendentalism, 2–3, 4; extreme, 5; and Marxism, 10; one-sidedness of, 14; predominance in E. Europe, 6
Transport and General Workers Union (TGWU), 83
Turkey, 184, 188

Ulbricht, Walter, 197

unemployment, and technology transfer, 247
United States of America (US), 6; and Cold War, 12; links with Europe, 181–90, 198–201; and multinational enterprise, 244, 245, 250
urbanisation, and state intervention, 58

Volksunie (Belgium), 44

Warsaw Pact (WTO), 181, 191–5, 199
Weber, Max, 14
welfare programme, 59; *see also* social rights, social security
Western European Union, 204
Wilczynski, Josef, on multinational enterprise, 246

Yugoslav Communists, League of (LCY), 159, 164, 165, 166; and Yugoslav self-management, 170–72
Yugoslavia, 34, 190, 256, 262; and COMECON, 219, 221, 225; economy, 144, 151, 255; nationality issues in, 125–30; origins of socialism, 158–61; problems of self-management, 170–75; system of self-management, 161–70

Zhukov, Georgi, 97